An American's
First-Hand View of
Living and Working
in China

RANDOM HOUSE
NEW YORK

IN THE
PEOPLE'S
REPUBLIC

Orville Schell

IN THE PEOPLE'S REPUBLIC

All rights reserved under International and
Pan-American Copyright Conventions.
Published in the United States by Random House, Inc., New York,
and simultaneously in Canada by Random House
of Canada Limited, Toronto.
Much of the material in this book appeared originally in *The New Yorker.*

Library of Congress Cataloging in Publication Data

Schell, Orville.
In the People's Republic

1. China—Description and travel—1949–
2. Schell, Orville. I. Title.
DS711.S288   951.05   76–53458
ISBN 0–394–49905–0

Manufactured in the United States of America

2 4 6 8 9 7 5 3

For my sister Suzy,
with love

Preface

There are few men in the twentieth century who seemed as immortal as Mao Tse-tung. During his long life of eighty-three years he not only survived the vicissitudes of a society in revolution, but was in great measure responsible for that revolution. Protest as he might that there was no such thing as individual "genius" behind social and political movements (only that of the "people"), his influence on the transformation of China appeared almost superhuman. It often seemed that Mao had become China. For many people who watched, China without a Mao seemed barely conceivable. The endless statues of Mao, the chanting of his name, the posters, the red books, and even memorabilia like the red cigarette lighters emblazoned with Mao quotes seemed to suggest to onlookers that China might be a country so firmly anchored by one charismatic personality that it might never survive his demise.

The book which you are about to read was written just before Mao's death. While in Peking, I often passed the brilliant crimson and gold gates of Chungnanhai, where Mao lived, and even then wondered what it would feel like someday for a Chinese to pass by the high walls of this compound knowing that their Chairman Mao no longer lived. I knew that they would of course feel grief, and probably also a sense of uncertainty and insecurity. For most Chinese today, there is no memory of a China without Mao.

But, while trying to imagine this Mao-less China, I was struck in a very forceful way by the fact that even prior to death, Mao had transcended his own personality. He was no passing rock star, no movie idol, or even a John Kennedy, who once taken from our midst was gone. For Mao had transformed his being, even his personality, into a series of carefully thought out and organized ideas. Mao was a thinker as well as a doer. He conceived of the Chinese revolution, and then helped cause it to happen. And, in the process, the thought of Chairman Mao became inculcated in almost every Chinese. The word almost literally became flesh. And it seemed clear, even before Mao died, that his death could not erase the way in which he had almost become transubstantiated in his people.

Today, September 10, news of Mao's death is on every front page of every publication in the world, and I too can not help but wonder if the centrifugal forces of a China without him will not just spin that country apart. Of course, one can not yet answer that question with any certitude. But as I reflect on my experiences in China, one predominant impression lingers, and that is that Mao not only gave the Chinese people decades of leadership, but that he also bequeathed them a whole unifying legacy. He left China with a whole world view, a uniform way of analyzing things and a common language. Through this legacy, he assured that his influence will persevere even after death. There will be factional squabbles and jousting among potential leaders. This is true anywhere. But I believe that the underlying unity of purpose laid out by Mao will essentially survive, that the political features of China and life for the average man will remain much as they were when I witnessed them.

And so, upon learning of the death of Mao, I have made virtually no changes in the text of this book, which recounts a rather unusual trip to China to work both in a factory and in the countryside. This experimental trip was arranged with ranking Chinese leaders for a group of Americans by the Hintons, an American family whose members have been involved with and interested in China since the end of World War II. The group was composed of both men and women, who ranged in age from eighteen to sixty, reflected a variety of occupations and political persuasions, and included several Americans who have lived in China for the last twenty-five years. As someone who speaks Chinese and has been intrigued by China for almost twenty years, I was offered an unequaled opportunity to see that country in a way afforded to few Westerners; from its fields and workshops as well as its guided tours. And I wish to thank both the Chinese people and the Hinton family for the energy they expended to make this trip possible.

I would also like to thank my good friends John Service, Tom Engelhardt, Richard Gordon, Carma Hinton, Burr Heneman and George Blecher for the time they took to help me fashion my experiences into this book.

ORVILLE SCHELL
SEPTEMBER 1976

Contents

I

TRAVELING

Departure

It is the last morning.

Everything is packed.

I head down to the post office and start walking out of town. The local realtor pulls up in his ancient black Rolls-Royce. His elderly gray head is peering up over the walnut dashboard, straining to see through the windshield with dimming eyes, as though he were driving in a dense fog.

"Where are you going?" he asks as he rolls down the window.

"China," I reply.

"Well, I'm going to Petaluma," he says without a pause.

I arrive in Oakland. An omnipresent roar of trucks and autos comes from the freeways which surround the Oakland Airport Holiday Inn.

The smell of deep-frying fat from a rooftop blower hangs over the empty swimming pool. A sign hung on a life ring says CLOSED FOR THE SEASON. A patio AstroTurf lawn turns into a real grass lawn so well mown it's hard to distinguish the demarcation line in between.

Part of our China Work Trip group is at the airport getting the frozen bull semen which is to be one of our gifts to the Chinese.

Slowly the various members of our twenty-person group arrive. Several of them relax around the closed pool in lounging chairs denuded of their cushions for the winter. They're wearing work boots, blue jeans and parkas. Other guests move purposefully in and out of the Inn's Galaxy Lounge, carrying briefcases and wearing plastic name tags on their suits. HI! I'M ED KURTZ. THE SINTREX CORPORATION.

The color TV in each of our rooms has a special channel featuring a program called "Listen and Grow Rich"—the Holiday Inn's answer to the guru craze. An earnest-looking businessman named Earl Nightingale delivers an inspirational message on "Self-development, salesmanship, creative thinking and successful living."

Can't sleep. Excited. Somewhat disoriented by the idea of our departure. The room is hot.

Try to open a window. Impossible. They are built only to be closed. I am forced to turn on the air conditioner, though it is cold outside.

A black woman on the graveyard shift moves past the window sitting astride a large, slow, noisy vacuum cleaner without a muffler. It inches up and down the parking lot, under neon lights, sucking up trash.

I turn on the TV for distraction. Johnny Carson is just finishing his monologue and golf swing. Ed MacMahon announces that one of *Tonight*'s guests will be Shirley MacLaine talking about her recent trip to China.

She emerges from behind the curtain in a slinky tight red dress slit from the floor to high on her thighs. She and Johnny start talking about "Vegas." Johnny is animated. Somehow Shirley gets the subject screwed around to China. "New man". . . . "Positive experience" . . . "Incredible energy". . . . "Changed our lives". . . . "Three women lost thirty-five pounds."

A look of thinly disguised boredom creeps across Johnny's face. He can feel the people nodding off all across America, or more horrible, switching over to ABC's *Wide World of Entertainment.* He tries to break. But Shirley keeps talking, groping, trying to find the words to articulate her experience in some way that will get through.

"I hate to interrupt," says Johnny finally, clutching a bottle of wax, "but we've got something to sell."

It is not easy to transpose myself from Room 148 of the Holiday Inn in Oakland, California, to rural China.

It takes two and a half hours to check in for our nineteen-hour charter flight to Hong Kong.

The Musak is merciless. As we board, it plays a bizarre version of a Clementi sonata with a rhumba beat.

We land at Anchorage to refuel. It is night, and our watches have long since lost touch with real time outside of the moving aircraft. Everyone is puffy and punchy. The whole airport is geared up for the growing influx of Japanese tourists and businessmen. Signs in Japanese direct travelers to the souvenirs: stuffed miniature polar bears, obscene ashtrays, midget Eskimo dolls.

Hong Kong

We land at Kai Tak Airport in Hong Kong, where three representatives from the China Travel Service await us. They provide our first glimpse of the world we will soon enter. They wear discrete black suits, white drip-dry shirts, dark ties and black shoes. We board a new Shanghai brand bus, and work our way through the crowded streets of Kowloon to the Golden Gate Hotel, a lusterless but clean and inexpensive hotel with which the Chinese communists do a lot of business.

There are jackhammers working everywhere in Hong Kong. The city is building, even though the lease runs out on part of this piece of colonial British real estate in twenty-three years.

The shopping areas around Nathan Road and the Star Ferry are filled with tourists and middle-class Chinese in exaggerated bell-bottom pants, thick cork platform shoes, rock-star haircuts, nose and eye jobs, and the latest women's fashions—a tenuous bridge between the refugee shacks which crowd the hillsides, and the world of Western fashion.

In a YMCA magazine shop, twelve-year-old Chinese girls in English school uniforms from the Immaculate Conception Missionary School pore over movie magazines with pictures of Western stars like Paul Newman and Burt Reynolds on the covers. The magazines are in Chinese.

Near Austin Road, a sooty flag of the First Battalion of the Royal Hampshire Regiment flaps listlessly over barracks on Gun Hill. The

British are the almost-forgotten caretakers of this Crown Colony.

In truth, Hong Kong is less a Colony than a free-fire zone for international business. It is bursting with commercial activity. Across the harbor on the Victoria side, the banks line De Voeux Road like Wall Street. Regal British lions cast in bronze lie sovereignly in front of the English-owned Hong Kong–Shanghai Bank, which retreated over the border with its name from its massive headquarters on the Shanghai Bund after 1949.

Not far down the line, two dynastic Chinese lions sit silently in stone in front of the tomblike Bank of China. There is no visible traffic passing through its grand front doors. On its roof are large illuminated Chinese characters reading "Long Live Chairman Mao." Immediately behind them is a tall modern building. In huge gleaming letters it identifies itself as "The Hong Kong Hilton."

The Crossing

Having been interested in China, and having traveled to Hong Kong often during past years, I had frequently eyed the old Victorian station of the Hong Kong–Canton Railway. The trains which left it dispatched people across a border which seemed impenetrable. There was a fascination with this station and its trains which no American could deny. For it led to one of the few places remaining in the world to which no amount of money or string-pulling could arrange entrance.

Today the trip takes about an hour. A few Nationalist flags fly over the shacks along the tracks. There are hawkers at each station in the New Territories. A beggar approaches the open train window, hands outstretched with the expression of a man who is about to be hit—a demeanor of almost stylized oppression. He seems to be so much in keeping with the natural order of things that one hardly takes notice.

It is Ch'ing Ming Chieh,* a spring festival when good Chinese on this side of the border go to "sweep the graves of their ancestors." Their hillside mausoleums honeycomb the landscape. The train is full of people traveling from the city to the countryside to pacify the dead.

The train stops. A Union Jack flies over the station house. Our passports are stamped DEPARTED by Hong Kong customs officials in Western uniforms. A hand-painted sign over a green doorway says, TO CHINA.

We walk down the tracks and cross the Lo Wu Bridge. Somewhere on that bridge we step over the line which divides the People's Republic of China from the rest of the world. It is the first international frontier I have ever crossed on foot.

The border has a relaxed provincial feel to it. Several men in blue tunics are sitting and chatting in the shade of a baggage cart. The crimson Chinese flag with five yellow stars flies overhead.

We are ushered into our first waiting room and given our first cup of green tea (the first of several thousand we are to drink before we return to this bridge on our way out). The waiting room is plain, and not calculated to impress anyone in the manner of certain countries which regularly repave the first few miles of highway just across the border.

We board an air-conditioned train for Canton. A red-cheeked young woman, fairly glowing with socialist health, moves down the aisle, swiftly and efficiently mopping the floor.

"It looks just like out of *China Reconstructs,*" a trip member whispers.

"Perhaps they copied it," someone else replies, and we laugh.

The train starts with a jolt. Soon we are gliding smoothly through the blinding green spring fields of the countryside.

---

*Throughout the book, I have used the Wade-Giles system of romanization, since it is more familiar to Westerners, even though a different system is currently in use in the People's Republic.

China by Air

There are no ads for airlines in China. The *People's Daily*, China's large national daily, does not run two-page spreads: "First Class Legroom in Coach" or "We Move Our Tail for You" or "Fly Me, I'm Comrade Wang."

All the commercial trifles which so consume the attention of the transportation industry elsewhere are absent here. Yet the flights leave on time, service is good, meals, which are usually eaten in airport restaurants during stopovers, are delicious. Moreover, the cost of flying is now dropping, beginning to be more competitive with train passage. Planes are almost always full. But as any Chinese will tell you, travel for private reasons is still unusual and costly. Most passengers are on official business for their factory, commune or organization.

The Chinese have one unique method of subsidizing transport for their own people. There are two fare schedules: one for foreign visitors, and one for Chinese. For instance, the cost of a one-way air ticket from Canton to Peking, about 1,300 miles, is 91 yuan for a Chinese. For a foreigner, it is 244 yuan.

Chinese airports are functional and unpretentious, although, in some cases they are positively bleak. The volume of air traffic which they handle is still small. Other than the foreign carriers like Japan Airlines, Air France, Pakistan Airways, Iran Air, Swissair, Ethiopian Airways, Royal Air Lao, and Aeroflot, which serve Canton, Shanghai and Peking, there is only one airline in China, China Airlines, run by the Civil Aviation Administration of China.

Besides the recent purchase of some English Trident jets and numerous older Russian-built prop and jet planes, China is now the owner of eleven new Boeing 707's. They are flown by all-Chinese crews.

Today, Canton's White Cloud Airport is filled with navy men in the blue uniforms with red and white trimmed hats. There is no indication of rank on any uniform. One of the English Tridents takes off. Everyone in the airport rises, walks to the window, and watches as the aircraft roars down the runway. Jet travel is still uncommon in China.

One of the Navy men catches me glancing at his ankles. Although the heat is stifling, the bottoms of a pair of pajamalike long underwear protrude from under his pants cuffs.

"Oh, I'm going to Peking, where it will be cold," he says, laughing at being discovered. As I am to learn, the Chinese have a passion for long underwear. They wear these individual furnaces (and often more than one pair) deep into the spring, long after most foreigners are sweating. It keeps them from getting colds, they claim.

A Tchaikovsky-like piano concerto, playing with much static over the P.A. system, is interrupted to announce our flight.

We walk out onto the runway apron with the navy men to where a brand new 707 is parked.

"It's a beautiful plane," I say to the navy man with the long underwear.

"It's made in America," he says laughing. I feel foolish.

Inside, the familiar surroundings are almost unsettling. All the brightly upholstered green seats are filled with men and women in Chinese military uniforms and caps. My initial feeling is something akin to that of imagining Viet Cong in the White House.

I see my first strikingly lovely Chinese woman. She is a cabin attendant. She is passing out Unity candy and gum as we take off. I can not take my eyes off her. As she moves down the aisle, I watch the eyes of the Peoples' Liberation Army (PLA) soldiers. Their gaze does not linger on her. Is anyone else in the plane thinking the thoughts I am? Is there a notion of "good looks" here?

She makes a second swing down the aisle, handing out small boxes of White Cloud brand cigarettes. I have heard that smoking is one Chinese indulgence about which Chairman Mao (himself a fanatic smoker) has said nothing. Soon the whole cabin is lost in a haze of smoke.

It is nighttime when we land in Peking. Flying is still a very special thrill for most Chinese. Everyone is craning to look out the windows. There are lights below, but no congested areas of the blinking neon so characteristic of our cities.

The airport is strangely quiet. There are hardly any other people —no bustle, no noise, no other flights arriving and taking off. Outside, as we board several mini-buses for the hour-long trip to downtown Peking, it is so still I can hear crickets.

The Peking Hotel

We are lodged on the top floor of the new wing of the Peking Hotel, a huge new building, beautiful in an awkward kind of way. Everything on the seventeen floors of this luxury hotel has been made in China, and the Chinese are recklessly proud of this accomplishment. It is strange that our first contact with this proletarian nation should be opulence, a trait so alien to the rest of China.

It is dawn. I look out over the tiled roofs of the old Foreign Legation Quarter, once surrounded by the open fields of the glacis, designed to give foreigners an open field of fire should trouble come, as it had during the Boxer Rebellion in 1900. Then foreigners barricaded themselves in the British Legation to ride out the final antiforeign spasm before the fall of the last Imperial Dynasty.

There is a wonderful feeling of exhilaration for me, being at last in Peking, after so many years of reading, studying, writing, teaching and thinking about China, a country which had existed for me much as the Forbidden City of the Emperors must have existed for the Chinese peasant over the centuries.

This morning, the Forbidden City, with its sloping roofs, is bathed in a mixture of smog and the orange light of the rising sun. The city is beautiful below me.

The Peking Hotel is divided into three sections like three archeological strata. The oldest section, once the Grand Hotel de Pekin, was built during World War I. Its massive creaky hardwood floors and dark-stained interior lobby evoke visions of Chinese warlords in their buffoonish medal-bedecked German-style uniforms. Like so little else in Peking, this architectural remnant summons back China's past, when warlord armies swept to and fro across China, and the titular seat of government in Peking was little more than a political plum for whichever warlord was in military ascendancy at the time. The regimes came and went like Latin American dictators, the names now long since forgotten.

Then, there is a newer section of the Hotel built in the nineteen fifties; a nondescript wing in the genre of "Polish Modern" constructed during the heyday of socialist bloc solidarity.

Finally, there is the new wing, seventeen floors of rooms with large plate glass windows and balconies. It is the tallest building in Peking. All day long one can see faces of passers-by peering in through holes in the outside shrubbery to gaze at this new socialist monument and the strange foreign guests and limousines which issue forth from it. The Peking Hotel is inhabited exclusively by foreigners. There are smaller, less grand hotels for the domestic trade.

The foreigners live in splendid isolation—a privilege which the Chinese afford them/us. Foreigners are grateful for the comfort. But it is also circumscribing; one is hardly in China in the Peking Hotel.

There are languages spoken here that I have never heard before. Albanian, Persian, Serbian, Finnish, Korean, Portuguese, Japanese and African dialects of every kind. At the moment there are a large number of Swiss, French and Belgians doing some sort of trade. The French have apparently just left in a huff because they were unable to work out an acceptable agreement on living arrangements for their petro-chemical technicians in Northeast China.

"They were turned down on rights of free travel and the duty-free import of food," says my French friend. "And, you know, wine is so important to them."

The ambassador to China from a certain Arab satrapy, who frequently hangs out in the Hotel's billiard room, manages to convince three female members of our group to join him for a late-night soirée at his apartment. They drink Black and White whiskey, listen to Frank Sinatra tapes, dance, and ward off the good ambassador's entreaties for sex.

Back in the lobby, twenty Japanese file out of the Shanghai-made elevators. They are wearing uniforms and red armbands. They form two neat columns and march off to breakfast. They are described as "friendly leftists." I can not help but wonder if they do not still summon up some bitter feelings among the older generation of Chinese who remember the occupation of their country.

Today, trade is expanding between the two neighbors, and of late, relations have grown friendlier, after a passing phase of Chinese fear over a resurgence of Japanese militarism. Numerous groups of Japanese businessmen, students and political personages now visit China.

"Most Japanese are very apologetic when they come here," says the floor attendant.

With the exception of some students, most of the visitors are men. They are neatly attired in dark Western suits, dark ties, and small lapel pins indicating their industrial affiliation. At airports, and in lobbies such as this, there are prolonged scenes of seemingly involuntary bowing. The inferiors back up before the step of the advancing superior, sometimes right into crowds of people or plate-glass windows. It is a kind of nervous prostration left over among the older people of Japan, which seems as out of place as burlesque in this land of upright equality.

On our way down, our already-full elevator stops at another floor. Three people squeeze in. One man is a tall, graying, Caucasian with a distinguished corporate demeanor. The second is a shorter graying Caucasian, jacketless, with a button-down shirt and necktie. The third is an even shorter Chinese man with well-combed hair, who speaks English with an American accent. He carries a sheaf of documents.

The bell rings. The elevator refuses to move. The taller man graciously leaves the overloaded elevator, telling his two protesting assistants that he will meet them downstairs. Their polite shoving and tugging match to see who stays in the elevator is suddenly interrupted by the automatic door, which, relieved of the weight of the taller man, suddenly closes. The elevator begins to descend. The shorter executive turns to face the multinational assemblage in the car.

"I hope you all realize that was the president of the Bank of America who just got out," he says, deadpan.

At the hotel magazine stand, there are two Australian businessmen looking hopelessly through the racks for some reading matter. But there is no *Time* or *Newsweek*, not even a London *Times* or a Washington *Post*. There are only copies of *Peking Review* (in Arabic, French, German, Esperanto, English, Spanish and Japanese). There are also copies of the works of Mao and the new Chinese Constitution. The magazine racks are otherwise filled with obscure foreign publications from overseas leftwing political groups currently in favor in official Chinese circles. One can buy a copy of *Revolution* (a U.S. publication of the Revolutionary Union), *The People's Voice* (New Zealand), *The Vanguard* (Australia), *La Voce Operaia* (Italy), *South Vietnam in Struggle* (The National Liberation Front), *Nhan Dan* (North Vietnam), *Roter Morgen* (Germany), *People's Star* (Japan), *Octobre* (Switzerland), *De Rote Vlag* (Holland).

Business is not brisk.

All Waste Is Treasure

Today I learn that all garbage from the Peking Hotel is collected each day, separated from inorganic waste, and finally taken by truck each evening to a suburban pig farm.

Most sewage in Peking is collected from each house by a "honey bucket man" *(fen-fu)*. Sewage from larger buildings in China, unconnected to sewers, is held in large holding tanks. It too is finally pumped out by large "honey trucks" and taken outside the city to agricultural areas, where it is ponded and allowed to anaerobically digest before being used as fertilizer.

Several larger cities like Mukden and Shanghai have developed larger sewers which recycle nutrient-rich treated effluent into the green agricultural belts around the heart of the city. Solids, or sludge, are used as fertilizer. The treated effluent is used for irrigation.

"All Waste Is Treasure," say the Chinese.

As the Tientsin Municipal Revolutionary Committee Writing Group noted in an article on waste:

"The process of production is one in which man knows, transforms and utilizes nature. But nature's resources can not be fully utilized by producing one product. In making one product, resources are partially transformed into this product, and the rest becomes 'waste.'

"The question is how to look at this waste; from what point of view, and with what attitude?

"From the metaphysical point of view, waste can not be used and should be gotten rid of. On the contrary, the materialist dialectical view holds that what is waste and what is not waste are relative. There is nothing in the world which is absolute waste. Waste under one condition may be valuable under a different one."

A Factory

Breakfast in the Peking Hotel is served in a large sunny dining room. Many of the white-clothed tables have condiments of different nationalities at the center. Imported olive oil for the Italians; some marmalade for the British; a half-finished bottle of French wine; a jar of instant coffee—perhaps for Americans? We eat yogurt, fried eggs, toast, plum jam and a very strange cup of coffee served from a thermos bottle.

Having finished breakfast, we gather in the lush red-carpeted lobby to meet with our six interpreters and ready ourselves for the day's outing, a trip to a printing factory.

To get to the factory, we travel through the back streets of Peking. Everywhere there are signs of construction. Large stacks of bricks are piled up in the middle of the streets next to temporary brick kilns. Clay is brought in from the suburbs in horse and ox carts. Bricks are fired right on the construction sight.

"It's practical, you see," says Lao Chao, one of our interpreters. Farther down the road, several hundred middle-school students plant trees along the street, even though it is Sunday. "This is their day off," says Lao Chao. "They are volunteers." He speaks as though this were the most natural way in the world to spend one's day off.

The cities, like the barren country mountaintops, are being covered with trees. Shade trees, trees for wood, fruit trees. China, for centuries deforested by a fuel-hungry people, is just beginning to be tinted with a suggestion of springtime green here in Peking as all these new trees begin to bud.

We are greeted at the printing factory by the "responsible comrades." In a gray almost-dark meeting room, we are treated to our first "brief introduction" (B.I.), a form of discourse with which we are to become all too familiar as the weeks and months go on.

Since 1966, we are told, this factory has printed thirty-six million copies of works by Marx and Lenin, eighty million copies of Mao's works, two hundred and twenty million copies of *H'ung Ch'i (Red Flag)*, the official Party theoretical organ, a billion and a half pictures of Chairman Mao and eighty-eight million copies of *China Reconstructs*, China's glossy color-photo *Life*-style periodical which comes in numerous languages. The factory uses ten thousand tons of paper a year.

We are pleasantly but firmly herded through the massive plant. Some of us try to take notes. Others struggle with photos as the tide of the tour sweeps all before it. I am not sure what it is that we should be learning here. What I do know is that we quickly lose all sense of where we have been and where we are going.

"Sorry. We must move faster. We have more workshops to see," says a guide.

A short worker in a blue factory uniform has been walking beside me. We have been exchanging smiles.

"What is your name?" I ask him.

"Ch'ien," he replies.

"Ch'ien?"

"Yes. It means money," he says, exploding in laughter.

"Are you a big capitalist?" I ask.

"No! No! Not me," he says, laughing and waving his hands as though the idea might bite him. "And this . . . This is Comrade Chin —Mr. Gold," he says introducing a friend whose surname is the same character as that for gold.

Comrade Chin is now also laughing. "We are a good pair," he says.

We return to the meeting room for questions. We are asked to write down all our questions before the session begins, an annoying habit which the Chinese sometimes seem addicted to. Upon occasion, they later ask us to write down questions before we even arrive at the factory, commune or meeting hall. This procedure tends to guarantee a certain kind of thorough answer (if they want to answer at all), while robbing any discussion of the spontaneity and free flow to which most Americans are accustomed.

"In our country," says a woman worker, "people aren't working for themselves or company owners. They are working for their country and socialism."

"When we work, we really feel good," says my acquaintance, Comrade Ch'ien. "And, you know, when we can't fill our quotas, we don't feel good. So, if someone doesn't do his or her part, they will feel badly. You remember the chart we saw on the wall where everyone but one man had a plus sign in front of his name? (He refers to a work chart in one of the workshops.) Well, everyone will get together and talk to that comrade, talk things over and try and help him."

A factory leader answers a question on the position of women in the factory. "Confucius used to say that if a woman boarded a boat, the boat would sink. Then they said that if women flew in planes, the planes would crash. Well, you came on a plane. And weren't there women on it? It didn't crash." He laughs. "And now, in new China, women are even pilots. Yes, there are really five women pilots."

He turns to a question on the Cultural Revolution, an almost unavoidable subject in China.

"Before the Cultural Revolution, we used to think about profit all the time," he says. "If we couldn't turn a profit for the factory, we just didn't print something. I remember once we ran off a whole bunch of flower-print tablecloths for decoration. But then we asked ourselves, Why? Yes, we could sell them, but what help were they? So, we made a criticism of this line. And we had to educate some who wanted to continue to print only high-profit items. Now our line is to print things for the workers, peasants and soldiers."

"For the workers, peasants and soldiers." This is one of the most common refrains in China.

Death

Tung Pi-wu is dead at age ninety. A landowner's son from Hupei Province, six years older than Mao, he first joined revolutionary activities before the fall of the Ch'ing Dynasty in 1911. He is one of the last survivors of the First Party Congress of the Chinese Communist Party held in Shanghai in 1921. Today the Chinese are mourning not only the passing of this one man, but the passing of a generation—a generation of men and women that brought about one of the greatest transformations in history. Tung's life bridged the poles: from the days of the cantankerous and aging Empress Dowager Tz'u Hsi to the days of Sun Yat-sen nationalism and the warlord strife which followed; from the heyday of Chiang Kai-shek to the birth of peasant communism late in the twenties; from the days of the epic Long March and life in the caves at Yenan through the dark years of World War II, the Japanese occupation, to the Chinese Civil War from which the Communists emerged victorious at last.

In recent years, the aging Tung had served as Vice-President of the Republic. But, in fact, with the removal of Liu Shao-ch'i from office during the Cultural Revolution, Tung had fulfilled the duties of President, alongside his old comrade Mao, who was Chairman of the Party.

Today, the flags hang at half mast around T'ien An Men. The sound of muted funereal music comes from the courtyard surrounding the ancient T'ai Miao in the Forbidden City. The stately T'ai Miao, once the ancestral temple of the ruling dynasty, now serves as a funeral site for China's revolutionary rulers.

There is a hush as we walk into the old cypress garden of the Forbidden City, now a park. On normal days, the courtyards and plazas are filled with working families strolling together on their days off. But today it is empty.

A seemingly endless line of students, factory workers and PLA soldiers in olive drab uniforms with red patches stand, waiting patiently to file through the temple and pay their final respects. Black bunting is draped on the last tile roof gate to the courtyard. Several young women silently give us black armbands as we move quickly past the waiting soldiers in a special line. In China, even at funerals, the foreigner is received as a privileged guest. We walk with Arabs, Africans and North Vietnamese under a black banner which is inscribed with the characters for THE MEMORY OF OUR PROLETARIAN LEADER WILL NEVER FADE.

Within the T'ai Miao, the ashes of Tung Pi-wu lie in an urn on an altarlike platform beneath a large photograph of him with his famous drooping walrus mustache. The urn is covered by a small Chinese flag. Beside it is a huge flowered wreath with a white ribbon inscribed with the three characters for MAO TSE TUNG.

Tung's aging widow stands in a receiving line to shake hands with the mourners. Her eyes are closed. She rocks back and forth slowly in the arms of a young family member who holds her gently by the shoulders, as if her frail body would topple over in grief if unattended. I ask Hsiao Yao, an interpreter, to help me translate a memorial message on one of the wreaths. His face seems unmoved as I whisper my question to him. He turns to me as if to answer, but he is unable to speak.

The Chinese do not dwell on the subject of death, even when asked about it. One almost never hears people, even old people, discuss death or identify with it in the manner of, say, the Irish. The only voluntary mention I have heard of death was when a cadre proudly proclaimed that the State guarantees the cost of a simple funeral for everyone. It is one of the Five Guarantees: Food, Clothing, Housing, Medicine and Burial. But this country is so busy being born that death seems to be little more than an unavoidable and passing intrusion, instead of an obsession or a pastime.

In the city, the dead are almost invariably cremated.

"Why bury a dead person and take up all that space?" says a Chinese student, when we later pass a cemetery which is being exhumed in Shanghai to make way for new housing. "Once you put people in the ground like that, it's not easy to get them back." He laughs at the apparent absurdity of digging up a graveyard, and then says, "Things aren't the way they used to be."

In the countryside for centuries before 1949, funerals had been the curse of the peasantry. The death of a family member, particularly an elder or parent, could push a family that was poor enough in ordinary times hopelessly into debt. The social and religious pressure to furnish an expensive funeral for a departed ancestor was enormous. It was a child's binding filial duty to his or her parent to provide a full brace of ceremonies and accouterments to usher the spirit into the afterworld. On numerous occasions afterward, recurring ceremonies had to be performed to celebrate good harvests or drive off evil spirits.

Those elaborate practices are often referred to as "ancestor worship." But it was not as though the deceased were granted godlike status through the funereal ceremonies. It was simply that even in death Confucian practices required correct relations with one's elders, on the assumption that they would somehow keep channels between the living and the unknown in good repair. It was commonly assumed that any insult to the deceased or desecration of the grave would bring repercussions on the family. In old China, a peasant could hardly suffer a greater sacrilege than the despoiling of the family graves. Chinese history is replete with calls to defend the land in war and "protect the graves of our ancestors." The process was costly and time consuming.

"All that has changed now," says Lao Geng, a peasant turned driver whom I later meet in the countryside. "You know, my father passed away last year. He was just a poor peasant. He worked all his life for a landlord. It was hard. But at least he had his old age after Liberation. Anyway, we buried him. In the countryside people still usually do not like to cremate their dead like in the cities. There is still a bit of conservatism, maybe even superstition, among some of the older peasants. We just aren't as used to the new ideas, and we don't like to see our dead family members burned up.

"When someone dies in this area, we usually call a meeting. The deceased is dressed in a new suit of clothes, and laid out on a pallet. Then, after a short gathering where friends might speak a few words of praise, the body is taken up to the hills to an arranged place, and buried in a small cavelike hole dug sideways into the earth cliffs. The family usually follows along. They bear brightly colored paper wreaths which they leave at the burial place. But nothing is expensive. They don't even use coffins now. Maybe in some other places they do. But not here. In fact, after they lay the body in the cave, they take the wood pallet back. And it's not like when each family had a plot right out in the middle of a good field because they worried about the geomancy *(feng-shui)*. No. That wastes land. So now the dead are just put into the cliff bank. Then the family will close off the mouth of the cave with stones and earth. And that's it. There are no mourners, no big procession, no one spends any money. That is discouraged."

Along a country road, I later observe a family bearing a body to burial.

A teen-aged boy and an elderly woman walk slowly down the shoulder of the road. They walk among the other foot traffic, donkey carts and hand tractors, pulling trailers of coal, stone and sand. They carry light wooden frames decorated with brightly colored crepe paper. They hold them aloft on short sticks—like picket signs. Two small children with miniature wreaths follow along behind. No one talks.

Coming down the hill a short way behind them is a young man straining to hold back a hand cart made out of rough wood. A red flower-print quilt *(pei-wo)* is spread out over the unseen body in the cart bed. The smooth clean white sheet sown to the underside of the quilt contrasts starkly with the gray splintery wood of the cart's sides.

Slowly they move down the road out of sight, bearing their departed to a final hillside resting place.

The Streets—Peking

Walking the streets of Peking.

People are curious. On the side streets they stop in their tracks and stare. Large groups of children follow Caucasians for blocks, their curiosity tinged with uncertainty. A camera aimed in their direction sends them giggling, running and screaming.

An occasional muted *"ta pi-tzu,"* meaning "big nose," can be heard from one of the braver smiling children, reminiscent of the times past when foreigners were called *yang kuei-tzu,* or foreign devils.

But times have changed. People are still curious, although not stupefied. The Chinese have indeed been isolated from the outside. In a real sense, particularly here in North China, they are untouched by the intrusion and confusion of the world beyond. Few tourists, few businessmen and few signs of the capitalist world outside have been allowed to permeate China. Mao has kept the Chinese people focused on revolution, and as much as possible, untempted by the world of money and things, seductions which would now be an impediment to his passion to build socialism. China is a land of possibility, but not variety. It is a nation where the word "communism" is *the* possibility. It is the only acceptable message. One does not get the sense that people who stop and stare are primitive or unintelligent. It is that they are not cosmopolitan, a trait which has no function in Chinese practical vision.

The main streets are full of shoppers and strollers. Everyone is dressed in the practical unisex clothes which are worn throughout China. These baggy uniformlike tunics—consisting of pants, jacket and cap—far from blurring people into sameness, seem to accentuate their faces. The question of the shape of a person's body is a moot one in China.

I sit and watch people pass by. And then, as if scripted by my own thoughts, a European woman walks through this flow of Chinese faces. There is an unmistakable air of self-consciousness about her. She is wearing a tight sleeveless yellow top, a rather short skirt and low heels. Her breasts protrude in an almost shocking manner. It is not that they are ugly or unattractive, but that they are utterly out of place in this busy street of comrades whose bodies and shapes remain so unannounced behind their sensible tunics. Hundreds of eyes are riveted on her dyed and set orange hair.

Further down the street, a line forms behind a newspaper vender selling the *People's Daily.*

I stop to look at a birth-control display in a drugstore window. Two young girls wearing Red Guard armbands notice me, turn toward each other, half amused, half embarassed.

Arching up behind Wang Fu Ching is the sloping roof of a massive building in the traditional architectural style. It was once Peking Union Medical College, built by the Rockefeller Foundation in the twenties. It was the finest medical facility in China. During the Cultural Revolution it was renamed "The Anti-Imperialist Hospital." Now it is the Capital Hospital, and still an excellent one.

Across the street, and further on, there is a steady flow of people moving in and out of one of the branches of the Peking City Department Store. Inside are several spacious marble floors filled with counters of goods. People walk around in a leisurely manner, doing as much looking as shopping. Cigarettes range from .15 yuan to .38 yuan.* Dark glasses sell from 3 yuan to 4 yuan. Fan or Panda Brand detergent sells for .53 yuan in the large size. Alarm clocks are 12 yuan. There is a great variety of photo equipment for amateur photographers. Leather soccer balls cost 19 yuan. Sweaters range from 20 to 30 yuan. Wool blankets cost 48 yuan; long underwear, 2.49 yuan; flashlights, 1.50 yuan; popguns, 1.10 yuan; plum wine, 1.30 yuan a

*One yuan equals $.45 in U.S. currency.

quart, and toothpaste ranges from .40 to .60 yuan.

Good-quality plastic raincoats cost 4 yuan. I buy one. Canned goods are expensive: pineapple is 1.99 yuan; apples, 1.24 yuan; mandarin oranges, 1.36 yuan, and jam is 3 yuan.

Long-playing records cost about 2.50 yuan and include such songs as "Militia Women in the Grasslands Bring Coal to the People's Liberation Army in the Snow," "An Ode to Peking," "Sailing the Seas Depends on the Helmsman," "Songs of the Great Leap Forward," "Chasing the Truck" and "Friendship Springs from the Ping-Pong Table."

It is strange how being physically here, watching people move about their daily tasks, removes the sense of coldness and remoteness in which, until recently, China has been shrouded for most Americans. China has been a political system, a world force, a military power and an abstraction. It is a relief to feel part of that abstraction reconstitute itself into a more concrete reality.

Tomorrow is May Day, or International Labor Day, as it is called here in China. It is celebrated as a three-day holiday, a time for families to reunite, one of the few times in China when work actually stops.

In celebration, lights fringe the tall buildings—a sort of Chinese Christmas. A warm night breeze blows through the budding trees. Almost all of the stores are closed now. The streets are full of people out strolling. A whole family on a bicycle cart pedals slowly down Ch'ang An Chieh. The mother, two children, and an old granny with bound feet sit together on the small flatbed behind the father, who pedals languidly. One of the small children wears a hat with the characters for HERO stitched on the brim. The eldest son, about twelve, rides alongside the cart on the family bicycle like a skiff next to a large boat.

A Passing

Today my French journalist friend tells me that Chiang Kai-shek has died on Taiwan.

His death represents the end of one of the great political struggles in history: the Nationalists vs. the Communists, Chiang vs. Mao. The event has not yet been mentioned in the Chinese press. I ask a waitress if she knows whether the news is true or not. She looks blank and confused at even hearing the name Chiang Kai-shek.

His death is finally announced in a minuscule notice in the *People's Daily.* No one rejoices. No one mourns. Here in Peking, the news is received with equanimity. Witnessing this passing is strange for anyone who remembers Chinese history. What is confusing for a foreigner is the apparent absence of any hatred, or even gloating, over the end of this much-reviled adversary. The Chinese seem to have a very special means of handling such situations. They hate what Chiang stood for and the misery he caused, but not Chiang as a person.

In any event, the Chinese are so preoccupied with politics of the present and future that they seem to have little time and emotional energy to waste on past feuds which have been won, and which are not likely to recur.

Teeth

I ask Lao Yao, from the Chinese Association for Friendship with Foreign Countries, to open his mouth so that I can look at his teeth. He laughs with embarrassment. He is reluctant at first. Then he attempts to satisfy my curiosity by opening his mouth—but only about halfway.

"Wider," I say.

He can't laugh and open his mouth at the same time. But I get a peek inside. He has no cavities.

I ask Shih Ch'eng-hui, an interpreter, to open her mouth. She waves me off, refusing even to speak, as if I could somehow pry her mouth open if she parted her lips. I ask her how to say "cavity" in Chinese. She finally relinquishes and answers. She tells me that she has none.

The Chinese eat almost no canned foods with sugar, since they are still much more expensive than fresh seasonal fruit and vegetables. They drink little soda pop and eat virtually no processed foods or junk food.

"Do the Chinese have a lot of cavities?" I ask.

"No," she says. "Some of the older people or peasant children may have some trouble. But now most people are conscious of how to take care of their teeth. There are health posters all over. We are told to brush them, to use toothpicks and not drink things which are too hot or too cold." (The Chinese make some of the finest toothpicks in the world—sturdy, slender and durable—from reeds and bamboo.)

"Do the children like to eat candy?"

"Oh, yes, of course."

"Do children get an allowance to spend themselves?"

"Well, you see, young children must first learn how to spend money wisely. They do not have money until they work. Their parents will buy things for them. Otherwise they would just go out and gorge themselves on candy and toys. Besides, candy is expensive. The children do not go out and eat a lot of sweet things, so their mouths are not always watering for candy and ice cream the way I think yours does."

She smiles, revealing a beautiful set of white front teeth.

"Fall" or "Liberation"

The May Day holiday continues. The streets are crowded, and the stores are full of people buying special holiday food. The only outward signs of anything unusual are the abnormally large crowds gathered around the display cases where newspapers are posted. The Vietnam war is over.

"When did Saigon fall?" I ask.

"No!" says Hsiao Yao, who is in charge of our trip. "Saigon has not fallen! It has been liberated!" He has the rather stern look on his face which he wears when he makes corrections on serious political points.

Members of the foreign community are either exuberant or relieved. But the news of the unconditional surrender seems not to have disturbed Peking much. As the city goes about its business, I wonder how the shock waves are hitting back home, filling newspapers with massive black headlines and preempting normal programming on TV. Here, there is a muffled quality to outside news. The victory is received gladly, but in stride.

Chairman Mao and other high Chinese officials have just sent telegrams to the Provisional Revolutionary Government of South Vietnam and to the Democratic Republic of Vietnam (North) extending their "warmest congratulations and highest salute for your firm resolve to fight and win."

They note that the sudden victory "Ushers in a new era, an era of liberation of Vietnam, and has great historical significance" which "inspires all oppressed nations and peoples engaged in struggle, and sets a brilliant example in the anti-imperialist cause of the people of the world."

From here in Peking, these official words seem to penetrate in a way which they can not when read from abroad. There is something about looking out over this city while reading even such clichéd language which gives it a different feeling and meaning. When the Chinese write that "a small country can surely defeat an outwardly strong enemy as long as they dare rise in struggle and take up arms in a just war to oppose an unjust war," and when that prophecy has just come to pass in its starkest form, one can not help but pay deeper heed to these words.

When the Chinese speak of Indochina, they are also speaking of their own experience in civil war against Chiang Kai-shek's U.S.-supplied and backed troops. And they too won their struggle, and the evidence of their continuing efforts to consolidate that victory are everywhere around us.

At a public park surrounding the Temple of Heaven, freshly made red-and-white banners have been hung up.

WARMLY CELEBRATE THE GREAT VICTORY OF THE
VIETNAMESE PEOPLE'S LIBERATION OF SAIGON.

Makeshift paper posters appear here and there throughout the city. A delegation of high-ranking Chinese shows up at the Vietnamese embassy in Peking. They are greeted with firecrackers and given warm hugs by Tran Binh, the Chargé d'Affaires, who tells them, "You stood by us when we were in need; you share our joy when we are victorious."

I hear that a larger mass rally is scheduled later in the afternoon at T'ien An Men Square. I walk out to see what I can learn.

It is a hot, glaring afternoon. In one corner of the vast square, several thousand people wait in line in front of the Great Hall of the People. They are factory workers. As they begin to file slowly up the stairway under the large stone columns, a group of about forty men in tan cotton shirts, pants and rubber sandals, emerge from a building on the other side of the square. They walk to the Heroes' Monument in the center, so unflamboyantly and inconspicuously that the other people in the square hardly seem aware of their presence.

They walk up the steps of the monument and pause silently before a stone frieze depicting revolutionary soldiers in combat. Above the frieze, written in Mao hand, are the large characters for "THE PEOPLE'S HEROES WILL NEVER BE FORGOTTEN."

Then, without fanfare, they descend the steps. As they approach, I notice that each man is wearing a minuscule pin on the breast of his shirt. It is the flag of North Vietnam, a yellow star on a red background.

People seem neither surprised nor jubilant. The monumental collapse of Pnom Penh and Saigon has produced no cathartic tidal wave of relief here.

"Oh, yes, we are happy," one worker says to me. "But it was always inevitable, you see."

Never having doubted for a moment that the war would end in the defeat of the Americans, the Chinese have accepted the conclusion of this war, much as they might greet the rising sun: they are glad, but not surprised.

"The real test of an analysis is not when a prediction comes true," comments another worker, "but whether it comes true."

University Encounter

"We want workers to be intellectuals and intellectuals to be workers," says Chou Chün-yeh, director of Revolutionary Education at the University of Peking. "Why should theory be divorced from practice? Why should students be locked up in school and kept apart from workers, peasants and soldiers? What we really want to do is run our schools with the doors open. We want our schools to be in society, not above it."

Peking University is the grandfather of Chinese universities. It was to Peking University that young Mao Tse-tung came as a library assistant in 1918. His real motive was to be near the center of politics and to study with Li Ta-chao, one of China's earliest Marxist intellectuals. Since that time, Peking University has undergone many changes, not the least of which was during the Cultural Revolution. In fact, I get the distinct sense, sitting here today listening to the brief introduction (B.I), that many of the issues raised during the Cultural Revolution are still unresolved and sensitive. There is a stiffness in the room—a formalism which suggests tensions that are unrelieved.

"Students used to study about literature," says the Vice-Chancellor of the Literature Department. "They memorized the poets Tu Fu and Li Po from ancient times. But what good did it all do? Old literature has a use, but if it is not related to socialist construction, it doesn't mean much. So our courses are not like they were before the Cultural Revolution, when most of them didn't relate to anything practical. Nor are the exams the same. Now we don't just want to trip up our students. The most important part of the exam, after all, is to help students learn how to analyze problems. So sometimes we don't even ask students to take formal exams. We just ask them to fulfill certain projects. There are no grades. In the past we graded students on questions we asked them. But maybe some students couldn't answer one question and failed. What help was that to anyone?"

We take a tour of one of the seven factories which the university maintains on campus as adjuncts to various departments. They, like the links the university maintains with some sixty-five other factories throughout the country, represent concrete evidence of the continuing effort to keep up contact with the practical world outside.

We visit a pharmaceutical factory, and tour the workrooms filled with temperature controlled vats and other equipment made and manned by the students.

"It used to be that students just wanted to write a thesis, get it published, and get famous," says our guide, looking at several students watching over the dials and thermometers. "And, you know, if they ever got into a factory which made what they were studying about, they wouldn't have had the foggiest idea what to do."

In another room there is a small display of medicines which have been manufactured at the university factory. There are bottles of round-worm pills, vials of anti-shock medicine and a new kind of anesthetic.

"We used to import this anesthetic from Russia at seventeen yuan an ampule. But then they cut us off in 1959. So we had to learn to make it ourselves. Now we make it at a cost of two yuan."

We are back in the meeting room again after our all-too-short and superficial tour. This is a frustration which is to occur again and again. It is a frustration of being able to communicate only on a level of formal political ideas. A coldness. An avoidance of real interchange. A scripted learning experience in which I collect facts and points about the "system." They are interesting, but, as these comrades around the table answer written questions and recite familiar litanies extolling the Cultural Revolution and the present campaign to Criticize Lin Piao and Confucius, I feel an absence. The exchange is too controlled. Questions go unanswered. Politeness seems to require that they not be pressed.

"It would be interesting to hear some of you discuss the problems you yourselves encountered during the Cultural Revolution," I say, hoping to steer the discussion toward more personal political descriptions.

There is a silence.

"Well, who would like to go first?" I say, smiling, hoping that perhaps a little levity will break the coldness. It does not. The question is still ignored.

What are some of these older professors thinking as they hear us getting "B.I.'d"? Some of them have lived through half a century of history. Do they secretly think of us as naïve and uninquiring? Does anyone else in the room, waiting his turn to speak, secretly yearn to reach out and talk more informally? I do not know. They are silent.

"There was a struggle over whether or not exams should be given by professors," says the vice-chancellor of the literature department. "In the mathematics department there was one professor nicknamed

'Leng Ping-ping' (Cold Ice). He was called that because he only did three things: he brought pieces of paper to class, used his mouth, and then used his feet to leave again. He only met his students when it came time for a class or an exam. He never cared whether or not his students understood him. The more confused a student became, the happier he was. And he loved to give hard exams. Once he wanted to give one peasant student a hard time, so he gave him a 59.5 just to make him barely fail."

We are given a long history of the Cultural Revolution at the university. Although most of the information is available in books, members of our group take notes. Some take notes regardless of what is said, feeling almost unconsciously that the Chinese would be offended if the note-taking were to cease. A strange transformation seems to occur in many Americans when they get to China. Leftists, in particular, seem to lose their sense of balance. They forget they are not Chinese. They have a willingness to believe that China works perfectly, a willingness that is enforced by the apparent weaknesses of their own country. Learning becomes not so much a matter of delving into the world around them, as of obediently recording what is said. And surprisingly enough, the Chinese, the apostles of experience, often seem just as relieved to escape with a recitation of words and ideas.

The history of the Cultural Revolution grinds on. Even some of the Chinese students have started yawning. How many times have *they* heard this before, as endless groups troop through this meeting hall from almost every country in the world? One student of English, whom I talked to as we visited the grave of the American writer Edgar Snow (which is on the university campus), begins to drift asleep. Her head falls slowly chestward. Her chin hits her collarbone, and she wakes up. The speaker drones on. He does not speak of immediate political battles and disagreements. This does not come easily to the Chinese. They speak of the past, but not of the present—the unresolved present. The Chinese rarely seem to speak of their individual reactions. Perhaps it is because their experiences are primarily group experiences. I keep wanting to try to draw the conversation into a more personal vein, into retorts and descriptions which will reflect their own feelings and judgments rather than the current political line. But today our hosts avoid such attempts. They let questions pass, change the subject and return to discussions of movements, political tendencies and ideas. There is a difference in the way we as two different peoples seem to communicate. There is also a difference in the way we experience, and what we extract afterward as of significance. In China, what is meaningful (at least, what is worth recounting to foreigners) is rarely one's individual experiences. People are fulfilled not by becoming themselves, but by becoming part of the collective whole. And thus it is perhaps not unsurprising that what they wish to pass on as significant to us is the broad social and political movements which surround them, and not the pain or joy of their private lives.

Humor

The Chinese laugh easily. But often one is perplexed at what it is they find amusing.

Tonight we are all sitting around a table. The Chinese are trying to think up jokes in Chinese, and we are trying to think up jokes in English. We have trouble finding any that we feel the opposite camp would appreciate.

Finally Lao Chao starts to tell us a story which he says is a joke (hsiao-hua). It is about a beautiful girl who is riding in a sedan chair before Liberation. She passes a monk.

"And, you see, the monk feels very depressed because he is unable to marry her," says Lao Chao. His face breaks into a smile, more because he sees the blankness on all of our faces than because he is amused by his "punch line."

"It must lose a lot in translation," he says, now laughing with a twinge of embarrassment.

Chinese humor is elusive to foreigners. Often it is of a political nature, or involves some play on words which is impossible to convey in another language. For instance, at a banquet in Canton, we are told the following joke by a jovial old veteran revolutionary.

"In olden times, there was this *chü-jen* [a scholar who has passed the first rank of examinations for government officialdom]. He is making a journey through the countryside, and he gets to a stream. He asks a peasant working in an adjacent field how to get across. The peasant says, 'Jump' [*t'iao*]. So the scholar foolishly jumps with both feet and lands with a splash in the middle of the creek."

No one laughs except the Chinese.

The point is that there is a difference between the words *t'iao* and *yao* in Chinese. The difference is something like that between jumping with both feet (as in the standing broadjump) and leaping with one foot leading. The scholar hears the word *t'iao*, which means to jump with both feet, and in his pedantic academic way, *t'iao*'s right into the creek, when any practical soul would have known that regardless of the word spoken by the peasant, one needed to leap or *yao* to get across the creek.

Then there is the joke about the peasant who lived in Shansi Province before Liberation. One day as he is just finishing work in the fields, he decides to count his plots before he goes down the mountain. He is a poor peasant and only has seven small plots. But count as he will, he can only tally six of them. Then, in despair, as he readies himself to leave without having located the seventh, he picks up his jacket from the ground. He finds the seventh under his jacket.

Humor in China rarely seems to involve cruelty, sarcasm or cynicism at someone else's expense. Indeed, one rarely sees anyone laugh derisively when someone else is awkward, hurt or foolish. The first reaction seems to be to help. There are, however, exceptions for well-defined and officially approved enemies who are unambiguously assumed to be beyond resurrection or redemption.

The anti-Russian (or anti-revisionism) jokes are in this black category. There are, in fact, endless Khruschev (pronounced *Ho-lu-hsiao fu*) jokes (which the Chinese will tell you were imported from the Soviet Union), like the one where he gets a craving for some pork chops at a time when meat is very scarce. So he tells his wife to go down to the market to try and buy a whole pig. Mrs. Khruschev starts off with a baby carriage for town, planning to smuggle a pig disguised as a baby from the market to her house.

Finally, she finds a pig, has its feet tied up, and gets some peasants to help her put it into the carriage with a blanket over it. Then she commences to push it home.

When she reaches their mansion, she tries to sneak in through a side gate, but an old gardener sees her and comes running over to help. Noticing the carriage, he says,

"My goodness, I didn't know you had a new baby."

She tries to push by, but the gardener won't let her pass unattended. Finally, he reaches into the carriage to cooch the baby. He pulls back the blanket, sees the pig, laughs and says, "Isn't he the spitting image of his father!" I also heard a Khruschev joke about the time he's told that a new postage stamp with his face on it is receiving a lot of complaints from people because it won't stick to letters. So he decides to dress up in a disguise and go down to the post office himself and see what the trouble is. Arriving at the post office, he buys a stamp, spits on the back and slaps it on the envelope. It seems to stick.

"What's all this talk about these stamps falling off of envelopes?" he asks the clerk.

"Oh," says the clerk, "most people spit on the other side."

Another great mine of humorous stories in China revolves around people misunderstanding one or another of the hundreds of dialects which are native to different localities. Sometimes people will mimic the accent of another dialect. Or they might tell a story in Peking, for instance, about someone from Hunan ordering a meal. Invariably he will be trying to order a simple bowl of noodles, but the waiter will misunderstand and think he is being insulted or sworn at instead. The resulting confusion cracks up the Chinese, who are still very aware of local and regional differences in language and food.

Another form of humor which one hears on the radio, at shows, or even over the P.A. system on trains (which *can* be turned off), is called "cross talk" *(hsiang-sheng)*. In cross talk, two men carry on a fast repartee. One man, usually a little slower than the other, plays a kind of fall guy. But often, he will get smart by the end of the routine and get a few laughs off his partner.

One of the more popular cross-talk routines in China now is about the Tan-Zam (Tanzania-Zambia) Railway, which the Chinese have just finished designing, financing and building to provide Zambia with an alternate route to the sea, thereby by-passing Rhodesia. In the routine, one comedian tells the other that while he was in Africa working on the railroad, he stayed in the finest quarters, with the most luxurious soft bed, and in an environment of exquisite color. After being asked by the fall guy where this luxurious place might be, he confesses, to the delight of the audience, that the fine quarters were the outdoors, that the soft bed was the grass, and the exquisite colors the earth and sky.

In Tachai (the rural commune on which we will work for three weeks), there is a joke circulating, allegedly told by Ch'en Yung-kuei (former leader of Tachai, and now Vice-Premier in Peking). Ch'en has worn the traditional headgear of the Shansi peasant all his life. It consists of a white towel-like bandana tied around his head. The peasants wear these bandanas for protection from the sun, wind and dust.

Someone was supposed to have asked Ch'en why he wore his bandana in Peking in the Great Hall of the People, if there was no *feng* (wind) inside. Ch'en is said to have replied that while there was no *feng* (meaning "wind"), there was a fair amount of *feng* (which also means "craziness").

"Watch Out for the Foreign Guests"

The May Day celebrations go on today. We drive through traffic-free Peking streets to the Summer Palace in the suburbs. Its antecedent, the Yuan Ming Yuan, was sacked, looted and burned by the British and French in 1860. It was rebuilt by the Empress Dowager Tz'u Hsi, at the turn of the century, with funds earmarked to build a navy. Her only nautical contribution was the famous stone boat which she had built in the shallows of a large hand-dug lake. The boat served as a teahouse.

Today thousands flood the courtyards, walkways and buildings. Students with bright-colored flags row on the lake. Their boats are tied bow-to-stern in long convoys, boys in one boat, girls in another.

Three of us become separated from the main group in the crush. We find ourselves alone with two interpreters. In my view, our separation is no great loss, since our group is large and unwieldy in such crowded circumstances. But our interpreters are possessed with the idea of regaining the group, whereas we three Americans feel comfortable and happy in this divided situation.

After several hours of intense looking, we finally meet up with the others. The interpreters are relieved.

We begin to wind our way out of the seemingly endless gardens and courtyards back to our waiting bus. The crowds are particularly dense near the main gate. A Chinese woman runs headlong into me.

"Watch out for the foreign guests," Lao Chang says firmly to her without a smile. The woman looks up, sees all the white faces, and retreats in confusion.

So often we receive rarefied treatment. We are handled by our Chinese guides like clumsy overbred children who might perish without close minute-by-minute attention. We have so many self-indulgent un-Chinese needs that seem to confuse our hosts. They try to accommodate them graciously, but in the process their impression of us as vulnerable and somewhat precious is evidently reconfirmed.

Many of us need coffee daily. Various members have not been sufficiently inspired by socialism to give up drinking. We carry an immense amount of luggage. We seem to get sick relatively easily. By comparison with the trim, well-exercised forms of the Chinese, our ungainly, fat, tall, slouched and awkward bodies look like those of some less advanced race—or a race on the verge of extinction.

Here in the crowded Summer Palace, amidst all these buildings from China's ethnocentric past, our presence provides a particularly stark contrast. One suddenly acquires new insight into some of the early Chinese descriptions of Westerners.

"They all look alike," wrote one Chinese scholar at the beginning of the last century, "though differing in height; some being tall. My present idea of them is ugliness and stiffness from their angular demeanor, perhaps due to their ungainly garments . . . Their cheeks are white and hollow, though occasionally purple; their noses, which we consider unfavorable, are like sharp beaks. Some of them have thick tufts of red and yellow hair on their faces, making them look like monkeys. Their arms and ears do not reach the floor as they are often depicted by us. And, though sleepy looking, I think they have intelligence."

Thought

Tomorrow we will leave Peking. I pack, and then take a last walk. It is night and the streets are almost empty. As I walk I mull over our stay of a week in this city. I am beginning to sense a difference in the manner in which Chinese and Americans go about understanding their universe. It is a difference I had not anticipated.

I find myself understanding systems, and even people, in terms of their weaknesses. My impulse is to scrutinize the theory by trying to see where it breaks down or runs into difficulty in practice. In general, I look for flaws, inconsistencies and failures, not just because I wish to debunk systems, but because I want to relieve my mind, if possible, that frailties exist.

But the Chinese seem to approach things from the opposite direction. They search out what works in a system. And perhaps this is because they have a system which by and large does work. They grope for overarching abstractions. They are interested in the functional whole rather than the more isolated dysfunctional parts. We want to see jails and mental hospitals, and ask about problem children, premarital sex and divorce. But they take us to factories, museums, dams, schools and ballets.

Yenan, Cradle of Revolution

Our twin-engine Russian-built plane skims over the barren, eroded mountains of the Northwest Province of Shensi. The land is poor and steep, so that even the rolling mountaintops are cultivated. The ploughed fields cap the rough hills, and extend down to the steepest, most inaccessible cliffs like a dripping fudge topping on a dessert. Small villages are niched into river valleys. The fruit and nut trees are just beginning to blossom, dotting the mountainsides with smokelike pink and white puffs. The caves in which the peasants live are tiered up the hillsides, so that those living at the highest altitudes must walk hundreds of feet down to fetch water at the river.

Our plane flies up the Yen River Valley, dropping low between the mountains. Oxen plough the yellow earth in the fields beneath. We land at the old Yenan Airport, with its runway of hand-hewn sandstone blocks.

Yenan is a small provincial town. Coming from a large city like Peking, one notices the slower pace. There is no train through the rough hills to Yenan, only a long winding road. Yenan prefecture, consisting of some fourteen counties, is still predominantly agricultural, raising wheat, millet, corn, beans as well as swine, sheep and fowl.

But Yenan is no ordinary provincial town. It is a Chinese shrine —in many ways, the birthplace of the Chinese revolution. Mao and his exhausted troops first arrived in Yenan in October, 1935, at the end of the famous Long March from the old Kiangsi Soviet area to the south, from which they had been forced to flee by Chiang Kai-shek's encirclement campaigns. In his abiding passion to exterminate the "Communist bandits," Chiang assembled a fifth and final campaign of seventy-five German-trained-and-equipped divisions. The slowly developing Red Army was forced to abandon its mountain strongholds or be destroyed.

On October 2, 1934, they left to seek a new sanctuary. One hundred thousand troops, including some thirty-five women and Mao's pregnant wife, succeeded in breaking through the encirclement. They began their legendary trek, which was to last three hundred and seventy days, and take them six thousand miles through some of China's most treacherous country. First they moved west through Kweichow, to the plateau country in Yunnan, and on to Tibet. From there they moved north to the deserts of Kansu and up over the formidable snow-covered K'un Lun Mountains, and finally to Yenan. All along the way they fought, were bombed and strafed by Chiang's air force, and had to contend with climates which varied from extreme cold to extreme heat.

When they finally arrived in Yenan, just below the Great Wall which separates China from Mongolia, they had sustained some forty-five thousand casualties, and undergone numerous leadership struggles. But they had established a legend of political and military invincibility, and Mao was in command.

Yenan is a monument to both the Long March and the ten years which the Communists spent here fighting first the Japanese (until VJ Day in 1945), and Chiang and his Nationalists in the Chinese Civil War, which ended in Communist victory in 1949. But like so much current revolutionary history in China, the entire period seems to be personified in Mao. Coming to Yenan is like coming to *his* special city. He looms even larger here than elsewhere, and that is large indeed.

Thus it comes as no surprise that, having settled into the guest house and eaten lunch, we are whisked away to a museum, The Yenan Memorial Museum of the Chinese Revolution Led by Chairman Mao. The museum is crammed with Mao memorabilia, which, while they are interesting, evoke for me a comment that Mao himself is alleged to have uttered about "them" wanting to turn him into a "living Buddha." "Them" presumably refers to the cadres and bureaucrats in dark-gray suits who stand like a solid wall between the often-spontaneous leaders at the top and the masses of common peasants and workers at the bottom.

The museum is deathly chilly. A prim, rosy-cheeked female guide with braids takes us in tow. The first stop is a massive multicolored glass map which stands up in the center of the first room like the back of a large pinball machine. By manipulating a hand-held console, our guide makes different red arrows light up on the map, indicating the paths of the Long March. The detours, switchbacks, crossings and circuitous routes of the various elements of the Red Army slowly turn the board into a stunning collision of scores of red arrows, not unlike the convergence of freeways on a Los Angeles road map.

Everywhere there are quotes by Mao, in Chinese and translated into English. There are also hundreds of grainy blowups of demonstrations, battlefields, soldiers and meeting halls where one or another of the many historical "wrong lines" was crushed. Try as one may, it is not easy to find photos or much information on any of the myriad other Chinese leaders. In recent years there has been a reduction in acceptable heroes. Whereas in 1971 the central theme at the museum had been "Mao and His Closest Comrade-in-arms, Lin Piao," now it is almost as though the exhibitors had decided to convert the whole Chinese revolution into a single biography. There is a sense here, as well as elsewhere, that some awful centrifugal force might set into the nation's political life, were the whole revolution not so firmly anchored by the gravity of this one charismatic man's personality. And perhaps their fears are justified. But to an outsider, this flamboyant hard sell of Chairman Mao seems to indicate an uncertainty which hardly appears justified. China seems far too viable to be so possessed of one man, one symbol, in such an intense and relentless fashion.

Chinese high school students pass by us, writing feverishly in small red plastic notebooks with "Revolutionary Diary" on the cover. They go to the museum not to escape but to study.

Our guide stops abruptly in front of a display case showing weapons from the anti-Japanese resistance. "Now I will sing a song from this period," she announces, showing an uncharacteristic trace of embarrassment. She begins to sing in a quavering voice. But she is determined; she is singing for the revolution.

In the next display area, there is a sign which says NO SMOKING in Chinese but not in English. One of the members of our group who can not read Chinese asks whether she can smoke.

"Oh, yes," says the guide.

"We pass a glass case showing captured Japanese mortars and automatic weapons, a lesson in how the Red Army of resistance supplied itself. Nestled in between the armaments bearing Japanese markings is a small two-way radio set. The museum placard says that it was Mao's personal radio. In small black letters printed on the white enamel dial of the radio is the inscription "Made by Western Electric Instruments, Newark, N.J." I wonder whether anyone at this company knows that one of its radios is a celebrity in China.

As we move chronologically through the museum, it is strange to see Mao growing older in the photos. He starts out in the first rooms looking boyish, with a shock of black hair across his brow. By the end he has become the balding patriarch of his last decade. Then, suddenly, near the end of the long display, I come upon a tall upright glass case containing a white horse. It is stuffed and wears a saddle and a bridle. It was Mao's horse while he lived in Yenan.

"The horse died in a Peking zoo in 1962," says our guide, deadpan. "Sometimes Chairman Mao rode, and sometimes he walked."

I see several people trying to conceal smiles. I can not help wondering what and who will get stuffed as a historical object here in the China of the future.

The Chairman's Works

Downstairs in the Yenan guesthouse, a movie about Chinese acrobats is playing for our edification. Outside on a knoll overlooking the river, the ancient Pao An Pagoda towers in the darkness. It is ablaze with lights, and looks like some overgrown Christmas decoration from a Saks Fifth Avenue display window.

I am sick. Fever, chills. I stay in bed all day reading some of Mao's recent talks and writings, which are still officially unpublished here in China. They were, however, printed during the Cultural Revolution as underground pamphlets, and subsequently smuggled out of China and commercially published abroad in translated form.* If and when they are officially approved and published in China, they will doubtless be sanitized, and purged of their earthy content.

In talking to an assemblage of the Chinese leadership about the weaknesses of the Great Leap Forward, Mao speaks of who must bear responsibility.

"The chaos was on a grand scale," he says, "and I take responsibility. Comrades, you must all analyze your own responsibility. If you have to shit, shit. If you have to fart, fart. You will feel much better for it."

Or, again, "Those of you who shirk responsibility or who are afraid to take responsibility, who do not allow people to speak, who think you are tigers, and that nobody will dare touch your ass, whoever has this attitude, ten out of ten will fail. People will talk anyway. You think that nobody will dare touch the ass of tigers like you? Well, they damned well will!"

There is real life in Mao's writings, particularly those which are unexpurgated. Perhaps it has been because he was the one man in China who could speak completely freely, with utmost confidence and intelligence, quoting the classics (even the present supreme *bête noire*, Confucius) with abandon. There is a quality of frankness and good humor in Mao's speeches, writings and interviews which is sadly —and at times, almost frighteningly—missing from those of many of the lesser leaders. While there are startling and refreshing exceptions, there is a tendency in many of the responsible cadres at lower levels whom we've met to avoid difficult or embarrassing questions—to hew to the present party line with a lifeless tenacity. But relentless curiosity has long been one of Mao's hallmarks.

He repeatedly speaks of the unity of opposites, of the need to

*See *Mao Speaks to The People,* edited by Stuart Schramm, New York, Pantheon Books, 1974.

understand and even tolerate both sides of many contradictions in China. He has lectured assembled officials on "struggle," "divergencies" and "splits" as natural and healthy, and as part of the process of releasing tensions and gaining new consensus and unity.

"We can not talk of monolithic unity alone," Mao says, "and not talk about struggle, about contradiction . . . to talk all the time about unity is a pool of stagnant water; it can lead to coldness . . . Things can not only possess unity and common features, without also having independence and distinctive features. For instance, after this meeting is over comes independence. Some of us will go for a walk, some will study, some eat. Each has his own independence. It would never do to keep the meeting going without a break. That would be the death of us. So, each unit of production, each individual, has to have initiative and a certain degree of independence. All must have independence which is linked with unity."

In fact, in Chinese, there are really two separate terms for our word "individualism." Individualism in the sense of each person's individual characteristics is *ko-hsin-chu-i*, or literally, that "ism" which pertains to "the heart of each person." Individualism in the sense of selfishness is *ko jen chu-i*, or literally that "ism" which pertains to "each person for himself."

Mao of course does not believe in *ko-jen-chu-i*, or the individualism of the Western world which sanctions the rights of people to do what they want whenever they please. He has drawn careful philosophical distinctions between antagonistic contradictions (those, for instance, between friends and outright enemies) and contradictions "among the people" (those between friend and friend, which can be worked out through discussion and negotiation). But he clearly seems to recognize, and repeatedly stresses, the need for people to be assertive, to disagree, to question and maintain a certain critical awareness. One senses that Mao has been no lover of yes-men or people who try to find which way the wind is blowing before they speak their minds.

"Many of our comrades," he says, "when confronted with numerous codes and conventions, do not consider whether there might be an alternative formula . . . They do not make any analysis, or use their brains. They do not make comparisons."

I am relieved to stumble across Chairman Mao stealing the words right out of my mouth. I think of the stuffed horse and wonder whether being elevated to such a position was not distasteful and trying for Mao. Such suspicions are borne out by various of Mao's comments, as well as those of confidants. Before his death, Chou En-lai told interviewer William Hinton, "If you make Mao Tse-tung thought absolute, how can there be any development? Such a theory would freeze all social progress. It is quite wrong. We would end up in a passive position . . . "Then, there are those Mao Tse-tung pictures and Mao Tse-tung statues that have been put up all over the place without regard for time or circumstance. This is also wrong. This turns a good thing into its opposite. There is much too much of this. Mao considers it *t'ao-yen* (a nuisance)! All this display is not genuine, nor is it respectful."*

Mao himself was always a prolific writer, constantly surprising one sector or another of officialdom with sudden directives or terse, biting analyses.

It is worth reprinting one such document in its entirety, for it gives an important sense of Mao's mind. "The Twenty Manifestations of Bureaucracy" was an internal document which surfaced in China sometime in 1967.

Chairman Mao Discusses Twenty Manifestations of Bureaucracy

1—At the highest level there is very little knowledge; they do not understand the opinion of the masses; they do not investigate and study; they do not grasp specific policies; they do not conduct political and ideological work; they are divorced from reality, from the masses, and from the leadership of the party; they always issue orders, and the orders are usually wrong; they certainly mislead the country and the people; at the least they obstruct the consistent adherence to the party line and policies; and they can not meet with the people.

2—They are conceited, complacent, and they aimlessly discuss politics. They do not grasp their work; they are subjective and one-sided; they are careless; they do not listen to people; they are trucu-

*New China, Vol I, #2, 1975, p. 28.

lent and arbitrary; they force orders; they do not care about reality; they maintain blind control. This is authoritarian bureaucracy.

3—They are very busy from morning until evening; they labor the whole year long; they do not examine people and they do not investigate matters; they do not study policies; they do not rely upon the masses; they do not prepare their statements; they do not plan their work. This is brainless, misdirected bureaucracy. In other words, it is routinism.

4—Their bureaucratic attitude is immense; they can not have any direction; they are egoistic; they beat their gongs to blaze the way; they cause people to become afraid just by looking at them; they repeatedly hurl all kinds of abuse at people; their work style is crude; they do not treat people equally. This is the bureaucracy of the overlords.

5—They are ignorant; they are ashamed to ask anything; they exaggerate and they lie; they are very false; they attribute errors to people; they attribute merit to themselves; they swindle the central government; they deceive those above them and fool those below them; they conceal faults and gloss over wrongs. This is the dishonest bureaucracy.

6—They do not understand politics; they do not do their work; they push things off onto others; they do not meet their responsibilities; they haggle; they put things off; they are insensitive; they lose their alertness. This is the irresponsible bureaucracy.

7—They are negligent about things; they subsist as best they can; they do not have anything to do with people; they always make mistakes; they offer themselves respectfully to those above them and are idle towards those below them; they are careful in every respect; they are eight-sided and slippery as eels. This is the bureaucracy of those who work as officials and barely make a living.

8—They do not completely learn politics; they do not advance in their work; their manner of speech is tasteless; they have no direction in their leadership; they neglect the duties of their office while taking the pay; they make up things for the sake of appearances. The idlers [e.g. landlords] do not begin any matters, but concentrate mainly upon their idleness; those who work hard, are virtuous, and do not act like the officials are treated poorly. This is the deceitful, talentless bureaucracy.

9—They are stupid; they are confused; they do not have a mind of their own; they are rotten sensualists; they glut themselves for days on end; they are not diligent at all, they are inconstant and they are ignorant. This is the stupid, useless bureaucracy.

10—They want others to read documents; the others read and they sleep; they criticize without looking at things: they criticize mistakes and blame people; they have nothing to do with mistakes; they do not discuss things; they push things aside and ignore it; they are yes men to those above them; they pretend to understand those below them when they do not; they gesticulate; and they harbor disagreements with those on their same level. This is the lazy bureaucracy.

11—Government offices grow bigger and bigger; things are more confused; there are more people than there are jobs; they go around in circles; they quarrel and bicker; people are disinclined to do extra things; they do not fulfill their specific duties. This is the bureaucracy of government offices.

12—Documents are numerous; there is red tape; instructions proliferate; there are numerous unread reports that are not criticized; many tables and schedules are drawn up and are not used; meetings are numerous and nothing is passed on; and there are many close associations but nothing is learned. This is the bureaucracy of red tape and formalism.

13—They seek pleasure and fear hardships; they engage in back door deals; one person becomes an official and the entire family benefits; one person reaches nirvana and all his close associates rise up to heaven; there are parties and gifts are presented. . . . This is the bureaucracy for the exceptional.

14—The greater an official becomes, the worse his temperament gets; his demands for supporting himself become higher and higher; his home and its furnishings become more and more luxurious; and his access to things becomes better and better. The upper strata gets the larger share while the lower gets the smaller; the upper strata gets low prices while the lower gets high prices; there is extravagance and waste. This is the bureaucracy of putting on official airs.

15—They are egotistical; they satisfy private ends by public means; there is embezzlement and speculation; the more they devour, the more they want; and they never step back or give in. This is egotistical bureaucracy.

16—They fight among themselves for power and money; they extend their hands into the party; they want fame and fortune; they want positions, and if they do not get it they are not satisfied; they choose to be fat and to be lean; they pay a great deal of attention to wages; they are cosy when it comes to their comrades but they care nothing about the masses. This is the bureaucracy that is fighting for power and money.

17—A plural leadership cannot be harmoniously united; they exert themselves in many directions, and their work is in a state of chaos; they try to crowd each other out; the top is divorced from the bottom and there is no centralization, nor is there any democracy. This is the disunited bureaucracy.

18—There is no organization; they employ personal friends; they engage in factionalism; they maintain feudal relationships; they form cliques to further their own private interest; they protect each other; the individual stands above everything else; these petty officials harm the masses. This is sectarian bureaucracy.

19—Their revolutionary will is weak; their politics has degenerated and changed its character; they act as if they are highly qualified; they put on official airs; they do not exercise their minds or their hands. They eat their fill every day; they easily avoid hard work; they call a doctor when they are not sick; they go on excursions to the mountains and to the seashore; they do things superficially; they worry about their individual interests, but they do not worry whatsoever about the national interest. This is degenerate bureaucracy.

20—They promote erroneous tendencies and a spirit of reaction; they connive with bad persons and tolerate bad situations; they engage in villainy and transgress the law; they engage in speculation; they are a threat to the party and the state; they suppress democracy; they fight and take revenge; they violate laws and regulations; they protect the bad; they do not differentiate between the enemy and ourselves. This is the bureaucracy of erroneous tendencies and reaction.

This document is harsh and clear and doubtless made a goodly number of bureaucrats tremble.

The Chinese are far from being without initiative and imagination, which are officially encouraged at every turn. But people seem to feel most free expressing themselves in practical or technological ways.

Political imagination, such as Mao evinces, appears to be very risky —sometimes even for Mao himself. For China has an abundance of middle-ranking leaders and cadres who seem genuinely confused and afraid (at least with foreigners) of the possibility of innovative political expression. There is a subtle, but nonetheless deep and repressive sense of hierarchy which still exists. It has little to do with money, better houses, clothes or more expensive cars, because these kinds of class distinctions have largely disappeared. The hierarchy tends to congeal around the question of authority.

For instance, when our group arrives at some new destination, the awaiting officials relentlessly seek out those leading us, often brushing by everyone else as though they did not see them—the Chinese are deeply uneasy when they can not identify the leaders in any given situation.

The concomitant phenomenon is the manner in which lower leaders often demur when in the presence of higher leaders. This would not be a particularly salient feature did it not contrast so sharply with China's impressive efforts toward an orthodoxy of egalitarianism.

Although our trip has blessedly been spared a lot of meetings with high-ranking officials, we did meet with one Vice-Premier, Ch'en Yung-kuei, because he comes from the farming community to which we are to go and work. Ch'en is a marvelously affable, earthy and direct peasant, whose leadership abilities were so transparent that he was elevated to a high-ranking position right from his village.

On the night of our meeting with Ch'en in Peking's Great Hall of the People, all the Chinese interpreters with our trip arrived in their very best dark cadre suits. They (and we) sat in audience with Ch'en like cowed servants before a wrathful king, as Ch'en valiantly struggled to melt the ice and get some kind of free-flowing dialogue going. There was a stilted atmosphere in the room—people whispering, toadying, making sure that Ch'en's teacup was full, and looking around for the slightest indication that perhaps Ch'en wished to get us out of there and use his time for more important matters.

In spite of all the rhetoric and endless stories about "daring to rebel" and "bombarding the headquarters" the Chinese often remain reticent to challenge authority. In fact, they seem uneasy with people who do. Perhaps it was recognition of this very problem which helped generate this kind of rhetoric—an effort to cure the problem. Perhaps also the key to the Cultural Revolution, which was indeed a massive challenge to the new and growing bureaucratic class in China, was that it was sanctioned by Mao, rather than springing from any innate or cultivated quality of Chinese rebelliousness. For Mao has long distrusted complacency. His writings are replete with derogatory references to people who view the world from behind a desk or a book.

"Only two emperors of the Ming Dynasty did well—T'ai-tsu and Ch'eng-tsu," he says. "One was illiterate, and the other only knew a few characters. Afterwards . . . in the Chia Ch'ing reign, when intellectuals had power, things were in a bad state . . . To read too many books is harmful."

One can not help but wonder, sitting here in Yenan, so much the symbol of Mao's kind of ceaseless revolution, who will be around in the future to lead such assaults on the middle-age spread of the revolution.

"Whenever the mind becomes rigid," says Mao, "it is very dangerous."

Dining Alone

Fever and chills again today—one of those continuing unfamiliar maladies which strike in foreign countries, and whose course is so difficult to predict.

Lao Chang, an interpreter, is also feeling unwell. We both stay in, missing the day's excursion. Around noon, he appears in my room to wake me up for lunch. We chat awhile. He sheepishly asks me the meaning of several four-letter words he has heard used around the group. I define one evasively as an expletive meaning "something people do when they want to have babies." He smiles knowingly.

We walk downstairs together to the dining rooms. For some unexplained reason, the interpreters have been eating separately from us here in Yenan. We reach the room in which our group usually eats.

"Okay," he says, squiring me across the threshold into the room. "I'll see you later." He begins to walk away hastily.

Inside on the table, there is one bowl and one set of chopsticks standing alone. "Hey," I say in disbelief, catching Lao Chang before he escapes. "It's pretty lonely in here. Why don't we eat together?"

He laughs nervously, and as though gripped by some higher command that he can not share with me, he says, "No. We can not. I'll see you afterward."

I eat alone, listening to the faint rattle of his china in the next room.

The Yenan Tour

In this mountainous part of China where wood is scarce, and other building materials hard to come by, most people have traditionally lived in caves which have been scooped out of the sheer earthen cliff sides around many of the mountains. This deep *huang-t'u*, or yellow loess soil, was brought down by dust storms blowing off the Mongolian steppes in prehistoric times. Warm in the winter and cool in the summer, the caves provide a practical living arrangement at no great cost. Some of the hillsides are veritably honeycombed with such caves, the less desirable ones being those that are high up and farther away from the fields and water.

From 1943 to 1945, Mao lived in such a cave, which is now a part of the Tsao Yuan, or Date Garden Brigade. Outside this two-room cave, there is now a small plaque on the adobe brick wall, noting the dates that he resided here. Inside there is a spare wooden desk with a small iron rod lying on top. We are informed that Mao used to strike himself to stay awake as he studied deep into the night. There are several simple chairs, a small oil lamp, and a standing wooden bookcase. Sunlight diffuses in through oil-paper windows.

In the adjoining room, there is a bed covered with a mosquito net. I ask our guide if these pieces of furniture are the originals. The reply is vague.

Often after seeing such historical sites or exhibitions, we belatedly learn that they were destroyed and later rebuilt, and that the objects are only "facsimiles." Thus we are never quite sure of the authenticity of what we are looking at. But it seems to make little difference to visiting Chinese, who appear as reverent before a mere copy as before a pan in which Mao actually washed his face.

In the meeting room, to which we go next, I sit down beside our guide, a young woman in her twenties who exudes earnestness. I watch her face as she describes the important meetings that were once held in the building in which we sit in the thirties and forties. All were led by Chairman Mao. Already they have attained the status of quasi-mythological episodes in history. She tells anecdotes of the past with a flourish of detail. It is hard to reconcile her relish for graphic particulars with the fact that the events she is describing occurred long before she was born.

She is slender, has pink cheeks and long braids, which are carefully plaited and tied with bright red plastic thongs. She wears a prim plaid jacket which is buttoned almost to the top. There is a small triangle under her chin, which is filled with the collar of her pink Peter Pan shirt, and three eye-catching green buttons. (I recall the comment of my French journalist friend in Peking, who declared that this small triangle was where "Chinese women express their fashion conscious-ness.") She has an aquiline nose, the tip of which moves slightly as she speaks a somewhat exaggerated Peking dialect that does not quite overpower her local accent.

She wears a wrist watch and smells faintly of sweet soap. (There is no deodorant in China. Nor do people seem to have severe body odor problems.) I have the feeling that if she were derailed from her well-polished talk, she might not quite know how to continue spon-taneously on her own. There is a suggestion of tension in her fingers, which keep creeping toward each other and engaging in brief encounters of entwining. I wonder whether she is pleased to have her obviously highly regarded job as a guide at one of Chariman Mao's former residences.

She is telling a story about the time Chairman Mao invited the surrounding peasants to dinner. "He actually poured wine for them himself," she says. "But they were too embarrassed to drink. So Mao proposed that they play the drinking game of casting fingers to overcome their excitement. When they lost, they had to drink. And then Chairman Mao said, 'Since you can drink so much, you must be able to work a lot.' "

"Educated Youth"

Since 1964 over ten million "educated youth" have gone to the countryside from the cities in China. This is a significant number when one remembers that only fifteen percent of China's population is urban. One woman here in Tsao Yuan reports that in her city graduating middle school class of sixty, only eleven stayed in the city. Some may have been children with elderly parents to be cared for, and a few may just have refused to go. But the fate of these few is one of extreme isolation. Their refusal cuts them off from jobs. They end up being idle in a land of endless purposeful work.

Everywhere in China you hear people asking one another if they have *"ch'a-tui"*ed," or not. Literally *"ch'a-tui"* means "to be inserted in" or "put out in." It is one of the many expressions in modern-day Chinese (like *hsia-fang*, literally to be "sent down") used to connote the process whereby intellectuals, bureaucrats and students in the cities get sent out into the country. All over China, these "educated youths" live and work in rural communes and brigades with the peasants. It is a wrenching experience for most of these young people from the city—one which they idealize, but also often find extremely painful.

The object is to bring the learning of the city-educated to the countryside, and to bring the practical experience of farming to the city dweller. And whereas many older professional people (agricultural experts, musicians, doctors, engineers, etc.) may get sent down for a year or two, most youths get sent down indefinitely upon graduating from middle school.

"We follow Mao's call to go down to the villages when we graduate," says one girl from Peking, who now works here at the Tsao Yuan Brigade. "We have come to be educated by the lower and middle peasants."

A national organization is responsible for making the initial arrangements for each youth's journey to the countryside. While preferences as to place and type of work can be expressed, a young person is basically bound by the final decision of administrators at his or her school. An allotment of six hundred yuan is made by the state to each educated youth to assist in the initial investments which must be made for housing and household utensils. After a year with a particular work unit, a young worker begins to be remunerated locally like any other peasant.

"When I first came here," says another young woman who has been at the Brigade a year, "I still really wanted to go to university. But I did not have a correct line. Then we had a series of really heated discussions among ourselves on how we felt about settling in a small place.

"After I had been here awhile, the Brigade members asked me if I would stay longer. I just answered in a vague way, still hoping I could somehow get away and back to my studies. I said that I would do whatever the revolution needed. But the comrades saw through my unenthusiastic reply." She laughs nervously, and sits forward on her chair. "I used revolutionary words to cover up my individualism.

"Of course, others had the same problem, and we talked about it in the fields a lot. The peasants would tell us that the countryside needed mechanization and needed educated youth to help. I gradually began to see how I was in fact using my revolutionary words to cover my own personal intentions. Now I know that I must alter my world outlook by tempering myself in the country. The change of one's outlook is a fundamental one, you know. It's not easy to change your class standpoint and outlook to that of the peasants. But I've made up my mind to do it, even though the process may be painful and difficult."

When she ceases talking, there is a silence in the meeting room. She looks to one end of the room, and then to the other. She is clearly interested in the effect her words have had on those listening. But it also strikes me that she is testing the effect of her own words on herself.

"I remember, there were two parents who thought their daughter shouldn't come to the countryside," says a young man. "They tried to persuade her to stay in the city. But she said that Chairman Mao had fought for many years in Yenan, and that the people of Yenan had made a great contribution, although the area was still backward. They had a big fight. The parents tried to shut her up in her room, and even brought meals to her. But she said, 'I am grown up now. And the Party and Chairman Mao ask me to serve the people. But you want to keep me locked up like a piece of private property. I have graduated, and now I must take part in socialist reconstruction.'

"Although we didn't know much about production when we got here," he continues, "the peasants have been very helpful and have taught us. I remember one time just after we had gotten here, we went out to hoe some fields. Somehow we chopped off the tops of a lot of seedlings. An older peasant came by and saw what we had done. He said that when we wrote characters we did them one by one. He said that we should do the same thing when weeding plants."

The caves in which these youths live are in the same blocks as those of the peasantry. There is a congenial atmosphere out in front of the caves when we visit at sunset. Children are playing basketball on the hard clay threshing floor. Two young women struggle with a bow saw, sawing wood for the evening cooking fires. Inside one of the caves of the educated youths, there are some cupboards, tables, chairs, with the usual posters of Chairman Mao adorning the walls. Cups and toothbrushes are neatly aligned in wash basins under each person's towel on a hook. There are several dog-eared sets of *The Collected Works of Chairman Mao*, on the tabletops. Laundry dries on an overhead line. One young woman is ladling grain from a basket on the floor for the evening meal.

In the middle of this domestic scene are two large targets hanging on the wall. They are in the shape of the human body, and have numbers marking various vital points. There are several bullet holes in each. An AK-47 hangs on a peg next to two bolt-action rifles of older vintage.

"Yes, we are in the militia," says one smiling woman, as she follows my gaze. "And we have regular target practice."

Somehow this little collage of weaponry on the wall has no threatening quality to it. The educated youths seem hardly conscious of the guns' presence in their home, whereas I almost have to force myself to stop looking at them.

Many of these youths, although they have been at Tsao Yuan only a year or so, are already cadres. They have assumed positions of leadership very fast. But they do not brag about their positions. In fact, they do not even mention them, although one can usually assume in China that in a formal meeting like this with foreigners, those Chinese in attendance will be of high position, or at least of "correct" political outlook.

Yet, despite all the cadres we've talked with, I still do not have a clear idea how leaders are chosen in China. Questions on the subject usually do not lead to useful answers. Certainly it is not a simple process whereby local residents vote them in. There is a much more complicated and (perhaps ill-defined) process which involves approval from the top (and often even appointment from the top), which is then discussed at the bottom.

To the question what would happen if the top appointed someone who was not acceptable to those on the bottom, the standard answer is "They could not. The people would not accept it."

In any event, the local leaders in the country do not all rise from the local ranks. Some do, but other leaders are chosen from the educated youth, who comprise a relatively small segment of the Brigade population. (There are thirty-two educated youth at Tsao Yuan.)

Do the peasants resent cadres in their midst who are both younger and imported?

"These students are sent down from the top to learn and to be leaders," whispers a local cadre next to me. "The educated youth are educated. The peasants are not. And so, the youths are expected to lead. This is an aspiration not shared by all peasants. The youths have received education and gained talent, and so they must use it. They must help bridge the gap between the country and the city."

China's leaders want to homogenize this country—to break down the traditional barriers dividing cities from countryside, manual from intellectual labor, educated and uneducated. These earnest youths sitting around the room talking are just a few of the millions of people who have gone into the centrifuge and been spun to distant parts of the country. In the West, pundits view this process and see broken families, disruption of expert research projects, and inefficiency. Devotees of Mao look at the same process and see the welding together of worlds which should never have been separated. They see a process of equalization—the antithesis of the old Confucian adage:

> Some labor with their brains, and some labor with their brawn. Those who labor with their brains, govern others. Those who labor with their brawn, are governed by others.
> Those governed by others, feed them. Those who govern others, are fed by them. This is the universal principle of the world.

Anger

Sian is the hub of Northwest China. Once called Ch'angan, capital of the ancient T'ang Dynasty, Sian was more recently enshrined as the place of infamy in which Chiang Kai-shek was kidnaped by angry soldiers of his own forces in 1936. They wanted to fight the Japanese. He wanted to fight the Communists. "The Japanese are a disease of the skin," said Chiang. "The Communists are a disease of the heart." Today Hua Ching hot springs, site of the famous Sian Incident, is a public park. Ordinary Chinese crowd the trail up the mountainside to look at the rocky grotto where Chiang was captured in his pajamas without his false teeth after an abortive escape on a cold December day.

Outside the gates of the hot springs, the road is clogged with carts and trucks. Finally our bus makes its way to a place in the road where two trucks are pulled off on the shoulder facing each other. The front wheels and axle of one truck are in a ditch filled with water. Several horse-cart drivers sit on their motionless carts in the middle of the road, staring transfixed at the unfolding drama. One of the drivers is standing on the running board of the other truck. He has been run off the road. He is furious. He is reaching in through the window, yelling and grabbing. The other driver has recoiled up against the far door. Three other men stand on the road clawing at the angry figure on the running board. The peacemakers are unable to separate the angry quarrelers, locked through the open window like dogs in battle.

Suddenly, the scene is gone. We move on down the road.

Lao Chao, who sits next to me, turns toward me. "You know, in China if one is unable to repair a car or a truck, he can not get a driver's license," he says, as if the irrelevant banality of his words might erase the poignant effect on us of the anger we have just seen. But for me, to see real anger in China, comes almost as a relief.

All along the roadway, the buildings and walls are adorned with the usual slogans. Some have been painted over. Half-hidden characters from the Cultural Revolution, when angry outbursts were not uncommon in China, begin to show through again. It is as if they had been written in invisible ink, only now revealing the slogans of long-since discredited enemies and wrong lines—recalling a time when passions were hot, and even suicides were not unheard of. The "right line" in China is an ever-changing canon, often like a vague shape in the mist. The "right line" is not always easy to discern in the intense political struggle of the moment. The "wrong lines" leave some faint traces—old slogans which are painted over, books which are discredited and disappear, and films which are no longer shown and extolled.

The past must constantly be weeded to provide credibility for the present.

*　　　　*　　　　*

There are big red characters hung above the ballet mirrors, reading REHEARSE FOR THE REVOLUTION. The mirrors are made from slightly imperfect glass, giving the effect of a fun house. As the B.I. progresses, I play with my reflection in the mirrors, moving one way or another in my chair so as to render my body headless or possessed of a huge tumerous bulge.

An orchestra waits. Actors, dancers and musicians stand in clumps by the door, listening and watching. Many have their arms around each other, or stand leaning up against another comrade with a naturalness which is striking. The boys are with boys, the girls are with girls.

"Students must go down to the masses," Liu Fung, Chairman of the Revolutionary Committee of the Sian Song and Dance troupe is saying. He is an older man. "They must try and write plays and songs based on the principle of 'Coming from the people's life, but improving the people's life.' They must try and meet the political and entertainment needs of the Shensi Province masses. All art and literature are for the masses of people, especially the workers, peasants and soldiers."

"We are opposed to works with bad political viewpoints," says another comrade sitting behind the leadership table. "But we are also opposed to works which lack artistic power. We are now trying to perform more works showing the heroic posture of the workers, peasants and soldiers."

"We have gone down into the coal mines three times," says another speaker. "We went four hundred meters under ground to work and discuss things with the miners in order to prepare material for a dance. When we want to write a long play, we always go down to the factories and fields and gather material. Then we analyze it in a three-in-one committee of writers, directors and performers. The idea is first discussed with our Revolutionary Committee. Then it is discussed with everyone. We feel that our art should help build socialism and social transformation, not weaken the Party's leadership. And, in fact, some performances are halted, because after they are shown to the workers and peasants, they might not approve. They might say something like 'This doesn't show the spirit of our time.'

"For instance, in one dance, a woman does a fluttery kind of a step. And, some people thought that it didn't really reflect the proper proletarian strength. So, we changed it."

A group of women ballet dancers take their positions at the bars around the room. They wear brown tights, loose bloomers and blue knit shirts. Their bodies are muscular, small-breasted.

The pianist plays exercise music. They start at the bar, and then move out onto the floor, doing pliés. They move easily and with discipline. One dancer muffs up a pirouette. She comes to a full stop, recomposes herself, and then begins again without grimacing or showing any sign of embarrassment. The teacher is a middle-aged woman who stands on the side of the room calling out suggestions and corrections in rhythm with the music.

A men's chorus is next, suggesting that this rehearsal is turning into a performance. They sing with an accordion. ("It's an easy instrument to take along to the countryside," says a young man sitting next to me.) A heavy Soviet influence lingers about their presentation. They stand shoulder to shoulder, with flawless expressions of proletarian defiance and sing "We Must Liberate Taiwan."

And then, to stress beyond a shadow of a doubt that Taiwan is an issue of importance, a soloist sings "People of Taiwan, Our Own Brothers." This is currently a popular song in China. In fact, a recent visit of a Chinese cultural troupe to the United States was canceled by the U. S. State Department because the Chinese insisted that they be allowed to sing this song in America.

The orchestra behind us tunes up. It is a Western orchestra with flutes, oboes, horns, clarinets, bassoons, double basses, other strings and a piano.

They play what sounds like some providentially lost Khachaturian score. The music is difficult, but the technique of most of the musicians is good. A group of dancers, all smiling those special Chinese stage smiles, appears.

The dance is ingeniously choreographed to portray the various stages of a harvest. There is the male lead dressed up in blue costume overalls and cap, who prances around the stage with his hands going through the motions of steering a vehicle. The women cut and thresh wheat around him.

"He represents a tractor driver," says my neighbor. "We must mechanize agriculture."

This is a standard role in Chinese ballet. I have seen it several times. This particular dance is called "We Are So Happy Because We Are Delivering Grain to the State." The Chinese do not fear repetition.

The final offering is a solo from a popular ballet called *Yimeng Mountain.* The ballet, set in the 1930's, tells an unlikely story of a young woman who has just given birth. While hunting mushrooms in the mountains, she comes across a PLA soldier who is dying of thirst. Nowhere can water be found. So, without further delay, the heroine does a grand jeté behind a rock, and emerges a few moments later with a canteen of milk from her own breast. The dying soldier drinks and lives.

The scene being danced now takes place the next day at the young woman's house. It is entitled "Cooking Chicken Soup for the PLA Soldier." Smiles caused by the announcement of this quaint title are almost immediately erased by the ballerina. She can only be called a prima ballerina, although I am sure the Chinese would frown on such an appellation. She is exquisite, a beautiful woman utterly in control of her body and the dance. What is startling, is that such a dancer would be with a provincial company.

In entertainment, as in sports (where the motto is "Friendship First, Competition Second"), the Chinese do not emphasize star performers. There is no real cult of celebrities in China. At a performance of any kind, one is constantly surprised to find that an actor or singer who holds a prop and dances unobtrusively in the chorus in one scene becomes the soloist in the next. Yet even here in China, where classes and distinctions have been whittled down to an all-time minimum, one senses the perhaps unavoidable tendency to give attention to those who perform exceptionally well, and who inevitably get the solos. Sometimes, even in a small grade-school production in the countryside, one notices how the prettiest and most talented children are usually up front. And yet it is distinctly taboo to single out any performer and praise him or her at the expense of the group. Perhaps there will always be an air of glamour surrounding performers. The difference in China lies in the unwillingness on the part of the Chinese to exploit this tendency.

The performance ends, and we leave the hall to visit a school-run ballet slipper shop. Word has somehow gotten around our group that today's visit will be to a school here-to-fore unvisited by foreigners. This notion of virgin territory has somehow caused a small increase of enthusiasm among our members. (People in groups like ours tend to face visits to factories and historical sites which others have already visited, and even written about, with some resignation.)

At any rate, I casually ask a woman in the ballet slipper shop if they ever receive visits from other foreign delegations.

"Oh, yes," she replies. "Lots of foreign friends have visited us. From North Vietnam, America, Albania, Germany and Japan."

I am curious to know who started this rumor, and also a trifle irritated.

We move on to a prop room.

"Since we often take our performances to the mountains," says our guide, "we are experimenting with ways to make props lighter and more compact. Sometimes we work out elaborate ways that they can be folded up. Since the Cultural Revolution, we have been making all our own props rather than buying them. We try to run our troupe in an industrious and thrifty way."

All around us are collapsible swords, styrofoam eggs and cardboard water urns.

We return to the practice hall for a question-and-answer session, where once again we are asked to write down our questions ahead of time. We sit and listen for a long time. My mind begins to wander. The chairman of the Revolutionary Committee is saying something about "bourgeois feudal artistic rubbish," but I have caught the eye of one of the male dancers with whom I had earlier chatted briefly. He stands by the door in back of the orchestra.

I make my move. I head across the hall and out the door as if in search of the bathroom, feeling somewhat like a student whose only officially permissible relief from class is the lavatory. Magically, this same dancer intercepts me on the path outside. He introduces himself, and we begin to talk while walking slowly down the path. I feel furtive, although there is nothing secret being said. But somehow the quality of the direct encounter is more satisfying than the exchange inside.

"Every year we go into inaccessible areas to perform," says Hsieh Han-min with great animation. "We break up into small groups and go to places where we have to walk for days carrying our props. There are no trucks or anything. But we like the trips a great deal and always have a good time."

"Where do you live on such trips?" I ask.

"Well, we live with the peasants. We sleep in their caves or houses with them. It's never more than a day or so in each place. We have the Three Togethers: Eat Together, Live Together, Work Together. The peasants welcome us. They love our performances because most of them rarely get into the cities."

Hsieh is speaking very fast. His excitement is infectious. "We like to go to the countryside. We must go to answer Chairman Mao's call," he says, emphasizing the word must. "Because if we don't go, art will become separated from the masses."

"Do foreigners ever come with you on these tours to the countryside?" I ask, fantasizing for a moment.

"No, no!" he laughs. "But you would like to go? It's hard. It's not easy work. But anyway, we welcome you."

We both laugh at the idea.

"Ah, but your time is short," he says, consigning the idea to futility.

Just then, Wang Chien, the soloist from the Chicken Soup ballet happens down the path. She stops. Hsieh introduces me. I struggle to find some acceptable Chinese expression of admiration and appreciation for her dance. But I realize I should be praising the whole troupe, not just her. All I can say is "You dance very well."

She acknowledges my compliment with a silent nod of her head. I'm madly in love with her. But, it's too late—a functionary, who has noticed my fifteen-minute absence from the question and answer session, is speeding toward us. He is full of officious concern that I might have succumbed on the way to the rest room.

I bid a reluctant good-bye to my two new acquaintances, and am hastened back to the meeting room, where written questions are still being patiently answered.

Mao's Hometown

Shaoshan is a small village tucked into the lush green valleys between the rolling mountains of Hunan Province. Although the peasants of Shaoshan still farm and live much as peasants do everywhere in China, this village is in a category all by itself. It is the birthplace of Chairman Mao.

Most members of our group had requested that the visit to Shaoshan be cut from our itinerary to allow more time for the work section of our trip. The Chinese seemed upset by this request. Whether they felt slighted by our lack of interest in Chairman Mao's birthplace, or whether they thought that our trip (like almost all others) should go to Shaoshan for some unexplained political reason, I do not know. In any event, our request was turned down.

Shaoshan is another one of China's living museums;—a museum, which like Yenan, focuses almost entirely on Chairman Mao, the personification of all correct tendencies in modern Chinese history.

Chairman Mao's house has been rebuilt, and replica furniture installed. It is surprisingly spacious, almost luxurious, in fact, even by today's standards.

"Yes, this is a nice house," confesses one of our local hosts. "You see, Chairman Mao's father was a middle peasant." In common parlance, he was not poor.

We pose for a photograph in front of a small pond before Mao's house. We stand on tiered risers, as countless thousands of groups have done before us. We are given strange little three-dimensional plastic photos of Mao's house. They remind me of the cheap beer advertisements of 3-D waterfalls which hang over bars and move as you walk by.

I have difficulty getting involved in this political shrine. A sense of reconstituted history hangs over Shaoshan—an embalmed, rouged corpse. My interest is flagging, and it probably shows. My major energies are directed at preventing our "hosts" from detecting any signs of ingratitude.

There is a lecture being given at this moment on "The Ten Incidents of the Two-Line Struggle in Chinese History." I stay on my bed in the guest house. Quite simply, I am exhausted. But exhaustion is not credible grounds for surrender in China. The Chinese seem not to recognize fatigue as a phenomenon, even with their stress on preventive medicine. So I have reported myself as "tired and *getting a cold.*" The "getting a cold" puts me in a different category —the fearsome category of "yet another sick foreigner," who will need doctors, medicine, and maybe even hospitalization. For the Chinese, whose conscientiousness and concern over sick guests is unbounded, this possibility (which happens regularly with visitors unaccustomed to the climate and germs) is always taken seriously.

I lie on my bed reading a precious month-old copy of *Newsweek* that someone has received in the mail. The magazine reports the fall of Saigon several weeks ago. It is a kind of wrap-up issue on the war, like some end-of-season sports review. There are several pages of photos taken at different times throughout the long war. There is a photo of B-52's dropping necklaces of bombs on unseen targets. Police Chief Loan explodes the head of a Vietcong prisoner with a handgun in a downtown Saigon market place. Robert McNamara, hair plastered down, holds a pointer in front of one of his light-at-the-end-of-the-tunnel charts. A GI gropes over the body of a half-clad whore in Saigon. Diem lies dead in a soiled white Panama suit in a pool of blood. Students put flowers into the barrels of soldiers' rifles during a demonstration in front of the Pentagon.

Hsiao Yao comes into the room to see how I am. I hand him the magazine and point to the pages of photos without speaking. He looks. His brow knits together. He does not turn the page. Wordlessly he returns the magazine to the bed, and walks out of the room.

Our visit to Shaoshan wears on. We remain cooped up in hot rooms listening to the endless B.I.'s prepared for us by the reception committee. I yearn to be outside walking around. The only way to achieve this is to rise at five in the morning before the official program commences.

The dawn is beautiful. As the first gray light comes up over the mountains, the village begins to stir. The clusters of earthen houses with thatched roofs lie shrouded in ground fog. Wisps of smoke rise lazily from the chimneys as the peasants begin to prepare breakfast.

At first, villagers are surprised to see white faces. Although Shaoshan is besieged with visitors, tight schedules and short visits seem to keep most people from wandering far, particularly at this time of morning. The farm families are friendly. We are offered a cup of tea here, some eggs there. But not wanting to cause an uproar (which is easily done, since the Chinese cease all manual activity when guests arrive), we demur and walk on.

We follow a narrow dike between paddy fields down to a stream, past a young boy grazing an ox, past a man who is casting great clouds of white fertilizer out onto the green sunbathed rice.

My notes show little else about Shaoshan. About our interminable B.I.'s and discussions, I find only this:

"The Vice-Chairman of the Shaoshan Brigade Committee drones on. He seems to be unconscious of the audience which sits in a circle around him, trying to maintain a semblance of polite interest. He just keeps talking." (Now, upon writing this, I can not even remember the subject.)

"An old peasant who has come 'to tell his story' spits on the clean floor. He listens awhile, drinks some tea, and then falls asleep. A young cadre notices him after a few moments, head slumped over to one side, mouth wide open, and beginning to snore loudly. He wakes him up under the pretense of offering him a cigarette."

Shanghai

We pass into the old French Concession, land formerly leased to the French by the Chinese government. It was once the home of wealthy European traders, rich Chinese merchants and officials, and of course, the leaders of Shanghai's legendary underworld. The mansions here are grander than those we have just passed on the outskirts of Shanghai, huge dark gingerbread-laden ersatz European structures. Behind high walls rise Victorian turrets, Bavarian cuckoo clock balconies and ornate chimneys. They are built of brick, slate, tiles, stone —as if their colonial architects could not imagine a time when there would be no Europeans left in China to enjoy their luxury and spaciousness.

Now there is laundry drying out under porticos at front doors where limousines driven by uniformed Chinese chauffeurs once delivered their charges. Many of the well-manicured lawns of the past out under grand old shade trees have been turned into vegetable patches. No distinction remains between the front of the house and the former servants' quarters behind. The people whom the high walls once excluded now have the run of the whole house. Some buildings have been divided into apartments, although they are reported to be drafty and cold in winter. Others of these relics have become institutes, academies, headquarters for neighborhood revolutionary committees, and factories.

There is a faint suggestion of Hong Kong about Shanghai: the sidewalk vendors (now organized by the State), the bustle in the streets, the endless variety of small shops. We pass through different strata of smells as we move down the street: seafood, cakes baking, a honey bucket truck, food frying in oil. People do not stare at foreigners here. People from Shanghai are more cosmopolitan than those from Peking and the country. Their faces are paler. But they are much looser and gayer. They seem to laugh easily. One feels that it would not be an unpardonable sin here to get into an argument or a heated discussion.

Shanghai now has ten million people, and is considered by many to be the largest municipality in the world. In the fourth century it was a fishing village. By the fourteenth century, a small textile industry began to flourish in Shanghai. But it was not until the nineteenth century, when the Western powers forced China to sign the "unequal treaties," that it began to grow rapidly. Sitting as it does on the Whangpoo River, a tributary of the mighty Yangtze River which flows out into the China Sea, Shanghai proved to be the most prosperous of the new "treaty ports." Although it was filled with Chinese who labored in its factories, docks and mansions, Shanghai was never really a Chinese city before Liberation. It was a creature of foreign trade and foreign influence. It was ruled by foreigners and Westernized Chinese as a profitable trade access point to the great Chinese hinterland behind.

"In 1843 the imperialists forced us to sign an unequal treaty," says a member of the delegation greeting us.

"The imperialists did a lot of evil things in the Foreign Concession. Not only did they bring opium to China to sell in order to get silver to purchase tea and silk, but they extracted the special privileges of extraterritoriality from the Chinese government. If a foreigner killed a Chinese, he could not be tried and punished by a Chinese court.

"Our city was invaded militarily and culturally," he continues. "There were foreign warships out there on the Whangpoo River. There were foreign missionary schools throughout the city, which tried to turn Chinese students into the servants of the foreigners who dumped foreign goods onto the Chinese market, inhibiting the growth of our own industry. So many goods had foreign words marked on them that we started calling some things by new names, like yang-huo (foreign fire) for matches, yang-pu (foreign cloth) for cloth, yang-yu (foreign oil) for kerosene, or yang-t'ieh (foreign iron) for galvanized tin. And do you know why they were marked this way? Because they sold better. We Chinese felt better using something that had the word "foreign" stamped on it.

"Take this guesthouse where you are staying. The French built it in the 1930's. They called it Picardie Apartments. Yes, you can still see it engraved in the brass nozzles on the fire hoses. But this city also has a revolutionary history. The Chinese Communist Party was founded here. We held our first National Congress here on July 1, 1921. Our great leader Chairman Mao attended that session."

Shanghai was finally liberated on May 28, 1949. Since that time the industrial growth of the city has increased seventeen times. At present, one half day's output of steel is equal to a whole year's production during a peak pre-Liberation year. There are now sixteen universities and colleges, nine hundred middle schools, and five thousand primary schools. The Chinese recite such statistics with great relish and satisfaction. They represent the kind of irrefutable evidence of progress with which the Chinese feel comfortable.

Acrobats

Sometimes I feel the unmistakable strength and magic of this country in a way which momentarily eclipses all else.

Tonight we watch the Shanghai Acrobatic Troupe juggle, do highwire, trapeze and gymnastic acts, and stunts where fifteen people get on a bicycle as effortlessly as one. There is no honkytonk sideshow atmosphere. No freaks, no con artists, no snake oil. Just the consummate skill of the performers.

Before Liberation, the troupe lived as vagrants on the streets and performed on street corners for spare change. Now they perform in their own theater, an intimate round dome with a single ring in the center. There is a band on a platform which plays in perfect step, with muted drum rolls and trills, as one of the gymnasts gets ready to balance the fourth tray of full water glasses on a cone perched on his nose.

A man with a rouged face, a kind of dumb vulnerable grin and a powder-blue Liberace suit, walks out into the ring with his partner.

They extract long fluffy feathers from one of the hidden pockets in their jackets, and balance them horizontally on their foreheads. The feathers stick straight out in the air. The men move forward as the feathers begin to drop.

Suddenly, the man in powder blue produces a short and rather ridiculous little fishing pole. He heads into the delighted audience. A spotlight follows him. All of a sudden, the rod is shaking and bending. With a surprised foolish grin on his face, he reels a large orange goldfish in from the audience. Everyone is standing up trying to see how he did it. The two people from whose midst he caught the fish are looking at each other in wonderment, shaking their heads and appearing somewhat ruffled by the spotlight and all the attention that has suddenly and unexpectedly turned them from spectators into participants. Before the commotion has died down, the announcer says, "The next act is wrestling."

Two midgets dressed in clothes that look as if they might be worn by Eskimos, come bursting out in a clinch from behind a curtained door. These strange short men jump, trip each other, fall, roll, leap out of the ring, but they never break their clinch. The clown in the powder-blue jacket is refereeing. He keeps falling down, frenetically blowing his whistle, and generally unable to keep up with these two supercharged miniature wrestlers.

Then, just as suddenly as the mayhem began, it all stops. A human head pops up out of the tangle of fur and two costume heads and small bodies. The face is sweating and beaming. The two midgets instantaneously dissolve into the tall form of one acrobat who has been playing both wrestlers at once. The red-faced referee feigns dumb shock. The crowd goes wild.

Suddenly the hall is dark again. Two acrobats, now wearing blue tunics, appear in the center of the ring. There is silence. Then, almost imperceptibly at first, the sound of crickets in the evening comes over the P.A. system. The two men are making strange little shapes with their mouths.

"They must have some sort of gismos in their mouths," says a rattan-ware importer from New York who happens to be sitting behind us.

The two acrobats begin clucking, peeping and honking like chickens and geese. The clucking and honking get more intense, as though there were someone chasing fowl through a barnyard. Suddenly it stops, and there is nothing but the sound of one small captured chick being soothed. The laughter of a child rises above the acclaim of others. The lights come up. A mother hurries a small boy down the aisle to the bathroom. There are cries for more.

The lights dim. The two men return under a spotlight. They imitate a recalcitrant car starting, moving out, shifting, driving off into the distance, and then coming to a stop with a squeak and the sound of the emergency brake being set.

Then they imitate a battlefield with rifles, mortars, machine guns and a howitzer which fires, whistles through the air, and makes a dull distant muffled roar as it explodes. The sounds are done to perfection.

A sharpshooter appears. He shoots out the flames of candles with a .22 from a hundred and fifty feet away while looking in a mirror and facing the opposite direction.

As the show ends, the American behind me mumbles awestruck, "I hope we never have to go to war with these people."

Brain Surgery

Dr. Chu is a jovial, confident man. We sit in a lovely traditional-style garden house and listen to him discuss the changes Shanghai's Hua Shan Hospital has undergone since the Cultural Revolution. The Cultural Revolution is to the Chinese way of reckoning recent history what the division between A.D. and B.C. is for the average Western schoolchild. The fish ponds and lush gardens outside the reception center make one forget for a moment that we are in fact in a hospital.

"They once belonged to a rich capitalist," says Dr. Chu, with a certain impishness. "But that was in the past. We now have a staff of eight hundred here, with six hundred beds and a medical college which was established after the Cultural Revolution. The hospital is also affiliated with the Shanghai Medical College set up in 1907.

"Today we want to show you two operations done under acupuncture anesthesia: a hernia repair and brain surgery involving the removal of a tumor pressing on the pituitary gland. Since the Cultural Revolution, we have been doing more and more operations with acupuncture anesthesia. We have now used it in some three thousand five hundred cases. Over one thousand of these were for brain surgery. Our success with the anesthetic technique has been over ninety percent. Of course, we have other means of anesthesia standing by, because some patients still do have some sensation. The acupuncture technique is still not refined enough for some kinds of surgery.

"We have had to do some ideological work with new patients to help convince them of the effectiveness of the technique," continues Dr. Chu, "because when we first started using it, we too had great difficulty believing in its effectiveness. But now we know through experience that the technique has several very positive features.

"The first point is that acupuncture anesthesia does not trigger off any of the dangerous side effects of other kinds of anesthesia. If a patient has heart disease, liver or kidney trouble, hypertension or an allergy, using conventional anesthetics can be complicated and risky because they affect vital body functions. They slow down metabolism and make people nauseated at just the wrong time.

"A second positive feature, at least in surgery on the head, is that we have found acupuncture anesthesia to be almost ninety percent effective.

"A third, and simple, advantage is that acupuncture anesthesia is extremely simple, and we do not need a lot of complicated equipment. This makes the technique well suited for use in rural and mountainous areas which are cut off from sophisticated hospitals.

"The fourth point is that a patient has full awareness while he is undergoing surgery. There is no shock of coming-to or disorientation.

"Well, let's say no more. Let's go to the operating theaters. You can ask questions as you watch."

The operating room seems unusually bare and uncluttered. It is not filled with batteries of glittering machines and surgical tools which one might imagine are essential for such complicated surgery.

The patient, a twenty-one-year-old woman worker from Hunan Province, lies in sterile robes on the operating table. Her eyes are closed. A large brown cross has been drawn with iodine on her forehead and shaven cranium. It indicates the line for the incision. The patient is being monitored on an American-made polygraph. A long thin strip of paper moves through the machine and is etched by needles which bounce and report her vital functions like a small seismograph. Seven long needles, connected to fine electric wires, are inserted in her brow and feet. These acupuncture needles are attached to a weak electric pulse, which doctors have now found more effective than the traditional method of hand-twirling the needles in the acupuncture meridians. The patient's lips chatter involuntarily from the oscillating electrical pulse emitted from a small console on a table, which is powered by a forty-volt battery. Otherwise she is motionless, but fully conscious.

"Sometimes we give patients tranquilizing drugs," says Dr. Wang Wei-min, a neurosurgeon who sits beside me. "But we find recoveries are easier and there are fewer complications without sedatives or tranquilizers. This woman has a cystic pituitary tumor. It is nonmalignant, but in 1972 she began to have headaches and obscured vision. One eye could see only vague outlines. She was diagnosed, and as it turned out, she had one of these relatively common kinds of tumor. What we usually do even for the most ordinary surgical procedure is to talk with the patient at length before the operation. We describe the illness in detail, how it can be treated, and the necessity for the surgery. Because according to Chairman Mao's directive, we doctors are responsible to the patient. It is our job to make both the patient and his family feel secure and informed."

The nine men and women in the surgical team have assembled now around the operating table. They have scrubbed up, put on surgical gloves, green robes, masks, caps and sterilized sneakers. As they prepare the operating field, they chat with the patient. Then her face, from the eyes down, disappears under a white cloth. A small tentlike fabrication is erected over it so that she can breathe and talk.

The acupuncture needles are removed from the woman's head. A nurse adjusts the flow of glucose solution dripping from the overhead

I.V. bottle. The patient is given shots to guard against hemostasis and to minimize the possibility of hemorrhaging.

There is an incredible tension in the room. But the doctors are utterly cool.

"Yes, we perform about two of these every day," says Dr. Wang with a reassuring smile as a nurse prepares for a quick transfusion, should it be needed.

A woman neurosurgeon from Nanking is performing the operation. She lines up her surgical tools like a dentist. And then, suddenly, she is drawing the scalpel down the brown iodine line on the patient's forehead where the hairline once was. The incision immediately fills with blood. Bright red. It is the only color in the operating room. The skin is peeled back like a piece of inner tube. It is gray now. The blood is being soaked up with sponges. The skin is clamped back to hold it and prevent further bleeding. The clamps bristle up out of this great red crevice, making her head look as if it is festooned with some new kind of hair curler.

The doctors are talking to the patient. Does she feel anything? They reassure her as they peel back the lower flap of skin over her eyes, as though they were removing a cap.

They cauterize some of the smaller vessels. They cut through the fatty white subcutaneous tissue to the skull. Then the chief neurosurgeon takes a tool not unlike a brace and bit, and begins to drill four holes in the skull. The patient rocks a little from the pressure. The bone dust from the turning bit sticks to the damp bloody skull.

The four technicians maintain their vigil over the polygraph. The anesthesiologist sits over the blinking light of his pulsing oscillator. The chief surgeon begins her second hole. Our interpreters stand in stunned silence. Many of us are white as sheets. I find I have grasped the seat of my chair in a vise-like grip.

"How does she know when to stop drilling?" I ask Dr. Wang, who has performed many of these same operations.

"It's completely up to the touch of the doctor, who must know by feel when to stop," he says with matter-of-fact confidence. I have a sudden image of the way a bit finally breaks through a piece of wood, and plunges up to the chuck.

It is exhausting watching the delicate repair of this human body, watching these craftsmen of consummate skill laboring over the head of a factory worker.

Dr. Wang looks at me and smiles indulgently at the intensity of my involvement. "Before the revolution," he says, "workers never had brain surgery."

My attention is riveted on the small dark dots being drilled in this skull.

"Now they are sawing the bone," says Dr. Wang, as the surgeon inserts a shiny surgical wire under the skull from one hole to another. She pulls it back and forth through the two holes the way someone might dry his back with a towel.

Three sides are sawed. The fourth side of this square patch of bone is then cracked uncermoniously with a pair of plierlike instruments. This side will provide the ragged edges through which the bone patch will knit back together.

The bone square is swung open like a small hinged trap door. There is more blood now. It is sucked away with a vacuum hose.

"You see the gray-blue layer?" asks Dr. Wang. "That is the meninges, membranes around the brain." He is speaking in Chinese, patiently and slowly, aware that only one tenth of my concentrating powers are now focused in my ears. I miss much of his detailed description, although he knows many technical terms in English. I am staring into this incredible cavity in a woman's head, wondering what her exposed brain is thinking now, reminded of that pickled cauliflower-like display in a glass jar in my high school biology class.

The open brain cavity is squirted with a saline solution from a tool that looks like a kitchen baster.

"Before we expose the brain, we must sterilize it," says Dr. Wang. "We must also apply a kind of bee's wax to check hemorrhaging from the bone marrow."

A robed and masked aid walks up to the operating table with a plateful of peeled sliced apples for the patient to eat.

"Perhaps the patient is thirsty or hungry," says Dr. Wang, with a pleased smile on his face, not unaware that this moment is going to impress us as the tour de force in the acupuncture anesthesia drama. "Sometimes we give them apples, or maybe some cake and orange juice if they feel like it."

A needle on the polygraph takes a big jump.

"No, that's all right," says Dr. Wang, sensing my consternation. "You see, it is mostly even. A jump or two just means some slight sensation. It's all right. It's going fine. She won't even need a transfusion."

The chief surgeon is reaching deep into the skull cavity now. She is aspirating, or removing the fluid, from the tumor. The aspirator brings back black coagulated blood.

"Ah, good," says Dr. Wang, nodding his head. "We suspected this. It won't hemorrhage. Now they can just cut up the tumor and take it out."

Someone asks who will pay for this operation.

"Well, the patient will pay something," says Dr. Wang. "We always discuss these matters with the patients. If they are fairly well off, well, then they can afford more. And, of course, the cost depends on the severity of the operation, and how long the patient must stay in the hospital. The person's factory, brigade or organization will also help. But, of course, if there is no money, it doesn't matter. It's free, or the State will pay. Or perhaps the person will pay part in installments. But, there is no fixed price or procedure. We simply discuss it with the patient. It's not something that people worry about."

The surgeons are probing deep inside the dark square hole, with long, sharp, unfamiliar-looking instruments. They bring out pieces of tumor and place them in a white pan, as though engaged in some miniature mining operation.

"They must be gentle," says Dr. Wang. "They don't want to damage the pituitary gland."

The tumor is slowly excised, piece by piece. The patient's bare feet stick out from underneath her robes at the end of the table, with the acupuncture needles still inserted. The plate of apples remains like some misplaced still life under the bright overhead lamps. The apples have started to discolor. Somehow it is the presence of the apples, more than anything else, which demystifies this operation.

The tumor is out. The doctors and nurses begin to sew the head back up, layer by layer. One doctor holds his finger on the bone patch while another sews, the way a person might hold his finger on a string while tying a package. The white gleaming bone is sewn through its soft outer surface.

The patient's toe twitches, as if in rhythm to some unheard music, as they begin to suture up the last layer, the skin. They remove all the clamps, and draw it back as though performing some final Frankensteinlike restoration. The bloody linen of the operating field is removed. A nurse reaches over and takes the patient's hand. We see her eyes now, awake and blinking. She smiles. They wipe her face with a cool damp cloth. The doctors chat with her as they wind a turbanlike bandage around her head.

A nurse blocks one of her eyes with a hand and holds up two fingers. The patient sees both. The operation has been a success. The patient raises her head, looks all around her, squinting a little in the bright light. She sees us. She waves and says something we can not hear.

The nurses move her from the operating table to a mobile cart. She waves again, smiles, and then is wheeled out the door.

Old Shanghai/ New Shanghai: Drugs and Prostitution

"Shanghai used to be an adventurer's paradise because of all the corruption and the reactionary rule of the Kuomintang," says Wang Shih, a member of the Shanghai Municipal Public Security Bureau. (The Chinese do not use the word police.) He wears a white uniform with red collar patches.

"When the Europeans started bringing opium to China, Shanghai turned into one of the first ports in China fully open to the importation of drugs. It was this drug trade, forced on China by foreigners, which finally started the Opium Wars (beginning in 1839). It continued under the Japanese, who occupied Shanghai in the thirties. It was legal to smoke opium.

"It was not long after the Europeans began to bring opium to

China that it extended into the countryside away from the Treaty Ports. Even the police got into the drug traffic. They used ships, planes, trucks, boats and soldiers in their network. They even sold opium at the so-called drug-abuse centers. The addicts would come in the front door for treatment, and then there would be people selling opium as they left through the back door.

"All during this time, the Kuomintang was levying taxes on opium. The opium dens outnumbered the grain stores. People bankrupted their families for drugs, and then died on the streets, destitute. After a cold snowy night in winter, it was not unusual to find corpses in the streets."

Wang pauses, shifts his weight and mental gears.

"In 1950," he begins again, "the Shanghai People's Government issued a decree prohibiting drugs. Drugs started being smuggled secretly into Shanghai. It was not until after a thorough campaign that people's consciousness on the subject was raised, and the problem fundamentally solved.

"There were three important elements in our drug program. First of all, we carried out the correct line of the Party and Chairman Mao. We adopted a policy of combining punishment with reeducation. It was a policy of leniency toward those who acknowledged their crimes, and severity toward those who stubbornly refused to confess. We made clear distinctions between sellers, manufacturers and addicts, because many addicts were just laborers who started smoking because of illness or depression. We saw them as victims, as children. So our main efforts with them involved giving reeducation, and asking them to help expose the traffickers. If the traffickers stopped their activities willingly after Liberation, well, then we would treat them leniently. Then we would ask them to help expose other large dealers.

"Our second effort was aimed at mobilizing the masses fully to expose the problem. We spread the Party's policy to everyone, to every house," adds a middle-aged woman, a leader of a neighborhood committee. "We organized everybody. No one remained ignorant. We explained to everyone how the imperialists had brought drugs to China and used them to exploit and enslave the Chinese people. We talked with family members, and taught them how to deal with addicts. The families often hated the addicts, and would not even let them live at home. So we had to get them to take a positive approach.

"There was one man named Chu. And I remember his wife wouldn't let him live at home because he was an opium addict. We had to persuade her to try to help him. Finally the family was persuaded to move to their native town to change surroundings. Chu recovered and got a job. The family was indeed thankful for the Party and Chairman Mao.

"We finally asked that all opium pipes and other implements be turned over to the government," continues Wang. "Those who were less addicted stopped smoking voluntarily. The more serious cases were turned over to hospitals for treatment.

"The Kuomintang wouldn't solve the problem in all the years they ruled because they were profiting from it. Theirs was not a people's government. But we did succeed in solving the problem. And we succeeded in transforming Shanghai from an adventurers' paradise into a paradise for people."

"Was there a phased period of time allotted to addicts to shake their habits, or were substitute drugs ever used?"

"No. There was no such period. They had to stop immediately. And we did not use any substitute drugs, because then, those available were the same as the old drugs. The regulation said: If you take drugs, you must stop immediately. The important ingredient was the degree of the person's determination and his political commitment."

"Were there accusation meetings?"

"Yes. There were mass meetings where unconfessed criminals were accused and sometimes sentenced. Addicts and their family members would speak about the harm drugs had done them. If the criminals confessed, they were pardoned. Otherwise, they received severe punishments.

"We now no longer even allow people to grow opium poppies just for looks. At first, you see, the addicts smoked just opium. Then they moved on to heroin, which started after the Japanese occupation. And many prostitutes became addicted."

"Were many dealers executed?"

"We never try and solve problems by killing people. There were only five people in all of Shanghai who were executed. Our policy is to arouse the masses of people and raise their consciousness. It was only a few of the big shots who received death sentences."

There is a pause.

"I was a victim of drugs," says a woman speaking for the first time. Ts'ai Yu-mei has been sitting impassively while Wang, the official, talks on. She is middle-aged. She speaks almost without inflection. Her face has a stretched, haggard appearance to it. She is one of the two women in China whom I have seen unabashedly chain-smoke cigarettes. I have been watching her face as Wang has been talking. It is a face that stands out starkly in this room of healthy righteous faces. There is a hardness around her mouth. No brightness in her eyes. She has been sitting without expression, listening as an actress might wait for her cue in a drama which has been playing for months.

"My first husband was also an addict," she continues. "At that time he was a clerk in a bank. I was in poor health as well. And when I became pregnant, he persuaded me to try drugs too. His parents had also taken drugs before he was born, and he was a very heavy user. After he married me, he became an even heavier user. It got so that he was not even able to work. Finally, he died from drugs.

"My child was born. When he was seven, he got the measles and died. I was so drugged, I couldn't take care of him."

Her hoarse voice stops, still betraying almost no emotion. I find myself wanting to be moved by this woman. But she tells her story as if it comes from an outline. I wonder how many times she has told it before. The Chinese would say that this was irrelevant, and that what counts is the message behind her experience.

"It was only after Liberation that I really began to understand the harm drugs do. And I stayed home with a strong will and stopped. For three days and nights I drank and ate nothing. I just stared at the ceiling and lay awake. It was extremely difficult. I ached all over and shed many tears. My nose ran. I was exhausted but could not sleep. I tried to sit up. But I could not even do that. This pain just went on and on.

"Finally, three days later I began to feel better, and started to eat again. I ate a bowl of rice gruel. I began to work around the neighborhood. When the 1952 campaign to prohibit drugs began, I started telling my story to other addicts, trying to convince them to stop. I tried to explain the Party's policy of leniency to those who confessed. I wanted to make a contribution to this movement so that these things would never happen again, because my transformation is really due to the Chinese Communist Party and Chairman Mao. My transformation is due to the social change which turned me from a shadow into a woman. The old society turned people into devils. The new society turns devils into people."

It is the turn of a portly middle-aged man to speak. He is from the Civil Affairs Bureau of Shanghai. His corpulence reveals itself most evidently in his head, the sides of which have been shaved clean, lending a soft roundness to the rest of his body, which is hidden by clothes. He also speaks in a colorless matter-of-fact manner, which is broken only by self-satisfied little smiles, which come after he feels he has summed up some point particularly well.

He tells us that in 1949 there were thirty thousand prostitutes in Shanghai, many of whom worked in the eight thousand brothels licensed by the Kuomintang. (Prostitution is still legal on Taiwan.)

"Many peasants were homeless and helpless," says the official. "They had no alternative but to come to the city. But here in Shanghai, it was virtually impossible to find a job. Many people were forced into becoming vagrants and prostitutes. Most of the prostitution was controlled by the Kuomintang gangs. They used to say that the police departments and jails served as restaurants and hotels for these gang leaders. If they were arrested, they went in the front door and out the back.

"Not long after Liberation, our government published a decree against brothels and prostitution. Brothels were banned. The ringleaders were severely punished because they had committed real crimes against the people. But for the prostitutes themselves and those who committed lesser crimes, we used reeducation, and raised their consciousness through productive labor."

As he continues to describe the process of reform, which was almost identical to that used with drug addicts, I watch the faces of the various other Chinese women sitting around the table to see if the subject of prostitution or carnal sex might cast some unusual shadows. But their faces are devoid of either embarrassment or moral superiority. Several take notes. The others listen to this discussion of the sale of sex in much the same way they might listen to a discussion on Lin Piao and Confucius. And I make a mental note: they have arranged for us to speak to an ex-addict, but they have not arranged for us to speak to an ex-prostitute.

There have been recent reports of some amateur prostitution in both Peking and Shanghai. But they usually have been described as being in connection with the foreign community. And reading over some of these accounts later, I can not help but wonder at the tenacity of the Western reporters who filed these stories (usually from Hong Kong). For while it is of some passing interest that there may be a few quasi-prostitutes in China, it is of significant interest that there are not more. I can not fully explain the relish with which Western correspondents report these facts, unless it is that China's purity seems intolerable to those of us on the outside who live in a state of such permanent compromise and ambiguity. It is almost as though we can not allow the Chinese to become intelligible unless we can see them as flawed in ways which we have long identified as mortal and human—flawed that is, by greed, lust, selfishness and self-gratification.

Shanghai Haircut

There is a curtain over the doorway. A sign above says The Glorious Barbershop.

I walk in. All conversation stops. Heads in various states of lather and tonsorial disarray snap around to see what the cause of the silence is.

The room is an old one with discolored yellow walls. A portrait of a younger Chairman Mao hangs above dim mirrors in front of four aging barber chairs. The reflective surfaces of the mirrors are slowly peeling away behind the glass, as though they were being infected by some unspeakable skin disease. A few people sit waiting on the wooden bench behind the chairs.

One of the barbers finally turns to me like a head waiter. The expression on his face suggests that he would like me to speak, although I can see that he is clearly anxious over the possibility that he may be stuck with some incomprehensible foreigner with whom no one can communicate.

"Can I get a haircut?" I ask.

He looks quizzically at my longish coiffure, tucked behind my ears (unknown in China), and says, "Oh, yes. Please sit down."

I sit on the bench and try to read a newspaper as nonchalantly as I can. The uneasy silence in the room continues. The group of children who followed me to just outside the door is growing. They are trying to peer in through the cracks between the curtain and the doorway.

I can think of nothing to say just now—no way to break the ice. I feel intimidated too, by the way my presence has seemed to freeze the once-congenial atmosphere of the barber shop.

My turn comes up. A pleasant middle-aged barber with a white gown and a surgeon's mask over his nose and mouth directs me toward his chair. I am thinking of brain surgery.

He begins to cut with extreme caution, almost one hair at a time. Sometimes I feel as though he is just snipping the scissors above my head, vamping until he gets a clear notion of how to treat this uncharted territory. My hair is thick, blond and long. It is also dirty.

"Not many foreigners come in here," he finally says as he pecks around my ears, seeming to beg the question of what he should do with the ruin of hair on my head.

"Just cut a lot off, however you want to," I say.

He is not pleased with these instructions. Actually, I am tired of my longish (by Chinese standards) hair, and I am curious to see what the Chinese notion of a Western haircut is. I am not anxious to give detailed instructions. I do not really care what the outcome looks like, as long as it does not alarm the Chinese for the next month.

My barber begins as though he were doing a Chinese haircut—cutting everything off the sides, leaving a tuft on top.

Once this is done, he pauses with indecision over the top. My head now resembles a blond paint brush.

"Yes. Cut more off the top," I am finally compelled to suggest.

"Okay," he says.

"Who owns this shop?" I ask.

"It is State-owned," he replies. "Now we serve the people."

A rather severe-looking young woman takes a chair down the line.

"We do both men and women," says my barber, as the other barber begins to wet her already-short hair. She sits unsmiling as he cuts it into a bob.

The person immediately adjacent to me is a young man in his twenties. He has almost finished, and it is clear that he has some Shanghai style-consciousness. (Before the Cultural Revolution, Shanghai evidenced much more concern for fashion than other parts of China.) His hair is shaped back on the sides like "fenders," and is held in place by some oil, an unheard-of outrage in Peking or the countryside. He has carefully coached the barber the whole time. He holds a hand mirror throughout so that he can have a view of what is happening on all sides. Although his vanity stands out here in Shanghai, The People's Republic of China, he would doubtless be considered a model of modesty and self-abnegation in most of the hair salons of the West. It's all a question of proportion.

My own barber has hit his pace now. He is onto something, although it is not yet evident what it will finally mean to my new demeanor. He keeps sweeping back the long hair on top of my head as he cuts, suggesting that he plans this posture to be its ultimate repose.

A lady with a two-year-old child moves into the chair on my other side. The baby begins to howl. I laugh. Others laugh. The atmosphere is somewhat loosened by this small frightened child about to have his hair cut.

The manager suddenly charges at the door, snapping a towel as he goes. The mob of children scatters across the sidewalk in glee. There is a retarded child of about thirteen with them. He is not as agile as the others, and does not run. He just stands there in the middle of the sidewalk smiling a goofy smile. Some of the other children laugh and point at him, which almost sends him backing into a lit hibachi pot a woman is cooking on right out in the middle of the sidewalk. She swats him on the head with a wicker broom in a way which is only partially good-natured. The retarded child remains immobile, and gives her his goofy smile. The other children laugh mirthfully.

Back inside, my head is taking shape. The barber has definitely decided on the swept-back look; the Janos Misczek Czech freedom fighter of 1957 special! Early Toscanini!

I nod approval, and he squires me over to the wash basin, where he shampoos my head. Then he gives me a shave. He shaves my forehead, nose, ears, as well as my cheeks and chin. I feel like the kind of inordinately hairy foreigner described in the days of yore by Chinese who first encountered Westerners.

He gets out the hair drier, sweeps my hair back resolutely on top, and begins to dry it in place. He has lost all timidity now, and is wantonly shaping it and patting it with his free hand as he dries. It acquires a springy puffed-up quality, as though the hair had been immobilized in place by some magnetic force.

He places hot towels on my face. They feel wonderful.

I'm done.

I pay .25 yuan, shake hands, and leave through the sea of children at the door, who hastily part as if I were Moses.

I walk down P'ing t'ien lu past one of the more stately mansions of the old French Concession. I catch a profile of my new hairdo in a shop window.

I am transformed.

Courtship in China

Fishing family on the People's Liberation Commune

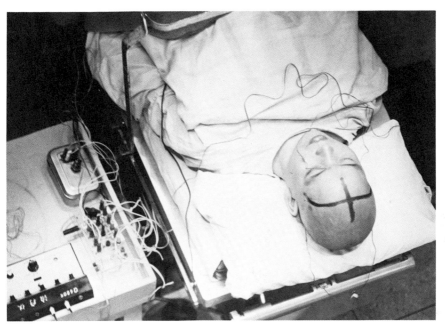

Woman awaiting surgery with acupuncture anesthesia

Shanghai dock workers

Dock Worker Liu Fu-chu

Physical education class at Peking elementary school

Lao Liu

Reception Committee at the People's Liberation Commune

"Educated Youth" in the Chung Non Central Co-op Canteen, Shanghai

Chinese High Camp

Tonight we are weary. But our usual agenda of three events a day—morning, afternoon and night—continues. This evening we visit the Shanghai Youth Palace. The Ping-Pong rooms, practice halls, dance studios, meeting rooms, and exhibition halls are housed in the old pre-Liberation Great World—a kind of Kuomintang Chinese Harrah's Club.

Just as I think we are coming to the end of the tour of youth activities, we are ushered into the Exhibit of Youth Heroes. The first exhibit is on Lei Feng, a young PLA soldier, who died in the early sixties, killed by a falling telephone pole. While living, he kept a diary of his exemplary life "serving the people," and has since been canonized as a flawless political saint and youth idol. It would be fair to say that there is not one young person (or old, for that matter) in China who has not heard of Lei Feng. He was a selfless composite character combining all desirable traits which China's young are supposed to emulate. There have been books, comic books, movies, exhibits, poems, and endless essays written about Lei Feng's shining example of selflessness.

The exhibit before me is almost bizarre. In its efforts to elevate Lei Feng to hitherto-unattained levels of exemplary behavior, the exhibitors have been forced to probe the surreal. There are tinted black-and-white photos of Lei Feng holding a rifle transposed over the Shanghai Municipal Revolutionary Committee building, once the British-owned Hong Kong Shanghai Bank, as though Lei Feng were some omnipresent spirit. A young Youth Palace worker is unclear whether or not Lei Feng ever even came to Shanghai.

There are gaudy oil paintings done in a heroic socialist-realist style which evoke Andy Warhol rather than Karl Marx. There are "replicas" in glass cases of Lei's cup, wash basin, straw sandals, uniform, and even a wax squash and pumpkin—representations, I suppose, of ones he ate!

The exhibit is seemingly without end. Replica notebook. Replica rifles. Photos of Lei Feng doing everything: studying, working, helping peasants, smiling. My companion from the Youth Palace and one of his friends are giving me a nonstop biography of the legendary Lei Feng. I can not help tuning it out. But I am looking at the exhibit. They are pleased. I am pleased for them that Lei Feng is such an inspiration. But how can I explain to these two helpful comrades that my fascination is more with the fact that I am witnessing one of the world's most definitive exhibits of high camp?

The Lei Feng display ends unobtrusively at an unannounced boundary, and a new exhibit of a more recent youth hero commences. I suddenly realize that although the message is the same, the face has changed in the tinted photos. The new hero's name is Chu K'o-chia. He is the twenty-fourth alternative member of the Central Committee. He is a native of Shanghai who has gone to the remote parts of Yunnan Province (just above Laos and North Vietnam) to "serve the people."

He is an earnest, intelligent nice-looking young man with benign patience showing in his bespectacled eyes. In almost every photo he is helping someone study or work. It is strange to think of Chinese youth holding this mild, sensible and probably kind young man in their hearts as a hero, while youth elsewhere dream fantasies of flashy detectives, reckless lovers, lawless gangsters and macho cowboys.

Chinese Marriage Problems à la Lao-Liu

We finally arrive at the end of the Youth Heroes Exhibit. We mill around awhile before arranging ourselves for one of *those* photos in front of a vast portrait of Mao surrounded by youths.

I feel that unique fatigue that sets in after long afternoons in museums. It is a relief to sit down in the dark bus. Out the window I see Lao Liu's beaming face bob up the steps, momentarily lit up as he gets into the bus past an outside light. He sits next to me.

Although Lao Liu is over forty, and in a position of some importance with the Friendship Association in Shanghai, he has the demeanor of an ebullient, overgrown and possibly naughty boy. He is of medium height and has a roundish face that ends in a surprisingly angular chin. At almost any moment he is liable to make some joke, and then laugh wantonly and wonderfully at his own humor. His pleasantries are usually followed by an arm draped over your shoulders. His good spirits are a joy.

Often he talks so fast that his jokes are lost on me, and he has to go back and recap them so I can understand. Then he watches me as one might watch a burning fuse on a stick of dynamite. At the first sign that I am beginning to grasp his punch line, he himself explodes with a roar of laughter.

Lao Liu speaks only ten words or so of English, which he often uses with great comic effect. But he is a man who seems able to be uninhibited, even around people with whom he cannot communicate. He enjoys telling stories immensely. Indeed, his tales of guerrilla warfare when he was a child in Shantung Province against the Japanese are spellbinding.

Although he sometimes cracks off-color jokes, he is also a man of deep revolutionary convictions and experience. At fifteen he joined the Red Army and local militia units. After the war, he observed and participated in the process of land reform in his native province. He can talk forever about these years, about the fate of this or that landlord, and the uncertainty felt by many as China's two-thousand-year-old land system began to break up in the late forties.

But tonight on the bus we somehow get onto the subject of marriage problems, a subject with which few Chinese seem comfortable. Lao Liu runs headlong into the conversation, speaking so loudly that people several seats away can hear him over the sounds of the moving bus. I ask him whether all the work people do and the time they spend outside of their families and without their spouses ever creates tensions and problems.

"Well, yes. Sometimes," he replies. "Sometimes we feel a contradiction. I mean, if you're working all the time, and come home late every night, and your wife is late too, I'm not saying it is always easy. But, you know, things are quite different now, compared to the past. For instance, if you're late and don't come home, your wife won't worry about you. Why should she? What can happen? I mean, no one's going to murder you. And it's not like before when she might have thought that you were out playing around with someone else. That doesn't happen. Well . . . I won't say never. But not much. And, it works the other way around too. If your wife is out, you know that she is working, serving the people.

"So, like now, you all are here. And, of course, I'll be with you all the time. Even when you go to the factory. How can I go home? I can't. So my wife understands. We just have to plan it all out ahead with the children."

He smiles, then continues to talk. One hand is on my shoulder. The other is gesticulating wildly in the darkness of the bus.

"Some of the older people still have the old thinking," he goes on. "They feel they have to separate how much time they give outside of their house for the revolution from how much they save for their families. I actually even have some of this. But we all really have a love of work. And if we get home tired, well, even the children understand. They help out."

"Do married people fight much in China?"

"Well, there are still some. But not so many. People marry late. Men usually wait until they are thirty, and women wait until they are about twenty-six or seven. They are more experienced, calmer. They are politically more advanced. If there is a disagreement . . . Well, you know about criticism and self-criticism. We try and talk about it and figure out the contradictions and problems. We talk it over. And, yes, it works.

"Let's just say there is a fight, okay? Well, everyone in the neighborhood or building will know, right? I mean, we all live so close to one another. How can you keep a fight private?

"Sure, we might feel a little embarrassed. But what can you do? And, actually, maybe it's better that way. The neighbors hear you and come over. And they might say something like 'Okay, now. What's wrong? What are the problems here? Take it easy. Let's sit down and talk.'

"It's mutual help. Very few people get divorced. But it's allowed in the new marriage law." He pauses and reflects a moment. And then with a smile, he says, "Well, you know, we have a whole different social system from you. It isn't like yours, is it? It's completely different."

Workers

Wang Fu-fa works for the Hsing Huo Day and Night Store in Shanghai. He sits with several young women from the store, a restaurant and a hotel. The Chinese see significance in our talking to workers such as these. As they talk, I conjure up the amusing vision of the American government's rounding up a bellhop from the Hilton, a short-order cook from a Kentucky Fried Chicken stand, and a check-out woman from Safeway to discuss political developments in the United States with a visiting delegation from China.

"Ours is a food store," says Wang, holding a small notebook in both hands. "We have thirty-five workers in it. Our store has developed through struggle against revisionist ideas. We have a motto: 'Think about whatever the people are thinking about, and serve them well.' "

Wang pauses as a preacher might, having given chapter and verse of the oncoming sermon. "At first we had only six types of commodities and two hundred different kinds of items in the store. We now carry twenty-one different types of commodities, and over eight hundred different kinds of items. This expansion happened after criticizing Lin Piao, and considering how we might better meet the needs of workers, peasants and soldiers. Now whatever the people need, our staff tries to provide. We run our store as a tool to consolidate the proletarian revolution, not for profit. In 1968 we began to stay open twenty-four hours each day as a service to people who got off their factory shift late at night and found it inconvenient to shop in the day. We have set up free services like an air pump for bicycle tires [bicycles are the main means of transportation in most cities]. We help send sick people to the hospital in a vehicle. We do little things like stock fuses, since we are an all-night store. Often people will blow a fuse at night when all the other stores are closed. And then, we do small services like helping people from out of town find a hotel room. We are trying to break down the old relationships between the shopkeepers and the customers. We want to help the customers.

"For instance, in our store we also have a refreshment service and a canteen. Once a comrade who worked in the canteen changed the name on some fish we were serving from white fish to silver carp. You see, people much prefer silver carp. White fish is not so popular. And so, when this old comrade switched the signs, the fish sold like wildfire.

"But then we asked ourselves, Why should we use such capitalistic techniques to sell this fish when we should just be serving the people? So we wrote an article in the canteen called "How White Fish Became Silver Carp," and we explained to the old worker and others what was wrong with what he had done.

"I remember another time, a very old man came into the store to buy cocoa powder. We wondered why he came alone. Were there not some younger people in his family to help him shop? Subsequently we found out that all of his family members live and work outside of Shanghai, and that his old wife was sick. We got his address and sent his groceries to his door. Later on, one of the comrades went to his house. He found that this time the old man was sick. So we just sent some groceries without being asked. They were deeply moved. The old man thanked Chairman Mao from the bottom of his heart, and he thanked the youths who were nurtured by socialism."

Fang Yin works in the Chung Nan Central Co-op Canteen, a small working-class restaurant in downtown Shanghai. The canteen is a long narrow room with a small charcoal brazier and kitchen at one end. Tables line the walls and windows facing out to the tree-lined street. With the exception of some posters on the walls and some overhead fluorescent lights, the restaurant is bare.

We visit in the morning. Several workers sit quietly at tables and eat bowls of soup and noodles. The attendants wear white kerchiefs over their hair. Many of the older attendants used to be street vendors and peddlers before Liberation. The canteen, which now employs forty-one people, was originally the result of a number of these street vendors organizing themselves.

"I first got sent down to work in this canteen after I graduated from middle school," says Fang Yin, who wears a "dress" jacket, which differs from work clothes only in that it is made of synthetic fiber, has bright-colored buttons, and shows faint suggestions of having been tapered at the waist. Fang is in her early twenties, and wears her lovely shiny hair back in braids.

"When I got assigned here, I felt very badly," she continues. "I felt that it was a waste of my talent to get sent to an ordinary restaurant like this. I was very unhappy. But after our Party Branch organized some discussion groups and we talked about it, I began to see that this outlook of dividing work into different levels was wrong. In the end, it all serves the people."

Her discussion reminds me how much easier the Chinese seem to find discussions on past issues that have been resolved than present issues that are still being struggled over. The Chinese talk openly and enthusiastically about problems which have already been laid to rest. But, with us at least, they remain utterly close-mouthed about present storms. The result is that a foreigner can gain a fairly clear idea about what *has* happened, but will be kept quite in the dark about what divisive problems are raging at the moment. Chaotic, or even violent, struggle is always talked about as a phenomenon of the Cultural Revolution, of land reform, or the Great Leap Forward—but not of the here and now.

The Chinese are forever looking at their past experiences and analyzing them in light of whatever current political campaign is under way. As the campaigns change, so do the features of their work and lives which they choose to stress. Right now, in the wake of the Cultural Revolution, the Criticize Lin Piao and Confucius Movement is the main focus of attention. Essentially, it calls on everyone not only to root out remaining class differences but to root out bourgeois tendencies (even incipient tendencies), from their thought and work.

A coworker begins to recount a story exuding a degree of uprightness which might strike one as ludicrous if indulged in anywhere else than China. And yet there is absolutely no sense of superiority in this woman's delivery—no trace of a desire to deprecate anyone else.

"There was this time" she says, "when we were serving an especially nourishing soup with eggs in it. One day while serving, an older comrade put two eggs in another comrade's soup. He said, 'You work hard, so why not eat one more egg?'

"The young comrade said, 'No. These eggs belong to the proletariat.' He gave back the egg because he saw how even these small things could engender insurgent capitalist tendencies. For it is from small everyday matters that bourgeois habits and ideas spring up. To get rid of these ideas, the young and the old must study together and see why we must exercise the dictatorship of the proletariat. For only this way will the new communal morality develop."

"We must absolutely obey the needs of the State," adds Chou Hui-ling, a middle-school graduate who works at a small inn. "All jobs are revolutionary. All jobs in China need people to continue doing them. Now, one might think that a canteen or a refreshment stand is insignificant. But if there are no canteens and refreshment stands, where are people going to eat and get refreshed?

"Socialist society is like a machine," he continues, "if one small screw is missing, the machine won't work correctly. So you can't divide up the jobs and say one is more important than another or better than another."

Beauty and Sex

There are no plastic surgeons in China to widen eyes, raise noses, lift breasts and sagging backsides. There is an obvious de-emphasis on the way people appear physically. The average person seems relatively comfortable and unselfconscious about his or her body. And yet, although one does not confront it every moment in magazines, books, TV, movies, and stores, there does seem to be a standard of beauty and physical desirability in China. It is, however, extremely low-key, and not easy for a Westerner to detect at first, since, like so much else in China, these standards are not traceable to those in the West. While our own notion of physically desirable traits has transformed the values of countries like Japan, China has been little affected. The Japanese spend millions of dollars each year on cosmetic surgery to alter prominent Japanese features to conform more closely to Western standards of beauty. While American women movie stars and models tend to be tallish, slender and well-proportioned, with prominent noses and other features, the Japanese tend to be short, squat, with flat noses and busts, and almost almond-shaped eyes. It would not be unfair to say that in the case of countries like Japan, a whole race of people finds itself saddled with a standard of good looks which is utterly in conflict with its own natural features.

The Chinese have not gotten themselves into a similar bind. No skin whiteners line store shelves, as they do in Hong Kong, Taiwan and Singapore. The Chinese have no fear of becoming sunburned and dark-skinned. In fact, in China, dark skin is considered to reflect one's attention to manual labor and proletarian dedication.

The Chinese do not talk a lot about physical features. There is little discussion of sex. Conversations on the shape of people's bodies are not bull-session events. Most people keep this kind of thing to themselves. What is played up in public is the notion of picking a mate because of "high political consciousness," and "revolutionary commitment." Such attributes as these, plus hard work, selflessness, admittance to the Party or PLA doubtless enhance one's desirability, regardless of looks. Just the way the captain of a football team often ends up with the prettiest girl in the class, so a model worker might end up with an exemplary cadre as a mate. It is altogether possible that in certain major ways, the Chinese have succeeded in fundamentally altering the notion of attractiveness by simply substituting some of these revolutionary attributes for the physical ones which play such an important role in Western courtship.

But even in China, physical features are not totally extraneous. As one long-time Western resident told me, tall slender people are still considered more appealing than short muscular people with peasant builds.

"There is something about the old stereotype of the helpless frail woman that must still have an almost involuntary attraction," she says. "These things still exist today. They die slowly. Even people with high political consciousness may find themselves with such biases. But the revolution has succeeded in changing many of the old, deep-seated attractions from our pre-Liberation society, which was full of backward customs from Chinese civilization, as well as vulnerable to the Hollywood movie image."

It is hard to get Chinese to talk about a subject like this. You draw blanks when asking such questions, as if you were seeking to draw them out in an area so tainted with bourgeois decadence that it would rub off on them through mere discussion.

"Yes, I suppose it's true," continues my woman friend pondering my interest in this subject. "China cannot be real for Americans unless they understand questions like this. Let me give you an example. Women who cut their hair off during the Cultural Revolution were not only considered 'correct' (because they did not need to spend so much time combing and braiding each day) they were also considered to be in the vanguard. They had an aura about them which was perhaps not unlike your hippies with their long hair. This style goes back to Yenan and the thirties, when women first cut their hair as a practical and symbolic gesture of liberation. And so even today, it comes with a suggestion of romance and the aura of those exciting days of living in caves and fighting the Japanese.

"And then, people generally seem to prefer square, angular faces with prominent jaw and cheekbones to rounder faces, which in prerevolutionary days people thought of as belonging to the peasantry. There was an expression, which is almost never used now, since it was one of mockery and derision. A *t'u-pao-tzu* (literally, "a ball or clod of earth") referred to a person just in from the country, a hick, with whom the features of round faces were associated.

"Then, in Tung-pei, in the Northwest of China people seem to prefer men whose heads are flat on the back. You know, babies often get flat heads from lying in one position. For some reason people like these, and they call them 'Tung-pei heads.' "

No doubt there are other regional preferences. One searches them out only to try to unravel the mystery of Chinese interpersonal relations. For Chinese do marry, have sex, live together, raise families and obviously care for one another. In variously complicated ways, a Chinese couple must be as individually attracted to each other as any two people in the world.

And yet, I often get the sense that the Chinese wish to convey, in some unspoken way, that they have learned to defy the sexual gravity which keeps the bourgeois world so preoccupied and earth-bound.

Americans are forever trying to get the Chinese to say something illuminating on the subject of their personal relations. They will sit at a tableful of commune cadres and officials and ask, and expect an answer, about premarital sex. Such questions by foreigners may elicit nervous laughs, but there is almost never any ensuing discussion.

Here is an example:

"Do you think that man is handsome?" a woman member of our trip asks a woman factory worker, pointing to one of her male comrades.

"Oh, no," she replies, warding off the question with some embarrassment and failing to deliver a judgment.

"Do you want to get married?"

"Oh, yes."

"When?"

"Not until about twenty-seven."

"Why do you want to get married?"

"To have children."

"How many do you hope to have?"

"Two, as suggested by the Party."

"Do the Chinese enjoy sex?"

Long pause. Finally a married woman sitting next to them answers. "Yes, of course. When we are married. But we do not talk about it all the time. It is not appropriate to discuss it in front of people who are unmarried."

Sex is indeed a private matter in China—one of the few areas in a married person's life over which the revolution seems not to make pronouncements. The Chinese certainly seem to have sexual energy like all human beings. (The recent rate of population growth has been about two percent annually.) But relations between the sexes have been shaped in a very different way from Western sexuality. The Chinese are not confronted with the daily barrage of subliminal sexual enticement which plays on people's weaknesses. There are no advertisements, books, movies or television programs suggesting that a certain level of sexual prowess and attainment is necessary. People are not goaded on to define themselves in purely sexual terms, to prove themselves or to close some imaginary gap between the achievements of their own lives and some mythical television figure. If there is any sexual manipulation in China, it is in the direction of de-emphasis rather than emphasis, just as China de-emphasizes the personal life of people in general, in favor of public or political contributions.

Another distinctly different feature of personal relationships in China is the role of work. It is the most important part of their lives, and they define themselves in terms of it. Consequently it takes almost all of their time. There is little extra energy to turn inward; there is little time and no encouragement for hedonistic activities. Leisure is not an activity high on the list of officially sanctioned pastimes in China.

In the West, many behaviorists tend to look on our intense pursuit of money, power, fame and career as products of a sublimated sex drive, as an almost dangerous substitute for normal sexual outlets. But in China an almost exactly contrary analysis has been rendered. It is considered normal to work hard (for the commonweal), and abnormal and "sublimated" if a great deal of energy is going into affairs with the opposite sex. The Chinese have taken Freud and stood him on his head. Many Westerners may be tempted to view China as puritanical, massively repressed, and suffering from some unexplained form of national impotency. All one can reply is that, although many of the causes may appear to exist, the symptoms of a tormented people are nowhere apparent.

Perhaps it is a question of values and not repression here in China. For whatever the Chinese are doing, they are clearly not afflicted with the crippling uncertainty and inadequacy which have somehow managed to become the hallmark of much of the Western sexual revolution. Whereas sexual attraction in the West often plays upon a kind of attraction-repulsion mechanism which both produces and feeds insecurity, the Chinese seem to find this alien. The notion of "playing hard to get" or exacerbating jealousies in order to win someone's love does not appear to assume such a prominent role. It is almost as though the defrocking of competition as an economic ethic has found a foothold in interpersonal relations as well.

As in so many other things Chinese, there is a directness and a matter-of-factness evident in relations between the sexes. There is a lack of the tension that both plagues and excites Westerners. Perhaps it is this absence which explains the feeling of flatness many Westerners attribute to Chinese personal relations.

The Shanghai Waterfront

The Shanghai docks comprise one of the busiest ports in the world. They line the Whangpoo River, which passes through the heart of Shanghai on its way to meet up with the Yangtze.

It is not unusual for the docks to be so crowded that ships are unloaded and loaded around the clock. Today there are twenty large vessels at anchor outside on the Yangtze waiting for berths. Ships of almost every country now call in China. But many of them fly flags most Westerners have rarely seen before. There are ships from North Korea, Albania, Somalia, Tanzania, as well as ones from the more familiar seafaring nations like Norway, Germany and Japan. I even note one small freighter flying a tattered hammer and sickle.

In the last ten years Chinese shipbuilding has proceeded at a pace which can only be described as previously unthinkable. China has been building ocean-going freighters in the ten-thousand-ton range, and now beginning work on larger ships in the twenty-thousand-ton range. China no longer buys ships abroad.

At Number Three Wharf, we board a large ship called the *Long March*, now loading cargo and passengers for the Manchurian port of Dairen. The captain is a plumpish man from Anwhei Province. As we walk around the decks, he holds my hand to guide me around more quickly. He is somewhat harried, and keeps apologizing for the hasty reception.

"We are sailing in a few hours, and there still is much to be done," he says.

The *Long March* was built in 1970 for both passengers and cargo; all materials used came from China. As with the trains here, the accommodations on ships are divided into classes. We did not see the fourth class, which I gather consists of porthole-less bunk rooms below the water line. Third-class accommodations consist of a cabin with six iron beds with mattresses, a desk, a spitoon and a porthole.

Second-class accommodations consist of a cabin with a sink, four wooden beds provided with linen, some chairs, a desk and a porthole. They have a touch of class, you might say. First class consists of a cabin with several rooms—one or more bedrooms, a sitting room, plenty of portholes and a private shower.

Out on the docks, men in hard hats made of rattan are operating fork lifts and off-loading fresh produce from trucks and bicycle carts. Large cranes swing nets full of produce, automobiles, and large earthen crocks of pickled vegetables into the hold of the ship.

The dock complex itself is like a small town. It employs two thousand workers, two hundred and sixty of whom are women. It provides canteens, kindergartens, and clinics for its workers, whose wages range from forty-two to ninety yuan a month.

Inside one of the buildings alongside the dock, we meet Liu Fu-chu, a retired dock worker. He is fifty-six. He has a week's growth of stubble on his chin, and wears a blue jacket. He talks with great animation, raising his voice for emphasis and rapping the table with his fingers. Periodically, he lights up a cigarette, which he clamps in his tobacco-stained front teeth.

"I really don't know where to begin," he says, taking his dock worker's cap off, and running his hand over his forehead and through his hair. "I have so much to say, and the time is short . . . I started work on the docks when I was fourteen. At that time people called us 'coolies.' " ("Coolie" comes from the Chinese k'u-li, or literally, "bitter strength.") "Everyone looked down on the dock workers as the lowest of the low. The foremen and the bosses called us vagrants. We had no status at all. We dock workers used to say that if there were eighteen steps to hell, then we were on the eighteenth step. We were beasts of burden. We ate like dogs and horses. And each day we feared for our work. At noon, we worried lest we would have nothing to eat. All night we worried about whether or not we could find a place to sleep. And then each day we had to wander from place to place trying to find work. We were particularly afraid of rainy and cold days because we had no place to go to get out of the rain."

A lusterless young dock worker in his early twenties interrupts. "Now there is no worry," he says smugly. "When it rains, the workers just go inside and study Marxism-Leninism."

"We had no umbrellas," says old Liu, having endured this contemporary footnote. "We had no clothing to speak of. We were hungry. So rain and cold were very frightening to us. Now young workers, because they've had no taste of the past, just say, 'Fine. If it rains, we'll go inside and study Marxism-Leninism.' " Liu turns benignly to the youth who just interrupted. "Or they go to the workers' club and play Ping-Pong, sing or read. It's not frightening at all. Now on a rainy day, we have hot water with sugar and ginger to drink. Or maybe we'll take a hot bath. But in our time, this was unimaginable.

Now the young can't understand why we have these fears.

"We feared sickness dreadfully, because we couldn't afford to see a doctor. One worker friend of mine, called Hung, was very strong. He could carry two hundred kilos. But because it rained for several days, he could not get work and could not get enough to eat. Finally, he just died in a public toilet. He was only forty-four years old.

"In the old days, if you caught a cold, you might be done for. Now the young people say, 'Don't be afraid. If you get a cold just get some tissues and go to the doctor. But they don't understand how it was. They don't understand how my good friend Hung died just because he hadn't eaten for several days . . . I was sick for four months not long ago. I went to the hospital, and I didn't pay anything! In fact, I got paid—in the hospital!

"Another thing we were afraid of was growing old. We knew that then we would be unable to find work easily, no longer being so strong. So we feared that we would just end up dead in the street. Now"—he laughs—"I have another worry. I am fifty-six, and the Party wants me to retire. But I don't want to! How could I just retire and lead an idle life, receiving money while doing nothing to improve the harbor? Maybe I am too old to add one more brick to the edifice of socialism. But at least I might be able to carry a few bricks to the site!" He laughs, again.

"The other worry we used to have in the old days was over holidays and New Year's. Those days were like climbing through a mountain pass for us. We had to borrow money to buy presents for the bosses and foremen. And you can imagine, if we did not have enough money to eat, how difficult it was to buy all this stuff to give to the bosses. Well, these worries are gone now. On holidays, we now have vacations too. We buy chicken and meat for our families. I even bought half a bottle of wine for Spring Festival last year!

"A lot of coal used to come into the docks in the old times. We coolies had to walk over piles of coal on wooden planks while carrying cargo from one place to another. Sometimes the workers would slip from one of these planks and fall down quite a distance, either seriously injuring themselves or getting killed. And you know what? When someone fell, the foreman would usually run over and get mad!

I had a coworker who fell one day. We all ran down to help him. When the foreman saw that he was dead, he yelled, 'Get to work! What does it matter if there is one less? With one call we can get a hundred more!'

"We used to say that if you were looking for a hundred dogs, it would not be easy to find them. But if you were looking for a hundred coolies, there was no problem."

Liu recounts another story about a friend who fell into the river while working. The foreman refused to allow Liu to help fish him back out, saying, "What's the big deal about one stinking coolie in the river?"

"Even single people couldn't make ends meet," says Liu. "People with families were in an unimaginable situation. We ate rice and rotten fish left over in garbage cans from the wealthy. Those were bitter years."

Another young worker unexpectedly jumps up and stems the tide of Liu's recollections. "We have become masters politically and economically of our docks," he begins. I glance around the room. I realize that, typically, almost all the Chinese who have come to meet with us will probably try to make at least a short declaration. Often these declarations seem to come out of nowhere. A subject is suddenly dropped as someone else takes the floor and gives whatever presentation he or she has prepared. Often this phenomenon breaks the focus of the discussion, derailing all of us. Here there are several young workers who have not yet spoken. I am sure they will. I assume that everyone who attends such a meeting as this has made at least a rough decision in advance on what to say.

No sooner have I thought these thoughts than one previously silent woman begins to talk. She is a welder who tells the story of building several of the large new cranes which have revolutionized the Shanghai waterfront.

She has hardly finished when another young woman begins to speak about Chairman Mao. She starts to describe an incident in which she got to shake hands with "The Chairman." Here in Shanghai, people seem to have the habit of referring to Mao as "The Chairman" *(Chu-hsi)* rather than as "Chairman Mao" *(Mao Chu-*

hsi). Her breathy delivery suggests that she had come with the intention of telling this antecdote and was suddenly unable to contain herself. She stands up, talking faster and faster.

"I was too excited to say anything to The Chairman. The people behind me didn't get a chance to shake his hand, so later they came by and shook my hand instead."

She continues on and on, not unlike a mid-sixties teen-ager rhapsodically describing an encounter with her favorite Beatle. Old Liu sits with his hands crossed in his lap, and stares out over our heads with a distant look in his eyes.

Pollution

Huang Hung-liang is an official from the Shanghai Municipal Office for the Treatment of the Three Wastes, something akin to the Environmental Protection Agency in the United States. The Three Wastes are waste water, gas and solid residues. Huang is a businesslike official and "wastes" no time getting to the point!

"During the twenty-six years since Liberation," he says, "we have attained great achievements in industry and agriculture. We have developed from a semicolonial consumer city to an industrial city. And along with the growth in production, the Party has had to take measures against pollution. We rely on the principles of overall planning, the rational distribution of industry and agriculture, multipurpose use, efforts to turn the harmful into the beneficial, reliance on the masses, the notion that each person must do something, protecting the environment, and doing good for the people." (These eight somewhat redundant points are a kind of official environmentalist credo in China, although no one in China thinks of himself as an "environmentalist" per se.)

"In accordance with the above principles, we try to stimulate the simultaneous development of industry and agriculture, of the cities and countryside, of economic development and environmental protection. Just as we relied on the masses to transform the old city of Shanghai, so we rely on them to transform the Three Wastes.

"In the past, many foreign countries imposed concessions on Shanghai. They carved up the city for profit. It was difficult to work out any rational scheme of city planning. And although these foreign and Chinese capitalists did open many factories, their sole purpose was to make money, even to the detriment of people's health and safety. They discharged a great deal of waste material. The situation was completely unchecked. And still, their production yield was low. One month of production now equals the total amount produced in Shanghai all during the year of 1949. Even though pre-Liberation production was low, our environment was seriously polluted. By 1930, Soochow Creek—which flows through Shanghai and meets with the Whangpoo River in the middle of the city—was so badly polluted that the public water works had to be moved from Ch'apei. The water was black and foul.

"Since Liberation, we have done some work in conjunction with the Plan for the Development of the National Economy to deal with some of these problems. Certain factories which used to discharge wastes into the creek have been redesigned. For instance, we merged some hundred small leather tanneries into eight larger ones. Then we mobilized the workers to transform the tanning process so that their wastes could be treated. Other factories—such as electrical machinery, steel and petrochemical plants—were moved out of the city proper into new industrial areas in the suburbs.

"Prior to Liberation, over one million people lived in slums with virtually no sanitation. In some of these places, like Fan Kua Lung, there were only small houses made with reeds. Since then, new residences have been built, and the old open sewage ditches, into which people also threw garbage, are now filled in. All in all, the city has filled in more than three hundred kilometers of these open sewers, which used to be breeding grounds for flies, mosquitoes and epidemics of infectious diseases. For instance, the park surrounding the Shanghai Zoo used to be only twenty hectares. Now it has been enlarged to seventy. These kinds of open spaces help purify the city air.

"Chairman Mao teaches us to hold ourselves responsible for the health of the people. New factories must be designed and constructed with treatment facilities for the Three Wastes, otherwise they can not open. And those old factories with pollution problems must form three-in-one groups to solve their problems."

In China, the battle against pollution is not so much a question of law as a question of responsibility—the responsibility of each person for everyone else. Although the Chinese are tremendously eager to develop industrially, they are also dedicated to the slogan "Prevention First," when it comes to health care. And thus, in the logic of Maoist analysis, developing and protecting the environment do not become an unalterably opposed contradiction. For in doing both, one is "serving the people."

"In Shanghai, we have taken three main measures to deal with pollution," continues Huang. "We are transforming technical processes of industry. If we can transform certain old processes, we alleviate some of the pollution. One common method is to search for nontoxic chemical substitutes for toxic ones. Here we have learned some lessons from abroad. As a result of the cases of mercury poisoning in Japan, some of our plants, like the Tao Pu Chemical Plant, have changed processes.

"The second measure we take is to implement multiple-use planning to regain valuable chemical resources from waste. One synthetic chemical fiber plant, which used to discharge poisonous gas, is now capturing it and making it into nylon. Their discharge of poisonous gas used to be thirty-five times higher than the standards now allowed by the State. Now they capture fifty tons of waste matter and produce two million nylon socks a year.

"Where we can find neither new substitute nontoxic chemical processes nor multiple-use reclamation programs, we have instituted various purification measures. For instance, petrochemical plants produce phenol. So we employ biochemical processes to treat the contaminated water.

"Of course, we have to invest a good deal of money and make no profit from pollution control. But we are a socialist country. We must prevent pollution for the well-being of the people.

"In spite of all our efforts, we still have problems. But actually there is no waste that we can not reuse. There are just some wastes whose reuse we can not yet visualize. And in the past, the old line of Lin Piao and Liu Shao-ch'i ignored this reuse, put profits in command. They did not pay attention to treatment of the Three Wastes."

Nine different people have come today to speak to our group about environmental problems in China. They have come from a variety of State agencies and industries. Those who are not speaking sit quietly and listen.

The next speaker is Chou Yün-ho, from the Liao Yuan Chemical Plant, which primarily manufactures polyvinyl chloride, caustic soda, hydrochloric acid and liquid chlorine.

"Our factory is an old one," begins Chou. "It was built in 1929. But since 1949 we have increased our output a hundred fold. Since 1970 we have instituted forty waste-control projects by organizing three-in-one groups, consisting of workers, technicians and cadres. For instance, one problem we tackled was the smoke from our coal-burning furnaces. We have a smokestack which is fifty meters high. We used to discharge four to five tons of particulate matter a day from the hundred and fifty tons of coal we burned. The smoke was hazardous for the surrounding residents, who made complaints. They said that in the summer when they came out to get cool, they needed an umbrella.

"Before the Cultural Revolution people had tried to solve this problem, but the effort came to nothing because of the expense and the management's concern for profit. It was not until after we formed our three-in-one committee during the Cultural Revolution that we came up with a simple method. It was a device that settles the unburned coal dust and allows the gases to escape. From this, we recover about four tons of unburned coal a day. It made everyone quite happy. Our neighbors said that we had succeeded in changing the black dragon into a white dragon."

Chou stops talking and rather casually holds up a glass bottle full of grimy black coal dust, which he says can either be reburned or used to make bricks. He passes the bottle around the table for everyone to inspect.

"It is true that there are other factories that have not implemented such techniques," he continues. "Development is unequal among different factories. We learn from the more advanced factories." This comment is delivered formalistically, in the manner in which the Chinese are accustomed to describing any current lingering problems which might have survived the all-solving powers of the Cultural Revolution.

After several more speakers discuss new technical pollution-control processes, it is time for a break. We walk outside to the veranda on the highest floor of the tall building in which we are meeting. Looking out across the city of Shanghai, we see a number of smokestacks sticking up through the green foliage and buildings of the city. They are belching black smoke.

"We still have a way to go," says one of the officials from the Shanghai Municipal Office for the Treatment of the Three Wastes. "But progress is being made, and new factories are not allowed to open unless they meet pollution-control standards. The older factories, like the ones you see out there, are catching up, although some are slower than others."

"Suppose the State desperately needed some product or other?" I ask. "Would they not let such a new factory open?"

"Well, yes. Perhaps," he replies. "If it were in the people's interest."

"Are there any inspections of factories in China by agencies that set the emissions standards?"

"In our factory," says a representative from an electroplating operation, "we are supervised at three levels. There is the sanitation department of the city and the various districts. They send people to inspect once a year. Then our leaders test and inspect from within the factory. And, of course, the workers themselves inspect. After all, they are the ones who are most familiar with what is happening. Then sometimes even the peasants and neighborhood people come and inspect.

"What does 'the rational development of industry' mean?"

"Well, first," says another factory technician, "this is a relative, not an absolute concept. But, for instance, if a factory discharged toxic wastes, we would not allow it to be built or expanded on the upper reaches of a river. Or we might locate certain industries downwind from large population areas. Then, of course, we often merge small polluting industries into larger better-organized factories where it will be more economical to treat wastes. Another technique is to decentralize our industry, as Chairman Mao teaches. It not only creates self-sufficiency, but means that we do not need to use so much oil to move goods all across the country."

"How will China solve the contradiction between her seemingly obsessive effort to expand industry and need for future protection of her environment and resources? Can China be the first nation to industrialize and not gravely threaten the quality of life?"

"Yes, we must pay attention to the contradiction between individual factory production and the development of the national economy, on the one hand, and the people's health on the other," says Dr. Fan Chien-hsing, a woman M.D. from an electrical materials factory. "Development can not just be for its own sake. It must be related to proletarian politics. Both aspects have to be connected and considered simultaneously. They must be beneficial to the people's health as well as to the national economy. No matter how much it costs to clean up pollution, we must do it. Didn't Chairman Mao say, 'Man is the most precious'?

"Our factory built a one-hundred-and-forty-thousand yuan wastewater purification plant. Now, did that benefit production? No. But it was for the people just as much as production. And if the costs go up, well, we just have to think of nonharmful ways of bringing the prices back down. We are not negative or passive about 'turning the harmful into the beneficial' or 'turning waste into treasure.' "

"Along with the great strides in production, has the gross amount of pollution increased in China in spite of the new pollution controls?"

"It's hard to make a comparison in a general way," says Fu Shukang from the Municipal Office. "For instance, we have solved sixty percent of the black smoke problem. But still, the remaining forty percent of the chimneys now belching smoke are more than during pre-Liberation. But at least now we are paying attention.

"And, of course, we have more transport than before Liberation, and thus have more noise and exhaust. We still lack experience in tackling these problems. But since the Cultural Revolution, we feel that the people and the government are cognizant of the problems. I am not confident that the capitalist countries will be able to solve their pollution problems. But I am confident that they can be solved in a socialist country."

Jail

Pieces of sharp broken glass have been painstakingly planted upright in mortar on top of the high brick walls. Two PLA soldiers with rifles and bayonets stand guard at either side of a large iron gate as our bus passes through to the inside of the Shanghai City Prison.

The prison buildings are dark brick, with thick gray steel doors. The windows are barred. There is almost no plant life growing within the perimeters of the prison. Our footsteps and voices echo off the concrete between the buildings.

We enter a cellblock. Even here, the walls are covered with slogans, providing one of the few common chords with the outside world. The thoughts of Chairman Mao also live behind these brick walls and guard towers, in an institution which must emphatically represent the end of the line in China. Even here there is talk of transformation and reform.

"We must keep up the policy we started in Yenan," writes Mao. " 'No executions and few arrests.' There are some whom we do not execute, not because they have done nothing to deserve death, but because killing them would bring no advantage, whereas sparing their lives would. What harm is there in not executing people? Those amenable to labor reform should go and do labor reform, so that rubbish can be transformed into something useful. Besides, people's heads are not like chives. When you cut them off, they will not grow again. If you cut off a head wrongly, there is no way of rectifying that mistake even if you want to . . . So, we should give all counterrevolutionaries a way out of their impasse. This will be helpful to the people's cause and our image abroad."

LONG LIVE THE DICTATORSHIP OF THE PROLETARIAT, reads a banner over the doorway to a long corridor of small cells. Each is about ten feet by ten feet. Each has an immaculately scrubbed, slatted-wood floor, a small storage chest covered in the daytime by the prisoners' straw sleeping mats, a bookshelf housing dog-eared copies of Chairman Mao's selected works and other Marxist-Leninist literature. Face towels are hung neatly on the barred doors to dry.

Three prisoners live in each one of these minuscule, orderly cells. Or perhaps it would be fairer to say that they sleep in these cells, since all able-bodied prisoners work each day in the prison factories, without pay.

Fastened to the outside bars of each cell is a small plaque bearing the names and prison identification numbers of the three inhabitants. I am reminded of the signs in Latin affixed to the bars of animal cages at the zoo. Prison regulations are posted in each cell.

One can hear sounds from other floors and other buildings— clanging metallic noises, echoes of distant factory machinery.

In the next cellblock, prisoners sit just outside their cells at tables laden with heaps of colored plastic parts. They are assembling toys. Piles of bright orange arms, green legs and unidentifiable chartreuse body parts. All eyes are lowered as we pass silently by. We have been told that we can not talk to any prisoner or take photos. I look at this wordless line of older men sitting behind their piles of toys and wonder what is going on inside those bowed shaven heads. I wonder why each has come to this end in China. Are some here because they have thought the very thoughts that often occur to me?

There is an eerie feeling about this place. There is no human exchange. It is like walking through an aquarium and seeing the fish behind their glass panels.

At the end of the corridor is a bulletin board displaying essays neatly written by the inmates. "Study Chairman Mao to Criticize and Reform Ourselves," "Remold Our World Outlook," "Correct

Your Reactionary Ideology and Become a Real Person." The titles read like Communist New Year's resolutions.

Police guards in immaculate white uniforms stand at all doorways. None of them carries a gun. And if a prisoner did succeed in getting beyond the formidable walls of this prison, where would he seek refuge? One can not just melt anonymously into China.

We file through several more factory shops. In one, prisoners are making labels for stamp pads, candy and packages of wrenches. The factory is completely run by the prisoners. The ceiling is crisscrossed with wires from which slogans hang like laundry.

DETERMINE YOUR SITUATION, HASTEN YOUR REFORMATION.

STUDY DILIGENTLY, WORK ENTHUSIASTICALLY.

REFORM YOURSELF FROM INSIDE OUT, AND YOUR FUTURE WILL BE BRIGHT INDEED.

On the next floor, prisoners are cutting, printing and binding exercise books. The covers read GHANA SCHOOLS. Each prisoner has a teacup beside him with a quote from Mao Tse-tung on it. They stand by their machines performing their rote tasks—no eye contact as we foreign voyeurs pass. Their skin is sallow. They wear inexpensive plastic sandals. A pale sun shines in through some of the windows and casts weak shadows on the concrete floors. The prisoners look almost like monks; the difference is that between abstinence and incarceration.

We enter the women's cellblock. They work right outside their cells in the hallway. There are many fewer women than men in this prison. They have the same small, clean, windowless cells. I can not take my eyes off the cells. I try to imagine three people sleeping on the wooden slats, under their quilts, with the door locked. I wonder if in this land with so little apparent deviancy, inmates succumb to homosexuality. I ask a prison official who is accompanying us.

"It is ideologically incorrect," he replies without expression.

STUDY THEORY. MORE DEEPLY RECOGNIZE YOUR CRIME. REFORM YOUR THOUGHT.

IF YOU REFUSE TO CONFESS, YOU WILL BE TREATED SEVERELY. IF YOU CONFESS, YOU WILL BE TREATED LENIENTLY.

The slogans are relentless.

The prison hospital has a Dickensian gloom about it. But it is clean, efficient and well-equipped. In the men's ward, eight prisoners sit in the middle of the room in pajamas and study a newspaper together. Several other sick prisoners lie in white metal frame beds under muslin sheets. Their eyes are closed.

In the women's ward, five prisoners are studying the works of Chairman Mao by taking turns reading passages out loud. Others lie in bed listening. A woman with a waxen face watches us with motionless, pained eyes.

There is a small operating room, an X-ray room and a pharmacy stocked with trays of herbs as well as antibiotics and other conventional Western medicines. Many of the nurses in the hospital are prisoners who have had medical experience. The hospital smells strongly of disinfectant.

We walk up a dark stairwell. There are old fire-extinguishers and brass-nozzled hoses set in glass-enclosed wall cavities. The directions for their use are written in English—another of the few remaining signs of the days when being British in Shanghai was better than being Chinese.

Ssu Kuo-hsiang, the prison warden, and several of his assistants meet us in a large room full of couches and chairs. The curtains are drawn. Tea is poured. Ssu welcomes us. He is a middle-aged man, dressed unpretentiously, who appears slightly nervous. He has a small notebook to which he refers as he talks.

"This jail was built by the British aggressors in order to suppress the Chinese working class," he says. "Construction was started in 1906, but was not complete until 1925. After Liberation, we followed Chairman Mao's instructions and reformed the prison. We turned the prison from one which oppressed people into one for those who spied, tried to commit sabotage on socialist reconstruction or committed serious crimes.

"There are two thousand eight hundred prisoners here at this time. This is the only prison in Shanghai, a city of roughly ten million people. Most of the prisoners are here for short-term imprisonment. Only a minority are here for long terms. However, some have received life imprisonment; others are sentenced to death, but their sentences are usually stayed for two years while they are given a chance to reform.

"Out of the two thousand eight hundred prisoners," says Ssu, "thirty percent are counterrevolutionaries. But regardless of whether they are counterrevolutionaries or not, all are sentenced by law. Our attitude toward all prisoners is to carry out reform through labor and Marxist-Leninist thought.

"All the criminals and counterrevolutionaries have bourgeois reactionary world outlooks. They seek comfort and hate labor. So to reform them, we organize them into physical labor groups according to health and age. Through work, the prisoners form new concepts and new habits of participating in manual labor. It changes their reactionary world outlook, and allows them to take the socialist road and become new men."

I am struck by the similarities in the way the Chinese treat prisoners and mental patients. Visitors to Chinese mental hospitals have noted that although mental patients are given a great deal more sympathy, neither is considered an individual problem. The difficulties of mental patients and prisoners are not seen as arising from innate personality defects or character disorders caused by family and various psychological stresses. They are seen as problems arising from a person's incorrect connection with the life-sustaining fabric of socialist society. Hence treatment lies not in traditional Western individual treatment but in reinvolving the person in the positive collective process of building socialism. There is only one definition in China of being sane and uncriminal, and that is to be part of the march of revolutionary socialism.

"Here at the prison," continues Ssu, "we do abundant ideological and propaganda work." (In China, the word propaganda, *hsüan-ch'üan,* has no connotations of insidiousness or deceit. It is a positive notion conveying the effort to deliver "the word" of Maoist and Marxist-Leninist thought.) "We take Chairman Mao's works as the basic material for education. We propagate information on the domestic and international situation, as well as the Party's policies on the reform of prisoners. We hold large and small group meetings to carry out criticism and self-criticism so that prisoners can deeply examine and criticize their decadent political ideologies and world outlooks. We use good and bad models. Those who behave are praised. Those who do not are criticized."

There is a tremendous emphasis in every aspect of Chinese life on "changing one's world outlook." It is a task of momentous and often painful proportions, even for Party members. Even in the group of six interpreters traveling with us, one can see and feel what a difficult and often agonizing process this change has been. It is not so much that one consciously refuses to "change" as that one simply can not facilely tear up a lifetime of needs, associations and responses, and trade them in for new ones—even when one might wish to. One senses this particularly among some of the middle-aged or older people whose lives were at least partially shaped before and just after Liberation. Perhaps they grew up relatively wealthy and well-educated, with tastes for Western music, dress, literature, leisure or other pastimes that are no longer acceptable.

Many of these people, possibly not unlike many prisoners, wish to serve China and the revolution—but perhaps in their own way and their own time. Remolding one's world outlook means to learn to serve China in a certain way—in a way which is very clearly delineated and often narrowly defined. It is simply not enough to act out the steps. One must change one's inner feelings and commitments as well. One must banish lingering bourgeois tastes and habits. One must, in short, literally become a new person. Perhaps this is a worthy ideal, but not one which is easily attained. And one to which, I must confess, I considered myself to be inadequate. This ideal—the total dedication of the self to others—left me feeling admiration for those around me who were wrestling with it. It also left me with mixed emotions as I observed people who either could not or did not want to so dedicate their lives. As Warden Ssu talks, I can not but once again wonder what thoughts (other than those of Chairman Mao) might still haunt the bourgeois-afflicted minds of some of the inmates.

"Our policy is one of punishment and leniency," says Ssu again. "We always allow a way out. We thoroughly forbid any kind of verbal cursing or physical punishment on the part of the guards. Prisoners are treated as human beings. But we separate prisoners for reform purposes, and adopt different policies for different groups. People who work hard to reform themselves are released on parole or have their sentences reduced. But for those who refuse to reform themselves, we add to their term of imprisonment. These people, however, are in the minority.

"For those released on parole, our staff members first go out and arrange a job for them. Our line here is that of the Party and the masses. In fact, we often organize workers and revolutionary neighborhood masses to come to the prison to talk with inmates. Sometimes those who do not behave well in prison are taken back to their villages or neighborhoods, where their own people hold meetings and criticize them. Or if family members come to visit, they might try to reeducate the prisoner and urge him or her to reform. We do not want the prisoners here to become divided from the masses. We follow Chairman Mao's directives. And under the powerful dictatorship of the proletariat, we can reform the majority of the prisoners into new men. It is only natural that there should be some diehards. But they really do not matter that much."

Ssu finishes his prepared remarks. Everyone in our group is eager now to ask questions. A tidal wave of curiosity. We visitors are at our most inquisitive when it comes to deviants. I have been overwhelmed by our fascination with any form of "aberration." We are obsessed with it—we also enjoy it.

"How old are most of the prisoners?"

"There are relatively few young criminals," replies Ssu. "Many of the prisoners may look young because their heads are shaven, but most are not. In any case, all the prisoners are over eighteen. People who are under eighteen and commit a crime receive education in the schools, family or neighborhood. In this prison, the eighteen-to thirty-year-olds comprise about forty percent of the prisoners."

"Are any of the women prisoners pregnant?"

"We do not take in pregnant women prisoners," says the assistant warden, who speaks very slowly and meticulously, bobbing his head up and down for emphasis. "Most of them are put on probation. If they confess their crimes before the birth of their child, they are pardoned and freed. If their term is long, they may not be required to begin serving until their child has finished nursing. Just because a woman commits a crime, that does not change the innocence of the child. There is somewhat special treatment for pregnant women. Otherwise people must ultimately serve their term."

And then as an afterthought, he adds, "Some of the women prisoners are counterrevolutionaries. Others are criminal."

"What is the definition of a counterrevolutionary?"

"We have limited-term sentence prisoners here as well," says the warden, who continues on with an answer which evades the question. "Most sentences are short term, less than seven years. Executions are not carried out at the prison. We do not have any statistics here at the prison on how many."

"Is there any suicide in the prison?"

"We have no physical isolation or solitary confinement. Solitary confinement is not safe. We keep prisoners together, two or three in a cell. This way they supervise each other and take care of each other. If one prisoner tries to commit suicide, he can be reported."

"Is there any homosexuality in the prison?" the question comes up again.

The interpreter, Lao Chang, has a difficult time translating the question. He fumbles awkwardly, looking for the right way to phrase it, almost as though the right words did not exist in common parlance in the modern Chinese language. Finally he stops and says to the assistant warden, "You know—men with men."

A faint smile spreads across the face of the assistant warden. It is a smile of indulgence reserved for these persistent and bizarre questions which appear so important to "foreign guests."

"We have found no homosexuality," he answers tersely.

"Do prisoners have rights?"

"Prisoners are sentenced because they have committed crimes. So they are deprived of their political rights. They have no rights to travel or organize themselves. For those who do well in reforming themselves and atoning for their crimes, we prepare a report. The report is sent to a higher level of the Public Security Bureau. They pass it on to the courts, where a judge may reduce or extend the period of imprisonment for a specific prisoner.

"Have there even been any prison rebellions?" asks a black member of our group.

The warden, who is sitting right next to me, laughs to himself, and under his breath says, "How can they rise up?"

Other questions about vicious guards, solitary confinement, prisoner mistreatment cause the same kind of head-shaking and puzzled disbelief. The interpreters again halt in confusion, as though they can not divine the proper way to even put these concepts in Chinese.

"Do many prisoners return to prison after once being released?"

"Very few prisoners are repeaters," says the assistant warden. "If they commit crimes after their release, they must return and once again undergo reform."

"What are the backgrounds of most prisoners?"

"Some are Kuomintang imperialist agents. Some are laboring people. Others are from the bourgeois and landlord class. Generally most prisoners come from the exploiting classes, although we do not have statistics."

"How are guards chosen?"

"Our guards are chosen from among the workers, peasants, soldiers and students. They receive short-term training in public security schools in politics and prison procedures. Most guards truly love their work and consider it an important part of the dictatorship of the proletariat."

"What are counterrevolutionaries?" someone asks again.

There is a pause. The warden breaks it. "Counterrevolutionaries oppose socialist revolution and construction. They sabotage socialist revolution. They murder people and commit arson. Simply said, the object of their crimes is to oppose revolution. They try to think up ways to obstruct the revolution."

"How do people get to prison?"

"Our conception of the dictatorship of the proletariat is different from what you have in capitalist countries, where it is the police who arrest a criminal. Here, we rely on the masses to expose, criticize, accuse and report a criminal. They will finally take their accusation to the Security Bureau. Or maybe a group of people will catch a criminal themselves and bring him to the bureau. Then both the Security Bureau and the court make investigations of their own. If the crime is not deemed too serious, the criminal is usually remanded back to the masses for further reeducation."

"How often are criminals executed?"

"This is rare in China," says the assistant warden.

"We believe in reshaping heads, not chopping them off," another prison official tells me later as we leave. Indeed, the only execution that I have heard about—and this in a roundabout way—while I was in China, involved a young Chinese man who attacked a member of the French Foreign Mission staff with a cleaver at the Peking Friendship Store. Sincere apologies were immediately made. The woman was hospitalized, but recovered. The assailant was executed the next morning.

The interview ends. It has been interesting, but in a way in which I can not quite articulate at the time, I feel unsatisfied. There is something about the vague way in which crime is defined which is troubling. So much of the notion of criminality seems to depend on what is held to be politically unacceptable at any given time. Crime is definitely a question of politics in China. The word "law" is hardly mentioned here at the prison.

In the bus on the way home, Lao Liu sits next to me. "Okay. You want to hear an example of why someone gets sent to prison?" he asks, sensing that our visit has raised as many questions as it has answered. "I'll tell you a case.

"There was this man who was sleeping with another woman. When his wife found out about it, she was naturally very upset. They had some fights. I think he promised that he would stop. But anyway, he didn't stop. So finally his wife reported him to the Security Bureau.

"After that, she subsequently got very ill. I don't think anything had been done about the situation in the meanwhile. Maybe the investigation was in process or something like that. Anyway the man bought some poison and gave it to his sick wife, telling her that it was medicine. And, of course, she got really sick, vomited and everything. She was rushed to the hospital, where they made some tests and found out that in fact she had been poisoned. In the end, she didn't die, and the husband was arrested and found guilty of trying to murder her. He was sentenced to death. But actually, he ended up being put in jail for life. The wife got a divorce."

Lao Liu gives a smile, as if to say, "See, it's so simple in spite of all your questions."

Theory

The only pastime in China which rivals manual labor in importance is the study of political theory. The Chinese read Chairman Mao, Marx, Lenin, Engels and Stalin the way a good Baptist reads the Bible. The Chinese divide their world analytically into "theory" and "practice." For they are firm believers that without the proper political theory, there can be no truly revolutionary practice. Yet all theory and no practice is equally repugnant to them. Mao has alluded to pure theory as no better than horse manure.

Today we talk with Wang Shao-hsi, who is introduced as a theoretician from the Shanghai Municipal Revolutionary Committee. His position is described to me in whispered tones by one student from Futan University as "of immense importance."

Wang wears a dark-gray cadre suit, which I am slowly learning to recognize as the hallmark of someone of position. (One would never see a peasant or a worker so clad. For them, blue- or khaki-colored cotton is de rigueur.) Wang is a smallish, compact man. He has not shaven for several days, which is not uncommon in China, where beards are light. He wears glasses. His eyes have an intense alertness and intelligence. He gives off an air of authority.

Wang chain-smokes. His yellow, nicotine-stained fingers clash with his healthy red cheeks. As he fields questions, he often gives knowing if cryptic smiles, suggesting that there is a lot more going on inside his head than he wants to let on.

"During the Cultural Revolution it was not always easy to understand what was happening," he says. "In fact, I'm still trying to understand it more thoroughly. You probably all read a lot about it in books and articles in America. Some gave an objective report. But others, because of the author's shallow understanding, turned out one-sided. And, of course, some were even distorted by bad intentions."

Wang begins to discuss one book in particular called *Shanghai Journal*, by an Australian writer, Neil Hunter. "I met with him later," says Wang, "and discussed his book with him. He admitted that there were limitations to his observations. For instance, he took some photos when he was in Shanghai. But they only reflected some of the truth, and not the essence. I'm not saying that he was bad, or counterrevolutionary, just that his views had limitations in spite of his good intentions."

It is always fascinating to me to see what foreign publications the Chinese read—what outside contacts they allow themselves in formulating their world view. With the exception of high-ranking officials on the diplomatic end of things, the average person sees very little material from the West. For instance, even the Friendship Association, which is one of the primary Chinese organs for dealing with visitors from the outside, receives only a few American publications at its Shanghai office. It subscribes to *The New York Times* and *Newsweek*, and receives whatever other books and periodicals visiting delegations leave behind or later send as gifts. But it does not seem to me that the Chinese, even those who read English, have what could be called a driving fascination with the outside world. Whatever information they do obtain is usually plugged right into their Maoist mode of analysis. They are not intrigued by aimless collections of trivia and information to which they can not impart a viewpoint. They never mistake the trees for the forest. One often feels that they read foreign books and magazines not so much to learn about the Western mind as to see whether the Western mind is getting any closer to real truth: their truth.

"Our Cultural Revolution is in essence not a cultural revolution but a political revolution," Wang is saying. "It is a revolution in the superstructure—a revolution under the dictatorship of the proletariat where the masses rise up and help the leadership solve bad political tendencies.

"It is, and has been, different from our revolution in 1949, or those revolutions in capitalist countries, because a transfer of the means of ownership had already transformed our situation into one where the means of production were owned by the people. The Cultural Revolution did not deal with these matters. It dealt with other theoretical issues like the two-line struggle.

"As Lenin said, the death of an old society is not just like the death of an old person whom you put in a coffin and forget. Even after a revolution, bourgeois culture and bourgeois ideology can still spring up and be disruptive. Bourgeois elements never take their defeat lying down. Struggle continues between the proletarian line and the bourgeois-revisionist line. We call this the two-line struggle.

"When we were fighting Chiang Kai-shek years ago, it was different. The struggle was clear. The enemy had different uniforms, different insignias, and different appearances. But struggles within the Party are now much subtler. Everyone dresses up like revolutionaries. Some good-intentioned people might even think that they are on a revolutionary line when they are not. It is not clear from the surface who is revolutionary and who is not. This is why we attach so much importance to the study of theory—to help us distinguish sham revolutionaries from true revolutionaries. Using the basic truths of Marxism-Leninism, we easily see the relationships between the two lines. We learn to distinguish one line from another."

Wang pauses, and holding his Phoenix brand cigarette half an inch from his rounded lips, inhales a long drag of air and smoke directly into his lungs. "Liu Shao-ch'i wanted to restore capitalism," says Wang, leaving no room for argument. Liu, the former President of the Republic, has been crowned the most poisonous of poisonous weeds. One never speaks of him as having done anything good or revolutionary in spite of his role in the Chinese Communist movement since the nineteen-twenties. His whole life has been retroactively reevaluated, and is now held as synonymous with all that the Cultural Revolution struggled against.

"Liu and his gang used their strength to propagate the line that there was no longer a class struggle, that it had died out. They used organs of literature, art, and propaganda to advocate this line of restoring capitalism. From 1961 to 1963, right here in Shanghai, you could see a lot of bourgeois movies and plays which corrupted people.

"Chairman Mao saw these problems and pointed them out. He said that our art and literature had already reached the edge of revisionism. Mao's wife Chiang Ch'ing came here to Shanghai herself and guided the artistic and literary revolution. She gave detailed and concrete instructions for the reform of the Shanghai Peking Opera, which was an old feudal form of art. The heroes in these operas were scholars, beauties, generals, emperors and kings. We did our best to occupy the stage with proletarian plays and productions."

Then, breaking into a big smile, Wang says, "I've heard about *Love Story* in the United States. At first look, it may appear harmless: a rich boy falls in love with a girl from a lower-class family. The boy may show a little rebellious spirit, but basically the movie shows that you will be defeated if you rebel. The girl just dies. So its final meaning is poisonous. And besides, it propagated class reconciliation (rich boy marries poor girl), and preached that the rich and the poor are not contradictory.

"I've even heard that Nixon and Agnew liked this book while they were in office. Why should they have liked it and propagated it? Well, because they liked the ideas in it.

"Of course, it's not easy in America to have literature and art taken over by the proletariat. Look how scared your government was when our Chinese art troop wanted to go to your country and sing songs about the liberation of Taiwan! It shows how nervous the capitalists who control your society are.

"In our own Cultural Revolution, it was the students who played the role of the vanguard. But they went to the workers and peasants, who subsequently became the main force. The rightists were afraid of the students. But they were more afraid of the workers. So they tried at first to hobble the workers with heavy production obligations.

"Many workers rebelled anyway here in Shanghai. Then the rightists, many of whom were in leading positions, tried economism; they gave privileges to obedient workers in the form of bonuses and special vacations, trying to make them 'worker aristocrats.' But the workers knew the meaning of unity. Comrades would try to talk to these workers and convince them not to sell out and forget the real enemy.

"In the midst of this worker-student uprising, some of the revolutionary cadres and higher-ups in the Party began to join the rebels. The revolutionary flames were kindled right in the backyard of the leadership against whom the Cultural Revolution had been launched."

Wang describes the Byzantine factional struggle that followed, a struggle that often left even the best-intentioned revolutionaries confused and uncertain about which line was correct. The account gets so involved that I have trouble giving all its permutations in recap form.

Two hours later, Wang stops talking. He has verbally refought the whole Cultural Revolution in Shanghai from beginning to end. Although he has said many interesting things, the surcease is not unwelcome.

Fish Farming

Huge dark-brick cathedrals loom up off the flat land which is honeycombed with canals, ponds, lakes and flooded fields. The cathedrals evoke a European ambiance which is disorienting here in the rural counties surrounding the core city of Shanghai. The city has been intentionally set in this planning pattern. It is the urban bull's-eye of an otherwise agricultural target. It is by means of these immediately adjacent food-producing regions that Shanghai attains a large measure of self-sufficiency. The churches stand like immovable archeological monuments of another epoch—temples of an invading spiritual army of the past.

"We suffered from imperialist religious beliefs here in Ch'ing-p'u County," says a local cadre. "Seventy-five percent of the fresh-water fishermen in the county had been converted to Christianity. We had seven cathedrals." He pauses. And then, as though delivering an original punch line, he says with a smirk, "Marx said that religion was the opium of the people."

He shifts in his chair, readying himself to make a more complete explanation. "The reason that the imperialists wished to set up so many churches was to politically rule our people—to perpetuate the notion that God rules people, and that there should be no resistance. This is like the fallacy of the old concept of *(t'ien-ming)* the will of heaven advocated by Confucius: that heaven rules and man must follow.

"The fishermen here were greatly exploited by the Church. They suffered the four exploitations. Three days after birth a boy child had to have water poured over him to be baptized. It cost twelve yuan. Then people were required to go to mass every Sunday, plus attend all the Christian holy days. Each time, a person had to pay a lot in either rice or money. They even let you pay these 'offerings' in installments if you were broke! Then the third exploitation came when one got married. You had to pay another twenty-four yuan. The fourth exploitation came when you died. You had to pay money for a requiem mass. So even after you died you had to pay the Church." This remark provokes some chuckling from other local Chinese in the room.

As we travel through this lush, partially submerged landscape, I ask Lao Liu what the cathedrals are now used for.

" 'What are they now used for?' " he asks rhetorically, barely able to conceal his usual impish smile. "Well, some are warehouses, and others are factories and schools. Why waste them? Who built them? The people paid, and they were poor. And what did God ever do for them? He certainly didn't feed them."

Before he has a chance to go on, we pass a wheat field which has just been harvested. There are hundreds of ducks waddling all over it, pecking at the ground. A small boy with a willow switch sits under a tree watching them.

"Hey, His-erh [a transliteration of my name, Schell]," says Lao Liu, tugging at my sleeve, and pointing to the field. "Do you understand that? After the wheat harvest, they bring out the geese," he says. "They glean all the leftover grain off the ground. Then after a few days, there are a lot of bugs and insects on the cut field. So for insect control, they bring out the ducks. The ducks love bugs. Have you ever eaten a duck that has been fed on insects?" He makes a gesture like a chef who has just sampled some fine cuisine. "Oh," he says, smiling. "They are much tastier than grain-fed ducks.

"This system is fine. The ducks get rid of the insects without any pesticides which we also use. It's not as dangerous and less expensive, too. We call this *ch'iung-fa yang-ya,* or "the poor man's way of raising ducks." Anyway, around here, we couldn't just let the ducks loose on the rivers and ponds. They'd eat all the fish, wouldn't they?" He bursts into laughter at the thought.

We turn down a dirt road to a small complex of gray-brick buildings surrounded by fish-breeding ponds. It is the meeting hall of the People's Liberation Commune. It's just beginning to sprinkle as we enter the whitewashed room. The usual inexhaustible supply of tea and cigarettes awaits us.

The People's Liberation Commune was formed in 1958 during The Great Leap Forward, out of the surrounding twenty-three fishing co-ops. It covers seven thousand five hundred and sixty hectares of fish ponds and lakes, including the massive Lake Ting Shan. The commune now consists of thirteen hundred households with five thousand and seventy-eight people, three thousand two hundred and ten of whom are considered to be in the labor force. The whole commune is broken down for organizational purposes into ten work brigades. Almost all the people on the commune are fishermen. The commune is now self-sufficient in breeding, hatching and raising young fish to insure that there will be an expanding rather than diminishing yearly catch in the surrounding waterways.

About ten members of the commune come to greet us. They speak with a heavy peasant Shanghai accent, which even several of our interpreters who hail from Shanghai have difficulty understanding.

"Before Liberation," says one commune member, "most of us were migrant fishermen going from here to there in our boats, trying to make a living fishing. We had a saying: 'With a broken boat, a torn net, and worn-out clothing, we must beg to make a living.' We fishermen were assessed with endless taxes, and were always prey to being conscripted into the army. But even worse, we were under the heels of the local money lender from whom most of the fishermen had to rent their boats. The fishermen even had to pay rent to use the rivers and lakes to fish. It came to about two hundred and forty to three hundred yuan a year just for the rights to fish in a certain area. And if they traveled back and forth from the waters of one pretty despot to another, they had to pay an additional toll.

"If a fisherman borrowed money from a money lender, he had to pay from fifty to one hundred percent interest a year. And when a fisherman finally did get a good catch, he could only sell it through a middle man. And often these guys had fixed scales.

"There was an old saying about poor fishermen. We said that 'They were so poor a cat would follow them for three li.' Their problem was that they smelled so bad. And the reason was that they were oppressed and exploited. They had only one suit of clothes. They never had anything to change into. From this, the nature of their exploitation can be seen.

"But after Liberation, and under the leadership of Chairman Mao, and the Chinese Communist Party, we became our own masters. We took over the whole fishing area, and we organized ourselves to fish in a collective way. In 1952, we started a democratic reform. We held meetings and poured out our bitternesses from the past. Then, in 1956, we set up twenty-three co-ops as outlets through which fishermen could sell their fish, and as a source of credit. We started an educational program, and began reforms in our own lives, like building housing so families would not have to live on their boats." And then, abruptly skipping from the beginning to the end of the story, without recounting all the intervening steps, he says, "Now our situation is better, since our production is done collectively. We are more mechanized, we live in new houses, and our lives grow happier and happier."

He then recites the usual litany of progress, which here consists of a great deal of new housing, eight primary schools, a hospital, several light-industry factories, one of which makes concrete-hulled boats. Many of these projects have been built with loans from the State.

As so often in China, the facts are indeed impressive. The progress is overwhelming by any standard. And yet, there is something about the recitation, the finality and glibness of it, which frequently fails to produce an impact commensurate with the facts. As I listen to the list of "newborn things," I find myself wondering at the equanimity with which we seem to have learned to absorb these endless lists of kudos. It occurs to me that perhaps one loses the ability to marvel anew at each example of progress, when in fact, the whole country is a kind of marvel of progress.

Lest there be any confusion in the minds of his visitors, this speaker ends his talk with a summation: "All of our commune members are determined to have a fuller command of Marxism-Leninism, to persevere in making continuous socialist revolution, and putting politics in command to promote production."

We board a shallow draft motorboat, and move out onto the muddy waters of Lake Ting Shan. There is water everywhere here at People's Liberation Commune, where the acreage underwater far surpasses that above. Most travel and transport is by boat. (In fact, the whole of Central China around the Yangtze River Valley depends on inland water transport.)

In the distance on this lake, so large that one can not see fully across at its widest part, there are small tugs slowly towing strings of barges. Some are headed toward Shanghai with cattle, produce, bricks, fish. Others return from the city with fertilizer, concrete, fuel. Each boat is marked with the name of its commune and the province from which it comes: Kiangsu, Chekiang, Kiangsi, Anwhei. We pass smaller fishing boats. The presence of a boat of white men induces their crews to stare; their wonderment is converted to smiles by our waving.

Our boat chugs off down the lake to a small harbor and docking facility where fishermen bring their catches and buy supplies. The docks are covered with large clay cauldrons full of water and seething with live eels. Large baskets, which serve as fish pounds, are suspended in the water off the docks. There is no refrigeration. Fish are often stored and shipped alive, although ice is sometimes used for overland transport.

As we dock and disembark a man grabs several eels out of a cauldron and holds them up until they writhe out of his hands and slip back into the water. Above him is a blackboard which records the daily catch of each kind of fish.

Not only does this commune raise and catch fish, it also has a mink farm, a chicken farm, a pig-breeding operation and an oyster farm. The connection between these various sideline operations is intricate and amazing.

"Through years of practice," says our guide, "we have learned to use fishery as our main undertaking, but also to raise mink, pigs, chickens and oysters at the same time. You see, what we discovered was that mink love to eat eggs, fish heads and guts. Chickens are very fond of mink droppings. And, in turn, chicken droppings make good pig food. It also just happens that pig droppings make good fish food. The oysters can be fed to the pigs or the fish, or we eat them ourselves, and the pearls we grind up to make traditional medicine, a very effective anticoagulant. Then, in the fish ponds, we have a system of tiered high-density production. We have black carp and Chinese ide living at mid-depth. The carp eat snails, and the ide eat grass. Their excrement nourishes microorganisms which feed the silver carp and big heads on the surface. Then, in turn, their excreta feed golden carp and common carp, which are bottom fish."

Our guide falls silent. I glance over at him to see whether he seems proud of what he has told us. He is looking down at his feet as he walks, evidently unaware that he has just described quite an extraordinary system of management.

A Banquet

Tonight is our last night in Shanghai. We have pleaded with the Chinese not to give us another banquet, of which we have already had several. Hsiao Yao, head interpreter and organizer of our trip nods with understanding but a noncommital smile. In China, banquets for departing visitors are as automatic and inescapable as farewell handshakes.

We are lounging around our elegant suites in the Heng Shan Guest House. Some of us are packing. Others are sipping glasses of hot tea provided by houseboys in white jackets and pants—an anachronism also reserved for visiting foreigners. Hsiao Yao arrives in the anteroom of our suite and announces with a barely concealed urgency that we are to meet upstairs before dinner in a large special meeting room.

Something is up.

We take the elevator to a large room with sofas and stuffed chairs covered with the ever-present clean Chinese slipcovers lining the walls. There is a thick handmade Chinese rug on the floor. There is a line waiting outside the door. One by one people are being introduced to someone. From the formal hush that pervades the room, it is clear that it is a comrade of some rank. The other giveaway is that all the interpreters have changed into their dark-gray polyester cadre suits. They stand around quietly and respectfully with their hands clasped behind their backs as each American is introduced.

The celebrity is a boyish-looking man in his thirties. He has a friendly smile. He shakes the hand of each entering person, and utters a pleasantry like a hostess at a society ball. We are told he is a member of the Shanghai Municipal Revolutionary Committee. Once a factory worker, he rose to his position of political preeminence in the chaotic days of the Cultural Revolution.

In spite of the many ways in which the Chinese have made

egalitarianism their hallmark, they still have more than a lingering fascination and respect for people of high rank. In their minds, there seems to be no contradiction between the notion of strong and revered leaders and egalitarianism, particularly if the leader in question does not "divorce himself from the masses."

Consequently when the Chinese arrange for a meeting with a ranking leader, they are making an offering—an offering which I did not always find informative or welcome.

The comrade from the Revolutionary Committee takes his seat at the head of the room next to our titular leaders. A profound silence falls over the room. People sit on the edge of their chair, kneading their fingers. The room is electrocharged with formal tension. It is clear that we will suffer through this stiff encounter like a speechless couple on a blind date.

"Well, how was your trip to the factory?" he asks.

Long pause. Silence. People look around the room at each other.

"I hear it was a success," tries the comrade.

Another pause.

"And Comrade Yao tells me that you have visited a prison, taken a boat trip and seen several factories here in Shanghai."

Another pause.

There is a prescribed length of time for these painful get-togethers. After about a half-hour of nervous tea-drinking and unanswered questions, it is suggested that we retire upstairs to the banquet hall. Relief floods the room as we break up and head for the elevators. Lao Liu comes up to me, puts his arm around my shoulders, and whispers, "Hey! Sit at table five." He winks and drifts back into the throng.

However, when I arrive upstairs, table five is full. Lao Liu gives me a disappointed shrug. I move to a table at the outer reaches of the hall. It is set with ivory chopsticks, linen napkins, beautiful china, and two wineglasses at each place—one for plum wine, and the other for Maotai (a clear liquor that tastes like a mixture of benzine and wood preservative). There is a third glass for Chinese beer (which is some of the finest in the world). Small printed menus list each course. Lazy Susans at the center of the table are laden with dishes of appetizers.

We begin to eat. Some begin to drink. Most Chinese are not heavy drinkers, and approach even toasting with great reluctance. Some go as far as to turn their glasses over, indicating that they want no part of alcohol. The possibility of insobriety occurs to them as uncouth and unnecessary. Others will drink if coaxed and cajoled with enough toasts to "long-lasting friendship between our two great peoples." This tactic often has powers which overwhelm abstinence. A very few Chinese do seem to enjoy the uninhibited comraderie which develops through drinking together.

"Perhaps it's because all Chinese immediately turn red when they drink," I remember Lao Liu saying earlier with a shrug. This is true. Lao Liu does not drink a drop.

As the banquet moves on, delegates from several tables appoint themselves to rove off to other tables to propose toasts. "We are representatives from table five, and propose a toast to the friendship between the two tables."

The room is noisy now. Several people rise and toast the whole room, thanking the students who have accompanied us, the intepreters and the officials who have worked on our trip.

One official, who has informally come to be known to some as the "Big Grinner," is caught up in the toasting. This elegant, tall and fastidiously dressed man can be triggered off into avalanches of head bobbing and grinning simply by having someone across the room catch his eye. It has become something of a preoccupation of mine not to glance his way at the wrong time—say, during a sober section of a B.I.—for fear that he will be provoked into responding.

The waiters pass continually among the tables, pouring wine and beer as soon as a glass is even partially empty. I glance at the head table, which is filled with our leaders and theirs. There is a suggestion of consternation creeping across the faces of several Chinese who, in any event, have never understood, and appear deeply distrustful of, the kind of spontaneous and uncontrollable energy which alchohol seems to release. Of all the people I have ever met, the Chinese seem the least disposed to losing their minds or drowning their sorrows in insobriety.

Nonetheless, I can not help but notice that the Big Grinner is reaching the point of no return. He arrives at our table with several other merrymakers, all holding wineglasses, and proposes a *kan-pei* (bottoms up). He has a silly glazed-over look on his face.

Suddenly, as though to reanchor the room, which is threatening to break down into revelry, some long-winded and interminable toasts begin to issue forth from the head table—toasts which everyone has already heard a thousand times before. Toasts extolling the "mass line," "friendship," the wonderous effects of the "Cultural Revolution"—and more "friendship."

The banquet hall is transformed. It's like a classroom just after the bell has rung, sounding the end of recess. Everyone is sitting down now. The comrade from the Revolutionary Committee goes on and on, as though to prove that the ascendancy of politics must be not only supreme but unceasing. Our leaders also make toasts. Some are heartfelt, others are fatuous.

When the toasts conclude, the room briefly returns to itself. People run into the kitchen, trying to capture shy or unwilling cooks and waiters to come out and receive a toast of thanks. One rosy-cheeked girl in pigtails is cornered and almost forcibly handed a small glass of plum wine. She is squirming, laughing, embarrassed. *"Pu-yao! Pu-yao!"* ("I don't want any!"), she protests. Finally she takes a timid sip and immediately retreats back into the safety of the kitchen.

The head chef is found and noisily toasted, then someone at the head table, feeling the need to reassert control, suggests that we all sing "The Internationale." We return to our places, stand stiffly, and begin to sing out over the messy array of food and plates on the banquet tables.

"Arise ye prisoners of starvation, Arise ye wretched of the earth."

The room sings drunkenly, like a record player slowed down.

"For justice thunders condemnation, a better world's in birth."

I glance over at the Big Grinner. His face has turned an ominous ashen gray-green. His eyes seem no longer to focus.

"No more tradition's chains shall bind us. Arise ye slaves no more enthrall."

Suddenly the Big Grinner topples over. He falls like a tree rather than slumping. Several comrades rush forward with tense, worried expressions. People go on singing automatically, their eyes riveted to the place where the Big Grinner once stood.

"The earth shall rise on new foundations. We have been naught, we shall be all."

The Big Grinner is carried to a curtained-off alcove as the chorus begins.

"'Tis the final conflict. Let each stand in his place. The international union shall be the human race."

The song is listless now. Those who do not know the words well, like myself, are just humming along. Only the leadership table is singing resolutely, as though the power of the music could somehow ease the human drama on the floor.

"We want no condescending saviors to rule us from their judgment halls," begins the second verse. It looks as if we're going to sing all five verses this time.

"We workers ask not favors . . ."

Elbows and legs are bulging through the curtain, indicating some kind of struggle. Suddenly the Big Grinner bursts out through the curtain like a rampaging bull moose.

"Let us consult for all, to make the thief disgorge his booty. To free the spirit from its cell."

He is standing in his old place, rocking and weaving back and forth. The assisting comrades stand awkwardly beside him, not quite sure what the next correct tactic is.

"We must ourselves decide our duty. We must decide to do it well."

He's on the floor again. They drag him back behind the curtain. This time he does not reappear. But no sooner is he gone than Allan, a towering six-foot-tall member of our group, crashes to the floor. Everyone continues to sing.

"The law oppresses us and tricks us. The wage slave system drains our blood."

He is carried off. The room is beginning to resemble a battlefield. Mercifully the song ends. Everyone heads for the door, soberer now.

II
THE FACTORY

Workday—Master Chang

At six o'clock "The East Is Red," comes on over the factory P.A. system. It starts very slowly, almost imperceptibly at first, like one of those alarm clocks which ring louder and louder until you wake up. Before the second verse, the music is booming out over the factory at full volume, with strange echoes coming back from the more distant speakers.

Men and women walk on the asphalt paths to the washrooms, sleepy and half awake. Their hair is matted from the night's repose. They wear long underwear in varied colors and carry their face pans containing soap, a toothbrush, cup and towel. Soon there are hundreds of people streaming out of the dorms toward the communal wash houses, where concrete sinks stretch the length of the building. Inside, there is a din of running water and tin pans bumping and scraping on the concrete. Above the background noise, there is an obbligato of gargling, spitting and throat-clearing noises, a daily ablution which the Chinese perform with gusto each morning.

The music stops. The news comes on as people move toward the cafeteria. Each person carries his or her own tin dish, cup and chopsticks.

The cafeteria is crowded. The workers line up and wait behind different windows as though at a bank. There is a small blackboard above each window, telling the dishes being served and their prices. Each worker holds a meal ticket. There are three squares for each day of the month. The prices of whatever one orders are written down in the appropriate square. Each worker pays for the whole month's meals at one time.

Breakfasts are not elaborate here at the factory. Most workers eat no more than a bowl of rice gruel or a few buns. Many take their food outside. Today there are a number of workers sitting in front of a dorm on the air shafts and entranceways to the factory's underground bomb shelters. They sit and eat under the green sycamore trees which have been planted throughout the factory grounds.

After breakfast, a sea of workers on foot and bicycle move off down the paths to the workshops. With them, we pass the huge billboard at the factory entrance that shows a beaming Chairman Mao standing in front of a large generator (he visited the factory in 1961). We continue over a bridge, which spans a small canal, to a circular area surrounded by display cases and bulletin boards covered with wall posters and factory directives. Here the crowd thins as people fan out in different directions to their respective workshops. Several young mothers, carrying infants, head toward the day-care center, where they will leave their children while they work. They periodically return to nurse throughout the day. The loudspeakers continue to boom.

Workshop Eleven is divided into six sections and twenty-odd work teams. It produces large D.C. electric motors. Our work team is made up of thirty-two workers and is called the Coil Inlay and Assembly Team.

When we arrive at the shop, the workers stand around a blackboard on which are written in impeccable script the words "Warmly Welcome the American Youth Delegation to China." The work captain is giving his daily briefing. It is hard to hear what he is saying over the din of the large machine tools which line the aisle, and the crane which rattles down the tracks overhead, delicately plucking up motor casings weighing several tons, and moving them down the workshop.

It is cool and drafty in Workshop Eleven today. Hundreds of small birds flutter in and out of open windows and fly up under the cavernous eaves of the shop to their nests.

I am introduced to Chang Yuan-k'ang, with whom I will work. Like many older workers in the factory, he is called Master Chang, an appelation which suggests neither rank nor authority, but is simply a title of deference given to veteran workers.

Master Chang appears to be a quiet, tentative middle-aged man. He speaks with a Ningpo accent, from his native Chekiang Province, which is difficult for me to understand. He shows me to a stool in front of a large lathelike machine which holds and turns the rotor of a 730-kilowatt motor as though it were a large ear of corn. It is the job of the workers in our team to assemble these rotors that turn within the stator, or casing, of electric motors.

At first Master Chang seems troubled by the prospect of his stewardship over me. We make little small talk as he hands me a pair of white cotton gloves and begins to show me how to place paper insulation behind the copper conductors in the rotor. He is embarrassed that I can not understand his Chinese as easily as he can understand mine. Like many older people in China, he can not speak the national dialect, a sign that he has had little or no education during his youth.

We sit side by side in front of our rotor, with a pair of pliers in either hand, bending down flanges. It is tedious work. Master Chang has done it for twenty-two years. We begin to chat, and Master Chang corrects my plier technique as we work. I, in turn, must ask him to repeat almost everything he says. Slowly he seems to grow intrigued and emboldened by my presence.

"In your country, does the State or factories give workers clothing?" he asks, pointing to my baggy blue factory uniform that has "The Shanghai Electrical Machinery Factory" and "Safety in Production" written in red characters above the left breast pocket. It is the first of his many questions, which begin with the assumption that the rest of the world must be somewhat similar to his own.

"Sometimes workers are given uniforms," I reply. "But factories are usually not owned by the State, but by private companies."

"They're run for profit," he half asks and half says. And then before I can answer: "Oh, yes. I know. It was just like that here before Liberation." He gives a shrug, and makes a funny face expressing feigned apology.

I ask Master Chang what his life was like before 1949. And as he begins to tell me, I think how strange it is that such hardship, which at the time had no redeeming graces, today ends up being one of the most important political assets an older worker has. He has the invaluable experience of oppression. It is the kind of experience which now exists only as history, but one which the Chinese tirelessly draw upon to remind their youth of the revolution's wellsprings.

"When my father died in the countryside, I was about fifteen," recalls Master Chang. "It was then that I came to Shanghai. My father and I farmed near Ningpo. We were poor though. Oh, so poor! We lived in a peasant house of earth and straw. Each day we worked in the fields. Of course, they weren't our fields. We had to rent them from a landlord. He was a real tub of rice. He never walked a step. He always had four men carry him in a sedan chair. It was from him that we also rented our oxen and plow. Very few people had oxen of their own. So renting the oxen also meant paying more money. If a person couldn't pay him back, he had to pay over more of his harvest, plus interest. Some people still couldn't pay. So the landlord's gang would arrive. Often they had guns. They'd take the person and lock him up. Then maybe there would be some kind of negotiations or something. Friends would help if they could spare anything. But usually we just had to borrow more money from the landlord at even higher interest rates. We were always poor. We never had enough to eat.

"Well, finally my mother came to Shanghai and stayed with some relatives," says Master Chang without expression. "She began to wash clothes for wealthy Chinese. Each day she went to a different house. You know, those big mansions in the French Concession. You can still see them in Shanghai. But they hardly paid her anything.

"Then I came to Shanghai too, although I was still pretty young. I was about sixteen. But we had nothing in the country. Finally I got a job as a tailor's apprentice. This particular tailor had several apprentices. And if one of us got sick, the boss would just tell us to go home and rest. Of course, he wouldn't pay us anything. Then when we came back after getting well, we would never know whether or not we still had a job."

I ask him when he first heard of the Communists. He pauses, thinking.

"Actually," he says, "I didn't hear much about the Communists until after Liberation. Shanghai was a Kuomintang city, and I couldn't read." Then, almost apologetically, he adds, "But I remember thinking that somehow all the workers and peasants should get together. Yes, I thought about that. Otherwise, maybe I would just have lost hope.

"Now if I get sick," he continues, getting back on safer ground, "there is nothing to worry about. I can get treated here at the factory, and the factory also pays for my family to be treated in Shanghai. They do not live here in Min Hang, so I go home on weekends. If they get sick, they just go to a doctor and get a receipt. I bring it here to the factory, and they pay for it."

Workday

The Shanghai Electrical Machinery Factory is situated on the Whangpoo River, about an hour upstream from the City of Shanghai. It is a large factory with some 4,000 workers that makes both electrical motors and generators. The massive ivy-covered brick workshops, the dormitories, cafeterias and sports facilities give the feeling of a university rather than an industrial complex. We ourselves are housed in a dormitory with some students from Futan University in Shanghai, as well as a complement of workers. The dorm is a two-story brick building which was recently inhabited by a group of North Vietnamese who were at the factory for an extended period of time receiving technical training. There are four double-decker bunks in each room. There are two small desks in the center, fluorescent lights overhead, some small clothes lockers by the door, and a rack in which our eight face pans are stacked like tires. Each bed has a mosquito net, a thick cotton pad, a quilt and a pillow. Other than these articles, there is nothing in the rooms when we arrive. The women live on the second floor, the men on the first. There is a lavatory with cold water on each floor. Baths are taken in communal bathing houses, where the hot water is piped in from a heating reclamation device which draws waste heat from the cooling system of the factory's rolling mill.

This morning we leave our dorm for breakfast at the usual hour of six-thirty. I arrive at Workshop Eleven just as Captain Chang is starting the daily "head-knocking session."

"Today we must remember our production schedule," he says. "Some of these rotors must be all finished by tomorrow so that we can take them and bake them in the ovens. And again I want to remind you of safety. Be careful. You foreigners are taller"—he smiles—"so watch carefully overhead for the crane moving machinery down the aisle. And always be mindful of keeping the area around your work place clean. That's important. Leave it cleaner than when you came."

The workers walk over to their toolboxes, unlock them, take out tools and white gloves, and return to the rotors at their benches. Another day has begun in Workshop Eleven.

From listening to the daily pep talk about production and quotas, one would expect a frenzy in the workshops. But the work pace is amazingly measured, even mellow. Workers don't loaf and connive to be secretly idle. But they do gather to chat for a moment, or just sit and watch the crane, which provides endless diversion. I sense little anxiety or pressure on any individual worker. I am equally surprised by the absence of any guilty speeches of self-criticism on the part of backsliding workers. On our work team the anxiety to produce seems to be shared collectively, even though there is a large measure of individual accountability for each piece of work.

The work pattern is in many ways the antithesis of the assembly line. Each worker sees a rotor through about twenty different processes, both large and small. Each works at his or her own bench, and when necessary moves the rotor from machine to machine with the crane. It may take as much as a week or two to finish the complete series of processes, depending on the size of the rotor.

There is a blackboard in the middle of the work area, just behind the soldering ovens. The names of the thirty-three workers are written on it. After each name is the kilowatt rating of the rotor that person is assembling. Strangely enough, the date work was begun on it is absent.

When a rotor is finally baked out and sent on to another team, it is identified as the product of a particular worker. It is this worker who makes the final test before sending it on. And while he may consult with others as he goes along—or even have some other workers help at various stages—when it moves on, it is essentially his craftsmanship that goes with it.

So, while there is tedium involved, it is not as repetitious as that of an assembly line. People set their own pace, and there are a great many breaks, both short and long, during the average day. If a worker feels that he is falling behind, it is common practice to return to the shops during spare time and catch up. "Volunteer labor" is not uncommon.

The Past

Like all other reception rooms in China, the one here at the factory is watched over by a large portrait of Chairman Mao. But unlike many other portraits, this one is not a simple reproduction. It is an original in oil paints, done in gaudy, almost luminescent, colors. It resembles an image from a color TV with the color tones out of adjustment.

We sit beneath it at long tables covered with white cloths, listen, drink tea, and munch candy which has been set out in small dishes. We listen to Wang Shan-liang, a bright man in his forties, who speaks with energy and numerous gestures to enforce his points. He delivers a monologue, but one in which he is so intrigued with what he is saying that he infects his listeners with curiosity.

"Before Liberation," he begins, "our factory was right in Shanghai and was rather small. It was on Tung pei Lane. There were only one hundred and seventy-three workers. It was called the Electrical Machinery Parts Factory Number Four. It couldn't even make large electric motors or machinery. It did some repair work and built some small motors. Under the Nationalists, China actually had very little heavy industry of its own.

"Our chief engineer, Comrade Ming, went abroad to study at that time. He tried to gather as much information as he could so that he could bring it back. And there was this one foreign professor who asked him why he bothered: 'The Chinese can't build electrical machinery anyway,' this professor said. And, in fact, when Ming returned to China, he did come back to a very backward situation.

"It was not until after Liberation that we really started to develop our industry. We wanted to continue production while we built our new factory. We wanted to 'walk on two legs.'

"I should mention that at that time we had help from our 'Soviet big brothers.' Russia was still under the leadership of Stalin, and they helped us. But we also tried to help ourselves. So we moved out here to Min Hang. And we succeeded in manufacturing our first six-thousand-kilowatt generator in 1954. All of the workers felt very proud and excited about this. For us, it had great significance, because it meant that at last we could make our own electrical machinery. At that time, one old man touched this generator and said, 'Well, I have worked for years, but I have never been able to touch a generator made in China with my own hands.' He was very moved, and even shed tears.

"By 1956 we doubled the output of electrical machinery, and began to make twelve-thousand-kilowatt generators. Because the electrical machinery industry must be in the vanguard of industrial and agricultural production, the workers in our plant started asking how we could keep pace with this rapid development. During the Great Leap Forward in the late fifties, we began to think about how we could make one generator do the work of two. In other words, we wanted to create a technical revolution in our area of production.

"What we did was to form a three-in-one group of cadres, workers and students to study and improve the cooling system of large generators. We thought that perhaps we could build a water-cooled generator. This had never been done before. It was needed because when the rotor turns inside a generator's stator, it converts mechanical energy into electrical energy. But it also generates heat. And if the generator gets too hot, it will burn out. We were able to use air cooling, by attaching a fan onto the rotor. This quite simply just blew the heat away. Then we also knew that we could cool generators with hydrogen. But if we used water, our technology at that time only allowed us to cool the stator—the outside part of the machine that did not revolve.

"We began to put our minds to the problem of cooling the rotor with water as well—a system of double cooling. We thought that such a system would be effective, even though we knew that the English had tried and failed to implement this method. In fact, we read an essay, written by an English engineer, that sentenced this technique to death. He claimed that it was impossible to use a double water-cooling process on generators which revolved at more than 3,000 rpm.

"But under the direction of The Chairman, and through the Great Leap Forward, we broke loose from this kind of fatalism. It was a worker who first suggested that we try to cool both rotor and stator with water. He had worked daily with generators and had had abundant practical experience. He looked on this whole dilemma as a day-to-day problem which even people have. When we sweat, we take off some clothing. And even if we take off all of our clothes, we may still have to fan ourselves for a long time, and we get tired. So we invented the electric fan, and it makes a breeze which is bigger than that from a hand fan. We feel more comfortable. But still, if the air is warm, we might want to have a cold drink or a popsicle.

"So this is the way this worker's mind operated. He and some other workers began to try some experiments from their daily experience, and they translated them into their work.

"Now, they deduced that using a hand fan on a person is comparable to using a mechanical fan on a generator. Using hydrogen coolant is like using an electric fan on oneself. Both cool from the outside, whereas drinking cold water or eating a popsicle cools internally. So this was the idea that the workers proposed: make a generator with double cooling of rotor and stator.

"Of course, we had difficulties. But we knew that we had to take our own road and liberate our own minds. So in 1958, we organized to study The Chairman's work *On Contradiction*. From there, we just started with a rough drawing done by a worker on a blackboard. We had no blueprints. We just gradually developed the idea.

"There was this one workshop—the minute you walked in, you could just feel the intense energy. There were wall posters everywhere. Technicians and cadres came out of their office for the first time and went to work with the workers. Whenever we had a difference, we wrote it out on a big character poster. Then people would form small groups to discuss and troubleshoot the problems. Four or five people might put their heads together to find a solution. And if they hit on a solution, they'd write it up for everyone else to read.

"Then we started sending workers all over the country to other factories to see what they were doing. For instance, while we were working on the inner water-cooling system, we tried to make hollow or tubular copper conductors around the rotors. But we were unable to make these ourselves. Another factory in Shanghai was set up to do it. When they heard about our efforts, they gave us full support. They had to retool to make exactly what we wanted, but they were willing. We brought them a lot of difficulties, too. So we can't say that our successes were ours alone.

"Anyway, even though foreign experts had said that water could not flow through conductors if the revolutions per minute exceeded 3,000, some professors and students at Chekiang University finally worked out a way to do it. After a hundred days of struggle and experimentation, we succeeded in making the first water-cooled 12,000-kilowatt generator.

"During the course of this struggle, the workers perceived that our success was due to our Communist spirit. We saw that there were always two lines. One is Chairman's Mao's, which gives support to newborn things, and the other is Liu Shao-ch'i's, which pours cold water on the people's imagination. His followers said that there was no way that we could succeed because we did not have enough expertise. They said that it was impossible, and that even the foreign countries had not succeeded in doing this yet. They claimed that we were just like children, and that a child must learn to walk first before it can run. They chided us for starting off with such big strides. But actually, we just went at it step by step, and the new generators were born. Now our viewpoint is to use these generators, find their laws and perfect them.

"After we got the first generator built, Liu's spiritual followers wanted to move it to the northwest of China. But we workers wanted to watch it, study it, and learn from it. Liu's followers wanted to 'exile it to Siberia.' They kept making comments about its potential dangers and that maybe it would blow up.

"Finally the generator was installed in North Shanghai. It is still there. It doubled that plant's generating capacity. So after the Cultural Revolution, we all deeply criticized Liu's line, and gave fuller play to the creativity and initiative of the workers. It led to another success at our factory in 1969, when we succeeded in building a 125,000-kilowatt generator with double cooling. In 1971 we surpassed ourselves again, and built a 300,000-kilowatt inner-water-cooled generator."

Wang pauses here. He clasps his hands and smiles out across the table. "In closing, I just want to say one final thing," he continues. "In old China we really had no industry. It was not until after Liberation that our industry began to grow incredibly fast. And we could only have done that under The Chairman's guidance. We still have a lot of shortcomings, so we must continue to try to follow the revolutionary line."

Hsiao Ti—
A Fellow Worker

Another workday. Master Chang and I sit in front of our rotor. My foot accidentally hits a pedal that activates the machine which holds the rotor. It begins revolving, showering the floor with the tools that had been resting on top.

Master Chang says nothing, and begins to gather the scattered tools. I look up in embarrassment to see whether anyone else is aware of my clumsiness. Hsiao Ti returns my gaze, then gives an elfin smile, puts his tools down and saunters over.

He leans on my bench. "It's okay," he says. "Just move your stool back a few inches. That way it won't happen again. We all make mistakes."

Hsiao Ti is almost thirty, but looks younger. He smiles a great deal —a smile which is somewhat exaggerated by his front teeth, which protrude, so that it is not easy for him to close his upper lip. He has been particularly friendly since we arrived at the factory. He lives in our dormitory. It is obvious that he has been delegated to spend time wth us, and help take care of any small problems which might arise. It is equally obvious that he is one of the politically trusted activists on our work team. Even after a day, the personality differences between him and Master Chang become apparent. For, whereas Master Chang's politics are essentially passive, Hsiao Ti's dedication to political affairs in the factory is almost aggressive. He readily engages in political discussions, and just as readily makes corrections or offers mild reprimands when he feels someone (Chinese or American) is off course. One feels keenly responsible for what one says in Hsiao Ti's presence, a feeling which is distinctly absent with Master Chang. Being with Hsiao Ti is pleasant, but it puts me on my guard.

"Are you married?" I ask Hsiao Ti.

"No," he says, putting a hand on my arm, and giving a partial smile. "I will not get married until after I am thirty. You see, these are the years when my body is strongest. My head is too full of factory things and building socialism to think of marriage and a family."

There is nothing pompous about the way Hsiao Ti describes his plans. It no doubt accurately reflects his state of mind. He does not belabor the point; he seems to feel the need to convince no one of its truth.

Hsiao Ti turns to six-foot-tall Allan, who also works with our team. "Hey," he says. "This guy is *really* tall! Let's call him 'slim,' okay?"

Everyone laughs. I ask whether it is common in China for people to joke about physical features.

"If someone's fat," says Hsiao Ti, "they're fat. They wouldn't feel embarrassed by a joke about it. Why should saying that hurt anyone? It's just in fun. Being fat has no bad meaning. It's just like being thin. So we say 'fatty' just in fun. *'Pang-tze!'* " he says, repeating the word as if to show that it carries no malicious meaning.

In our work team, Hsiao Ti lays conductors into rotors like everybody else, although he used to be a machine repair man, and has spent some time at a Red Expert School studying physics, drafting and electronics. I know these things because Master Chang has told me.

"Why do you no longer repair machines?" I ask Hsiao Ti.

He seems surprised that I know this piece of information. In fact, he seems somewhat miffed. I sense that his pique is not because I have revealed some sensitive fact about him, but because I have exhibited a tendency to ferret out information which goes beyond our planned daily diet.

"Whatever the factory needs, I will do," he answers with uncharacteristic coolness. "Anyway, isn't it better that we all have experiences in different things?"

Eating Lunch

It is ten forty-five in the morning. Suddenly all noise in the shop ceases. We remove our white cotton gloves, replace our tools in our lockers, and walk outside the workshop to a large tin sink, where we wash up for lunch. Other workers stand around waiting their turn, carrying their tin cups, dishes and chopsticks in small net bags such as French housewives carry at the market.

The cafeteria is crowded by the time we get there. We are in the first of three luncheon shifts, which are staggered at fifteen-minute intervals. Our work team separates as we move to different lines. Behind the windows, a vast kitchen hums with activity. Tons of food are cooked here each day. Women in white bandannas chop vegetables on large chopping tables. Baskets of fish and meat are being cut and prepared. Steam rises from a large cauldron of noodles, partially obscuring the attendants who stir it with oversized chopsticks.

Somehow the members of our small group manage to relocate one another and sit together at one of the long concrete tables which fill the room. I eat garlic shoots, cabbage soup and rice. Hsiao Ch'en, who works at a neighboring bench, eats a small whole salt fish and a bowl of rice. Hsiao Ti eats some broad beans and a five-ounce bowl of brown wheat noodles (noodles are sold by the ounce; five ounces seems to be the maximum a bowl will hold). There is some joking about Hsiao Ti's large consumption of noodles and his relative thinness. Master Chang is lost to what little conversation there is in his concentration on a bowl of cabbage soup.

The Chinese do not waste much time on eating. They eat in a businesslike manner, spitting bones and gristle out unceremoniously on the table beside them. One rarely hears exclamations over a tasty dish or announcements of anticipation over an upcoming meal. After eating, they usually do not hang around chatting or smoking. When they have finished with their meals, the workers take their dishes over to one of the several long concrete sinks. Here they rinse their dishes under boiling-hot water from the rolling mill. The water flows out into a gutter through a wicker basket, where the odd kernel of rice or scrap of food is trapped. This and other garbage is later sent to a neighboring commune as pig food.

P'eng Hung—"a responsible element"

I can not say exactly when I first became aware of P'eng Hung. Quiet and reserved, he hung back at the first, unlike Hsiao Ti, whose outgoing nature catapaulted him into the middle of most situations.

Chang Kuei-Li and coworker in Workshop Eleven

Factory workers taking a break in Shanghai

Children getting ready for daily athletics at factory school

Children's dance troupe at factory school

P'eng Hung and Work Captain Chang

Yü Shao-feng (seated, left) and friends

Master Chang and the author

Master Ch'en (left) and Master Chang in front of workshop

Hsiao ti bends flanges on a rotor

Our tug of war at factory school

P'eng is in his late twenties. He is very tall, strong and handsome. He usually wears heavy boots and a pair of machinist's overalls with a front bib and straps. Although a native of Shanghai, he comes from a Moslem family. More often than not, he eats at a special factory dining hall for minority workers. P'eng does not eat pork. But often he forsakes what seems by now to be an empty tradition, and comes over to eat with us in the main cafeteria.

P'eng works a large hydraulic drill press which drills out and threads bolt holes in large motor casings. Although he is officially attached to the neighboring work team, it is not uncommon for him to wander over into our shop area for a chat. As the days are passing here, I find us spending more and more time together. Although not particularly interested in America itself, P'eng is attracted to our group. Or perhaps he has been assigned to spend time with it. In any event, he seems to derive special satisfaction when given a chance to explain some political point or other. Although pleasant, he does not have a reckless sense of humor. When jokes are made, he usually smiles indulgently, and then steers the conversation back to whatever serious point the joke diverted it from. P'eng is his surname. *Hung* means "red." For a short while I started calling him Red P'eng. But red is a very serious color in China, like red, white and blue in the United States. One day he matter-of-factly asked me what "red" meant in English. I told him. Only the barest suggestion of a smile crept across his face. I did not call him Red P'eng again.

P'eng is both smart and politically ambitious. His fellow workers recognize him as a "responsible element." He often reads political essays or news analysis over the factory loudspeaker system, and in addition is the leader of a study group for work team discussion leaders. His serious manner, when it comes to matters of politics, marks him as a man who will doubtless rise to a position of some responsibility in time. In fact, he may already be a Party member. But I can not tell. It is not the kind of question that you just blurt out in China, any more than you might ask a college professor or a business executive of short acquaintance how much money he makes.

The Nursery

The nursery is a rambling two-story building directly adjacent to the workshops. It is literally brimming over with babies. In one room they lie two to a crib under brightly colored coverlets. They sleep in different baby poses, oblivious to the noises and voices around them.

In another room, ten small children all sit on potties, giggling, squirming, waiting to deliver in this collectivized toilet training.

"We don't really try to force them," says one woman attendant. "We just sit them down here. If they do something we praise them. If not, it's all right too. Eventually they will learn from the others." She picks up a small infant who has just awakened, and begins to change a cloth diaper through pants slit down the crotch.

There is a comforting hum of activity surrounding these small, yellow-brown babies with black hair and beautiful narrow black eyes. The attending women move slowly, picking up each child as it wakes or cries. They cooch it, rock it, kiss it. The nursery radiates a warmness.

In another room, two-year-olds play on rocking horses and with toy boxes on the floor. They stop and stare transfixed as we enter. It is a world of Lilliputians, where everything but the nurses is on a tiny scale. It is a scene duplicated millions of times all across China at every factory, farm or organization.

A woman comes in from the shops to nurse her child. She still wears her shop cap to keep her hair out of her face. She picks her baby out of a bright blue crib and raises it high in the air above her head. It gives a broad smile. She sits down, unbuttons her tunic, and gives the child her breast.

At Master Ch'en's Apartment

It is growing dark now, and the evening cool is settling as we walk out the factory gates to Min Hang, the vast apartment complex for married workers. In 1958, before the Great Leap Forward, Min Hang was a small rural village of three thousand. Today it is an industrial hub with thousands of square feet of new housing, department stores, swimming pools, four middle schools, fifteen primary schools, two hospitals and eighty thousand people.

We walk down a shaded lane between rows of five-story apartment buildings to visit Master Ch'en and his family. Master Ch'en works in Workshop Eleven, and his wife works in the factory store.

Apparently word has already gone out that foreigners will visit Master Ch'en at his apartment. We are met blocks away by a teeming army of small children, running, galloping, and tripping over one another to keep up with us as we walk. The children are laughing and cavorting, endeavoring to follow us as we move down the path. But they also leave a clearing around us, indicating a certain failure of nerve at the prospect of getting too close.

We near Master Ch'en's building. Faces are looking out of every window and doorway. By now, the courtyard is boiling with hundreds of ecstatic children. We walk up a dimly lit staircase to Master Ch'en's fifth-floor apartment. Families emerge on each floor as we pass, and clap us on as though we are in some sort of race. As we round the stairs to the top floor, Master Ch'en, his wife, and three children are also waiting on their landing.

Ch'en has a nervous habit of blinking his eyes continuously when he is uneasy. Tonight his blinking is ceaseless. His whole face squinches up as he squires us through the hallway into the bedroom. These two rooms constitute his apartment. (His family shares a kitchen with three other families on the floor.) In the bedroom, there are two neatly made double beds in which the whole family sleeps. There is no wall between them, only a wire on which a curtain can be drawn for privacy.

There is a spittoon under one bed. Several trunks are stacked in the corner next to a large stand-up wardrobe. A wooden table occupies the center of the room. The table is piled with carefully polished apples, candy, gum and glasses of tea.

We sit down. There is a moment of awkwardness. No one is quite sure how this visit should begin. Then, being host, Ch'en suddenly seizes the responsibility and says, "We've only lived here one year. But I have worked at this factory for twenty-four years."

Just to keep the conversation from halting entirely, one of us asks if he was at the factory when Chairman Mao came to visit in 1961.

"Chairman Mao?" he repeats. "No, I missed him. I was in the city. It was a weekend. But what does it matter?" And then, repeating a line from the song "The East Is Red," he adds, " 'Wherever the red sun of Chairman Mao shines, there it is light, and I can see Chairman Mao's presence.' "

This small man sits tensely on the edge of his stool like a child who has just finished a classroom recitation, and is waiting for a reaction from the teacher.

He still wears his blue factory uniform and sneakers. His wrist watch is attached to his thin wrist by a strap several sizes too large. His gray tufty hair fits his head like a cap. He has a small moth-eaten mustache, and wears thick glasses, through which his eyes can be seen only dimly, as if through ice.

Finally, he breaks the silence again by raising a dish of cigarettes, and, with an air of constrained hospitality, offering one to each person in the room. His hands tremble as he lights one for himself.

His young son, still wearing his crimson Little Red Soldiers neckerchief, sits quietly on the back of the bed, watching and listening.

Out of the blue, Ch'en begins to talk about his life, as if he knew that sooner or later this would be expected of him. It's a relief to everyone. Even he relaxes as he speaks. Then he is momentarily overcome with emotion as he describes how his mother was lost in the 1930's when the Japanese invaded Shanghai.

"We couldn't find her after the invasion," he says. "She just disappeared. It was not until 1960, with the help of the Party, that we relocated her." Master Ch'en's eyes become watery as he speaks. It is the only time I will see an adult even approach tears in China.

"When I was fourteen, I began to work for a man in a hardware store. He only let me sleep three hours each night. It was then that my eyes began to go bad." He points to his glasses. "My boss expected me to work like an animal. I knew that I could not survive such suffering if it continued. Finally, I ran away and became a small-time peddler. But it was not easy to sell my goods. People did not buy them. So again I was forced to move on.

"This time I went to the country and began to work for a man who kept cows. I had no choice. But I couldn't make a living working for this man either. There is an old Chinese saying: 'All crows are black.'

"Again I fled. By that time I was sixteen. I went to join my father in a town in Chekiang Province. He was a tailor. We went from house to house, making clothes, although we had almost none ourselves. Our income was meager, and we could hardly survive on it. People like me, or older, have a deep memory of those days. We have a strong hatred of the old society.

"For three years and six months after that, I worked in a stocking factory as an apprentice. Then it went bankrupt. The factory just couldn't get enough raw materials. So I was laid off again and back at loose ends. I couldn't find another job in a knitting factory. I couldn't find any job that I was trained to do. Finally I ended up as a janitor, mopping and sweeping.

"Then, came 1949 and Liberation. We stood up at last. It was then that I came back to Shanghai to work at the old Electrical Machinery Parts Factory Number Four that was still in the city."

Here, his manner of talking changes abruptly. Instead of staring at the floor, as though looking inward, he begins to address us as though we were a class.

"As Chairman Mao taught us," he continues, "we must work for our self-reliance through self-struggle. So at the factory we started to expand after Liberation. And over the next twenty years our situation improved tremendously. There is such a difference between the life of us workers before Liberation and now. Before Liberation we only had small shacks and huts. And now look! We have apartments. We only pay four yuan a month in rent. I make ninety yuan a month, and my wife makes seventy yuan. We even save a little money each month." Master Ch'en is effusive as he indulges himself in this Communist commercial.

Master Ch'en's wife sits behind her husband as he talks. She listens intently, leaning forward, as though the proper supportive posture of her body and undivided attention might help her husband speak. In spite of the impressive equality that exists between men and women in China, a man is still usually deferred to in his own house by his wife, who normally cooks, washes and cleans.

"In the evenings, I usually come home directly after work, except on Mondays and Tuesdays," says Master Ch'en. "On those evenings we have study groups. We are studying subjects on the dictatorship of the proletariat now. Other nights I just come home and read or listen to the radio." He gestures to a red plastic radio, which has been playing quietly in the background.

"I made it myself," he says, giving a large sleepy grin. His daughter takes the cue and jumps up to turn the volume up louder as a testimonial to her father's skill with electronics. The radio makes crackling shortwave noises, and then the sound of a Western orchestra comes booming out.

"Its tone is still not good. I must fix the bass," says Master Ch'en, repeating his earlier grin and blinking his eyes. "But I'm working on it. Some of the other workers like to get together and talk about international affairs and politics. But I prefer coming home and just being here with my family. And I like to listen to music."

The noise in the courtyard is picking up again, perhaps in anticipation of our departure. Master Ch'en turns to the open window, listening for a moment to the voices outside.

"Yes. You hear all the noise outside? It's the children. They all know that foreign friends are up here. They are welcoming you. The children now are so lucky. They never knew the bitter past."

Romance?

Yü Shao-feng is in her mid-twenties. She is quite tall, vivacious, and wears her shiny hair in two black braids. She is a woman who would be found extremely attractive by almost any man in a Western society. She is intelligent, and clearly a worker who is both politically trusted and active. Although I have talked with her on several occasions in a group, our most intimate activity together has taken place at the dormitory before we retire. She and a friend have been teaching us a song, written by a factory worker, called "Chairman Mao Meets the Truck Driver." We stand out in front of the men's washroom like ghetto kids on a Harlem street corner, snapping our fingers in time and learning this song. It is an agreeable, if somewhat distant, form of contact. (I recall that one member of our group suffered a temporarily broken heart during one of these sessions. A female comrade, to whom he had taken a shine, seemed to be directing too much of her song-teaching energy in the direction of another American male. Her unrequited admirer retired to the end of the veranda, where he pouted like a cuckolded husband.)

Today, as we go down the path to visit the factory clinic, I find myself walking next to Shao-feng. We begin to talk about the health-care system at the factory. Although other members from our group are all around us, she appears to grow more restive the longer we talk. Finally she breaks off in mid-sentence, turns around, and calls to her friend Chien-p'ing farther down the path. Chien-p'ing runs over. The three of us walk together. We continue the conversation. Shao-feng now seems completely at ease.

Futan University

"We are entrusted by the proletariat to attend this university," says Sheng Yüan, a young student at Futan University. "We have a responsibility to use our education for them."

It is raining today as we visit Shanghai's oldest university at which several Chinese students in our factory work group are enrolled.

Shen is studying Chinese literature. He is intelligent and direct, and not at all thrown off by the presence of foreigners.

"You know, here in China we don't just decide that we want to go to university. It's not like that. For instance, after I graduated from middle school here in Shanghai, I had to go to the countryside and work like all the other students. I had a choice of whether to go to Anwhei, Kiangsu (both in Central China) or way up to Manchuria. Well, I decided to go to Manchuria and answer Chairman Mao's call. I really had no idea whether I would ever come back."

We sit in the damp, cold university cafeteria—a large barnlike building with a concrete floor—and eat a lunch of fish, soup and rice.

"In 1969 I went to a large State farm where they raised mostly corn and wheat. At first I felt just like a guest," says Shen, laughing and shaking his head. "I didn't feel at all at home. I felt like I was off in exile somewhere. It took almost two years for me to get over that. There was different food, different climate, different language. But I got used to it. Finally I found myself beginning to get into the whole life-style. I made friends and slowly began to think that I wanted to stay there and work forever.

"I remember when we first arrived in Manchuria at the farm. The peasants had already built us a house. But we felt awkward living in something that they had built for us. At that time I was living with some other students from different parts of China. We decided to hastily build a temporary structure—it was a feeble thing of straw and mud. Then slowly as we learned more, we began to build ourselves a really proper house.

"So I spent four and a half years there. I didn't do anything special. I was not an expert in anything. I just worked in the fields. And after two or three years, I really didn't want to come back to the city at all.

"Then the possibility of going to university came up. Do you know how we choose students to go to a university? Well, it's not like it used to be. What happens is that the factory or farm will get word that it can send one, two or maybe three workers to a university to study. So the factory or farm will hold discussions and figure out whether there is any particular field in which they need to have someone trained. Then the workers who are interested in going will submit their names, or perhaps their names will be submitted by fellow workers who think that they would serve the people well. Then more discussions will be held, and it is finally decided who will be chosen. After that, the university reviews the choice. They could refuse a candidate, but they rarely do.

"Well, they chose me. As I said, by that time I really didn't want to go back to the city. But since I was approved, I came. I figured that I should take this chance to study and help out.

"When I arrived back here in Shanghai in 1973, it was still not determined what I would study. At first, I had chosen navigation. But later I found that my blood pressure was too high, maybe because I'm a little plump." He laughs, holds his hands out from his stomach, and puffs up his cheeks.

"Once someone begins to study one subject, it is almost unknown for him to change later on . . . Finally, I chose literature. I was interested in it, and I thought I could make a contribution, because since the Cultural Revolution, the whole concept of literature has been clarified. Before the Cultural Revolution, students and professors were incredibly bookish. Whenever they wanted to learn something, they would run to the library. They had no sense of the worth of practical experience. We have this expression in Chinese:

Ssu tu shu
Tu ssu shu
Tu shu ssu

Reading books as though one were dead
Reading books that are dead
Reading books and dying

"That's a good one, isn't it? Well, that's how it was. Students and professors did not connect teaching and learning with social needs or class struggle. It was not until after the Cultural Revolution that the new 'open classrooms' *[K'ai-men-ban-hsüeh]* became firmly established. For us now, it means that we students frequently go to work and make social investigations among the workers and peasants. We decide where we should go. Maybe to a farm, a factory or even an office. It all depends on what we feel we need to investigate and study, or where we can help. For instance, maybe a farm brigade will need some help in writing articles or analyses about what is happening to their brigade. We are glad to use our skills, and it is good for us as well, because it gives us a chance to talk with peasants, learn from them, and remold our outlooks.

"Or perhaps a publishing house will ask us to compile a book on some subject. Perhaps we will go to a factory and work with the workers awhile. Then we will write an essay or a novel with the workers. They teach us and criticize us. We all learn together. The point is to take the classroom out into the open. We want to take the intellectuals to the people so that our literature will grow out of our experience with these working people.

"We also write criticisms of various literary works. We hold discussions and write about the theory and justifications for literature. I mean, what is literature for? Just for fun? No! It is a tool for socialist reconstruction."

Shen pauses, and for a moment concentrates on shoveling down some food, which has become cold as he talked.

"What will you do after you graduate?" I ask. I am remembering that as far as I know, there is no one in China who makes his living solely by being a "writer."

"I don't really know," he replies. "I am willing to return to Manchuria. But in my case, the fact that I was chosen from there does not necessarily mean that I must return there. I will go wherever I'm needed, wherever the State wishes to send me."

We move to a large room to meet the Student Body President of Futan University and other teachers and students.

The president is a short, unprepossessing young woman. She wastes no time in getting to the point. Like someone with a practical chore to do, she launches right into her own life's experience.

"I remember in middle school before the Cultural Revolution, we were once asked to write an essay on your aspirations. Well, everyone wrote about how he or she wanted to be a big expert in this or that. But there was this one student—just one—who wrote that he wanted to be an ordinary soldier and go away out to the deserts in Singkiang and work like a normal person. The other students thought that this was a scream. They thought he was strange to have such low aspirations. Well, now it's all changed."

I ask Shen, who is still sitting with me, whether or not this woman was chosen for the job of Student Body President by vote.

"No," he says without hesitation. "She was chosen through discussion."

While we have been sitting around this large table listening and asking questions, I have not been able to take my eyes off one man. He has a distinctive look. Unlike many of the other students, who in spite of their dedication to manual labor, still have a somewhat bookish look to them, this man is short, wiry and swarthy. His hair sits on his head forming a kind of whirlpool effect—a giant cowlick. His face bears several small pockmarks. When he finally introduces himself, he does so with great pride and a smile on his face. He is a street sweeper. He speaks with a disarming confidence about studying "sweeping" at the university. And in this world dedicated to the glorification of ordinary work and the ordinary man, it seems completely natural to hear him talk as part of one of China's finest universities.

"I came to the university in a new department," he says, capturing the attention of every daydreamer and dozer in the room. "My

Department of Mass Work was a creation of the Cultural Revolution. I came right off the streets, and all my street-sweeping friends warned me that I better not forget that I was still a worker after I got here.

"So now here at the university we are organizing students to do this kind of work—to go down and sweep streets with other sweepers, and to work and learn from them.

"Now sometimes when there is a holiday, I just go back and sweep streets with my old comrades. And when I hear them say that I haven't forgotten my origins, I feel good. When I see that the streets are clean, I feel even better."

Factory Movies

Slowly the procession of dripping raincoats and umbrellas moves out of the darkness and pouring rain into the half light of the straw-roofed factory auditorium. Tonight there is a movie. It costs .1 yuan.

From the inside, the auditorium looks like an oversized Tahitian house. This large building, which seats over a thousand, is entirely made out of bamboo columns and cross-bracing lashed together with rattan. The roof is thatched. The auditorium contrasts oddly with the other surrounding brick buildings at the factory, all of which utilize more modern construction techniques.

"You see," says Hsiao Ti, crouching under a wet plastic poncho, "this is the auditorium that Chairman Mao came to when he visited the factory in 1961. So, naturally, even though it is old style, we did not want to tear it down." The structure, though caught in the kind of time warp of "backwardness" which the Chinese usually shy away from, has been hallowed by Mao's presence.

Master Chang, Hsiao Ti, P'eng Hung and I walk down the aisle and find four free spaces on one of the benches. We sit, chat and wait for the film to begin.

Someone sits down on my left. To my surprise it is Shao-feng. She is just as surprised (perhaps even unsettled) to find that she has inadvertently sat down next to me. It occurs to me that it is possible that she did not recognize me from the back in my blue jacket and cap. I toy (only briefly) with the other possibility—that perhaps she has purposely sat down beside me. In any event, I am not displeased by her presence. Master Chang is sitting on my right, and I know that it will be difficult at best to understand his dialect in the dark, should I need help with the movie. Perhaps I am also unconsciously looking forward to the thought of Shao-feng whispering quick translations in my ear. It is not much for our world of sexual revolution. But in the world of the Chinese revolution, it is almost too tawdry a thought to handle.

"Hello, Shao-feng," I say as casually as I can, hoping to expunge any suggestion of a leer from my face.

"Oh, Comrade Hsi-erh. What are you doing here? How are you you?" asks Shao-feng, quickly returning to her conversation with her girl friend. There is tension being emitted from her side.

The lights are dimmed. The shorts begin. The first is a documentary called *The New Face of Shanghai.* The managers of a Shanghai alarm clock factory "go among the masses" to find out what kind of alarm clocks the people find most useful and appealing.

Just as I am savoring the thought of my first question to Shao-feng, I feel a hand on my arm. It is dark. I can not see whose it is. It pulls me in the opposite direction from Shao-feng. Master Chang whispers something incomprehensible to me. He and P'eng Hung begin politely to tug me over toward them.

"Here. Take Master Chang's seat," says P'eng Hung, pulling me up awkwardly. Before I know it, Master Chang has slid into my seat almost beneath me.

The jig is up. I move compliantly now, aware that something of significance has occurred in this pas de quatre. Perhaps I have crossed the undrawn line of demarcation in China, where relations begin to become private rather than public.

As the shorts continue, I recall Hsiao Ti's having told me that if an umarried man and woman are seen walking alone several times, it is tantamount to a public declaration of marriage. Just today, one of the women in our group mentioned how modest she found her roommates in the dorm: "At nighttime when it is time to get ready for bed, the women usually get into their bunks fully clothed, drop their mosquito nets, and change into their pajamas out of view of the other women. Unlike the men's shower, the women's shower room is divided into stalls."

There is an old expression in Chinese for a person who is interested in romance, or is licentious. It is *feng-liu*. I look at Shao-feng's profile now, in the flickering light of the screen. She is beautiful. She is intently watching the movie. I wonder whether she knows the word *feng-liu?* I wonder whether there are any people left in China today who might be so described.

The main feature comes on. It is about the "two-line struggle" in a steel mill circa 1959 (just after the Soviet Union pulled all its technicians out of China, often taking the blueprints for unfinished projects with them). The struggle revolves around whether or not to import a special high-tensile steel for navy ships from a pointedly "unnamed socialist country" or whether to try to make it at the factory. The factory head is basically a good guy, duped by the wrong line of going abroad to buy steel. Finally he sees the light. He stands in his office with the good worker/cadre and criticizes himself, with tears in his eyes. He admits that he has taken the wrong line in renouncing self-reliance.

There is the usual assortment of other good guys and bad guys, or what Master Chang refers to as "bad eggs" *(huai-tan)*. He becomes uncharacteristically agitated when a "bad egg" is on the screen. As the villain slinks and skulks around, up to no good, Master Chang grabs my shoulder. He points to the screen as this particular "bad egg" is about to sabotage a blast furnace.

"See that! See that!" he exclaims. I am relieved to see Master Chang so engrossed. For until the movie had begun, I feared that he was accompanying me out of a sense of duty, not a craving to be entertained.

Often throughout the film as a character enters, P'eng Hung or Hsiao Ti speak their exact line, leaving the strange impression that the actors, who repeat the same words moments later, are mimicking *them.* I am reminded of Bogart festivals, during which Bogart seldom gets one of his heavy lines out before some aficionado in the audience beats him to the punch.

As the film ends with the camera panning across the smokestacks of the factory belching prolific amounts of smoke in psychedelic colors, I have an intuition. I lean over to P'eng Hung and ask him whether he has seen this film before.

"Oh, yes," he says. "I have seen it several times. It's a good film to study. The first time I saw it, I was so excited my head was spinning."

Workday

It is six o'clock and damp and gray. Barely light. The loudspeakers have gone crazy. They make nothing but unintelligible echoes and feedback noises. No one turns them off.

Walking to breakfast, I am reminded that while China is basically a very clean country, people still throw a good deal of stuff around. There is indeed some trash along the paths and grassy areas of the factory. People even seem to throw some things out the dorm windows. There are occasional piles of garbage on the banks along the canals. One of the real litter weaknesses of the Chinese is ice cream wrappers, which are strewn with reckless abandon around the factory store. Dotting the grounds are small spittoons placed next to public trash baskets. The spittoons are full of lime. But I have never seen anyone spit into one. The floor and the ground are still fair game.

Despite the endless campaigns to engender cooperative public responses, old habits die hard. And in a perverse way, I am pleased to find that the Chinese have a flaw so basic and human as littering. It reminds one (as they would be the first to admit) that their revolution is far from complete, and that the struggle continues against human imperfection.

It is almost seven o'clock. Out in front of Workshop Eleven the cardboard sign put up to welcome "American Friends" is still standing. Now it is blurred and soggy.

Hsiao Ti waits in front of it with his usual toothy affable smile. "You're a little late," he says.

Inside, the morning briefing is just ending with the usual admonitions about safety and production. I sit down with Master Chang next to the rotor we have been working on. We begin to tap small bamboo wedges into the coil ends to hold them in place for soldering. This factory is an unpredictable pastiche of hand labor and modern technology. It at first seems strange to be working with our hands and bamboo in this giant sophisticated factory. But in many ways, this contrast is the story of China everywhere today. The bamboo wedges are called *mao-chu* in Chinese.

"Is that the character for Chairman Mao as well?" I ask Master Chang, trying to identify which written character is used. (The character for Mao's surname has several meanings: feathers, ten cents and fur.)

Master Chang is silent. He does not even look at me. The name of Chairman Mao is a no man's land for discussion, comment or even comparison. Master Chang is not angry, he is just thrown off by even the remotest comparison of Chairman Mao's name with something of lesser status. There is an eeriness in the degree to which Mao, his thought and even his name have been canonized.

We are interrupted by the arrival of a short woman wearing a shoulder sack bearing a red cross on its side. She is a worker-doctor. Each day she makes her rounds through the workshop, dispensing prescriptions and referring workers who have an illness she can not treat to the factory clinic.

"Welcome to our factory," she says, as though she were a maître d' at a restaurant. And then in a reassuring way she says, "If you should feel bad, don't hesitate to let me know."

We shake hands. She beams and departs for P'eng Hung's drill press. P'eng Hung has a cold. His nose is noticeably red. The worker-doctor stands beside him awhile, and then pulls out a small pad and writes him a prescription.

I am just about to go and fetch some more bamboo wedges, when

Master Chang tugs my sleeve. "You see him?" he asks, pointing to a middle-aged man in glasses who is walking down the aisle looking up at the crane. He wraps a cable sling around a rotor weighing several tons, and motions the woman crane operator to pick it up.

"He's a cadre," says Master Chang. "Most of those guys used to spend all their time in offices before the Cultural Revolution. Now if you go to the office and look, you can hardly find anyone. They're all out here working."

Hsiao Ti smells a good conversation brewing. He leaves his bench and comes over, hammer still in hand. He leans on the machine holding our rotor and listens.

"Well, I wouldn't say all the cadres were like that," he says to Master Chang. "But there were a lot of bureaucratic types around. Some were sort of puffed up and proud. They thought that they were a notch better than the average worker."

"How did you feel about those cadres before the Cultural Revolution?" I ask.

"We felt nothing," says Master Chang. "It seemed normal. We thought that they were just doing some work. We thought, 'There's a cadre. A cadre is a cadre. Cadres don't do manual labor.'

"Then the Cultural Revolution started. At first I didn't realize what was happening, so it was hard to criticize the cadres. You know —they were above us. We weren't used to criticizing them so openly. We had to get our courage up slowly, and we didn't know whether it was right or not, but Chairman Mao says that every comrade must be responsible for his friends. So now if we think someone is taking the wrong path, well, we'll say something. We must."

The Chinese continually talk about the needs and virtues of criticizing those in command. But there is an axiom that I think one can postulate: whatever the Chinese talk about most is precisely what they have the greatest trouble doing. The Chinese talk about criticizing authority a great deal. In certain ways they have been successful. In other ways, the Chinese strike me as extremely obedient, almost paralyzed in the face of authority. Perhaps without Chairman Mao's forceful permission, there never would have been a Cultural Revolution.

"Sometimes people get mad," says Hsiao Ti, gesticulating with his hammer. "You criticize someone and he really gets furious. Maybe he takes it personally. But then after a day or two maybe he cools off. Then we can all sit down and talk."

"The point," continues Hsiao Ti, as if addressing a class, "is not to break them down and destroy them with criticism by saying bad things to them. What good would that do? It would just make another comrade feel bad. The point is to bring everyone closer together in ideological understanding. Unity comes out of struggle.

"So we must distinguish between someone's thought and life. Mostly we should be concerned with our friends' political thought. If they get wrong ideas, like trying to separate themselves from the masses, then we must say something. But we should be careful about criticizing a person's whole life, even though that too has a relation to politics.

"For instance, some people like to dress up a lot, make themselves up a bit, wear expensive or pretty clothes. We should say something here. Maybe they like to wear some kinds of bizarre individualistic clothes. I don't mean that everyone should go around in ugly worn-out clothes. But they should wear regular clothes." He pulls at his blue jacket. Master Chang seems lost in his work, as though all this analysis were somewhat beyond him.

"Now when we see something to criticize in a cadre," continues Hsiao Ti, gathering momentum, "we might go and talk to him."

I ask him whether most people would dare do this.

"Yes. Most people dare. Particularly in groups. Or we might write a wall poster saying where we think his faults are."

"But that was mostly during the Cultural Revolution," says Master Chang somewhat naïvely.

"We will sign our names to the wall posters," says Hsiao Ti, continuing where he had left off, as though Master Chang had not spoken. "If we don't want to sign our names, that's all right too. Then we would post the wall poster up at the entrance of the shop.

"Cadres don't usually reply. They don't have to. But they probably will think about the criticism, and try to understand whether or not it's true. And if it's correct, they must change."

We have been talking for almost an hour now. Hsiao Ti's rotor sits behind him untouched.

"Well," I say jokingly, "we haven't done much to up production this morning."

"We have been producing friendship," says Hsiao Ti with a slight sternness in his face. "Friendship—that's a different kind of production."

Factory School

The Shanghai Electrical Machinery Plant Workers' Children's School is a large multistoried concrete building set behind several blocks of workers' apartments. Its hard earth playground is surrounded by tall green poplar trees. Inside, sounds of children reciting their lessons in unison cascade out of each classroom and echo up and down the dark hall.

We are ushered into an English classroom. Soft music comes in over the loudspeaker system. A voice softly sings, "One, two, three, four. One, two, three, four."

The children sit quietly at the desks, eyes closed, massaging the muscles in their temples and other areas around their eyes. Each child knows the exercises.

"Every day we do eye exercises to improve the children's sight," says one of our hosts. "We consider it a kind of preventive medecine."

We watch an English class. Individual children rise obediently and repeat words and phrases after the teacher. The class ends with the teacher leading the children in an A–B–C–D–E–F–G song (to a slightly different tune).

"Aiya–Beeea–Ceea–Deea–Eea–Effa–Gee–Aitcha . . ." They sing with great spirit, like some final chorus in a musical which brings everyone out onstage.

The bell rings. The class has gone off without a hitch. All the questions have been answered. There were no naughty children. The teacher was a model of reason and good cheer. The display has been flawless. But there is something perplexing about it.

It is not that I feel we have been duped by some prerehearsed performance calculated to impress foreigners. It would indeed be easier to understand such a class if one suspected that it was simply a staged production arranged to hide some flawed inner reality. But actually I intuitively suspect that no reality exists other than what we have seen. I am convinced that this class, like others I have seen, is virtually as orderly and uncomplicated every other day of the year. Yet I find myself trying to ascertain how the Chinese have "solved" some of the problems which are endemic to our own schools.

What about truancy, disciplinary problems, slow children, delinquency, vandalism?

The teachers and school officials just looked perplexed and blank when confronted with such questions.

The children are out in the schoolyard now, standing in neat lines. It is the daily exercise period for several classes.

When the exercises are finished, the athletic instructor asks whether we would like to have a tug of war with the children. It is suggested that our six men pull against eighteen boys.

There is a great deal of excitement. The children are electrified by the idea. Immediately, in our group, there is much talk of winning and losing; our competitive sense is unmistakably piqued by this challenge. We line up along the rope—strutting, kicking heel-holds into the earth, and trying to organize ourselves as best we can. We decide to pull on cadence, and appoint one man as coxswain.

The athletic director stands at midpoint on the rope. He raises a track pistol and fires. The children heave into the rope with looks of grimacing concentration. They pull from low crouched positions.

We tug and strain, passionately trying to keep our cadence in rhythm. Suddenly, we are pulled off balance. Our bodies jerk upright, and we are dragged relentlessly across the line. Our group is crestfallen. All the children on the sidelines clap.

A second pull is organized against another class. We are eager and determined to win.The gun goes off. We grunt and puff. Our cadence is more effective this time. Slowly we can feel each tug dislodging the children a little more. We give a huge tug. We have them on the run! In a few seconds we have pulled them over the line. Again the watching children clap.

We feel satisfied with this great schoolyard conquest. We congratulate ourselves on our good sense and fast improvement.

I walk over to the sidelines to get my camera bag, suddenly feeling very stiff. A woman from our group sidles over to me. She wears the smile of someone who is about to share a wicked secret.

"Did you know that the coach went over and bumped three kids off the rope just before the second pull?" she asks, not without a tinge of triumph in her voice.

Doubts

Sometimes I just cannot make my mind up about this country. This morning, for instance, I have an interesting time working in the shop. I begin to feel that I see the human purpose behind hitherto obscure phenomena or prohibitions, as I see the country functioning smoothly around me. Walking back to the dorm I find myself wondering whether perhaps China is not some utterly new experience in history after all—one in which all the caveats against too much regulation, regimentation and organization ought not to be reconsidered. The old assumptions that human energy and imagination can only be released with liberal doses of freedom and self-expression end with question marks in my mind. Perhaps this is some new world as yet unfathomable by someone with Occidental experiences such as my own. Perhaps it is a world for which one must cultivate a new sense to perceive clearly.

Then suddenly the loudspeaker will come bellowing over the rooftops. Some oafish piano accompaniment plays behind an operatic soloist wailing on about Chairman Mao being a great red sun, a fearless helmsman and almighty creator. I feel myself freezing, doubts congealing. I find myself thinking back to accounts written with glowing enthusiasm by foreigners who first watched and experienced the Russian Revolution, but failed to see the seeds of brutality and sourness until long after they were full grown under Stalin. It occurs to me that perhaps the very strength of democracy is its supposed weakness: it is often so disorganized, it is almost impossible to get even half of the people to move fervently in any direction.

Are there any signs of a frightening future lurking here around me in this factory which is moving hellbent with hope and energy into the future? Can I detect ominous tendencies beneath China's proletarian optimism? Do I dare?

Work Captain Chang

Chang Hsüeh-tung is the captain of our work team. Just over thirty years old, he serves as captain over more than thirty workers. Each morning it is he who gives the pep talk. It is his job to make sure that our team keeps on its production schedule.

"He has been captain for a long time now," says Hou Pao-liang, whose job it is to tie the cables around machinery for the crane.

I ask Chang what the requirements are for being captain. He wrinkles up his nose and adjusts his glasses. "Well, a captain must have good political consciousness, and must be in touch with the workers," he says. "And, of course, he must be a good technician as well. We workers discuss who we want as captain, and then it is approved by the leadership. But this does not mean that a captain gets any higher salary. That is not the point."

Chang is lean and quite tall. He has short hair. His usual attire is overalls and a cotton jacket. His manner is standoffish. He rarely seems to interfere with any worker unless asked. In fact, although we are rare and distinguished guests, it was not until after we had worked in the shop for almost a week that I became fully aware of who Chang was. He works quietly, with a sense of competence and authority.

Today, we get into a long conversation at his bench, leaning over a half-finished rotor.

"The systems of our two countries are different," he says. "You come from a capitalist country, and we come from a socialist country. But, you know, we also criticize the Soviet Union as well as the capitalist countries. They are no longer truly revolutionary or socialist. We believe that under a socialist system people can work for something other than themselves. This was really what the Cultural Revolution was all about. It was trying to teach people not just to work for themselves, their factory or their country, but for all people. "What good does it do for a few people to get ahead and leave the others behind?" He makes a gesture of absurdity by opening up his two white-cotton-gloved hands and holding up the palms. "That's not development. In the long run, a system like that can't possibly do anything but bring about its own downfall.

"Take me, for instance. I get seventy yuan a month. I have a wife and two children. My wife makes another sixty yuan a month. I smoke and have a few other small special needs. Now, someone else may make just as much as we do, but also have more kids or perhaps old parents to look after. Or perhaps someone is single and makes seventy yuan a month. This equals a real difference in income. But still, it's not like it was before. Now we simply get salaries, with the older workers mostly getting higher salaries. Here in the factory it doesn't have so much to do with how much a person produces as it did before the Cultural Revolution. Then we got paid by the piece. However many rotors you turned out, you got paid accordingly. So what happened? People tried to find the easy jobs where they could do least and make the most money. Or some people spent a lot of time working for themselves. Maybe they made furniture or raised a few animals in their spare time. They rationalized that this was the way to raise production and development faster.

"Well, maybe in the short run you'll get some results. But what about the long run? Can you really build something for people with everyone just thinking about his or her own benefit?

"Now we have a fixed salary. That's that. The question has become, How can we change our thought? We must remember that it is the State that not only gives us a salary, but gives us a place to live, schools and health care. That's worth something too, isn't it? We must try to correct the tendency of all going out for ourselves, or we will end up as revisionists, and dog-eat-dog capitalism will follow. We don't want that. So we study to try to maintain high consciousness. We keep asking ourselves, 'For whom are we working?' We must do this because we are still marked with old thought."

Confrontation

It is a warm day with the sun shining colorlessly through thick, moist clouds.

After lunch I stroll down toward the Whangpoo River to enjoy the cool breeze. I take my cameras, intending to shoot some film of the factory and workers. But I soon feel clumsy, very much like an intruder. People along the way are shy, and not eager to have their photos taken.

I cross over the canal on the main footbridge. A string of small flat-bottomed concrete boats towed by miniature tugs is heading up the canal. They bring food to the factory and remove garbage. Boatmen stand on each end of the barges with long poles, helping to push the convoy upstream against the current. I take a few photos. A worker with a wash basin and a towel walks over.

"These boats and these people are not from the factory," he says. "They are from another commune." His face is expressionless, but his meaning is clear: don't photograph.

I walk on.

At the river, a fresh breeze is blowing in off the water. Large tugs are hauling strings of barges and rafts upstream. Junks under sail move rapidly downstream. I take a few photos, and begin to walk down the railroad tracks that run along the side of the river. A middle-aged man runs after me.

"What are you doing?" he asks in an unusually agitated and unfriendly manner.

"I am taking pictures of the boats," I reply.

"Why?" he demands.

I am about to reply that they are beautiful. Suddenly I know that this will be an incomprehensible answer.

"We don't have any in America," I find myself idiotically saying. Then, groping for something more practical, I add, "Using wind power is a sensible means of transport."

"It is rest time," says my interceptor coldly. "You should be resting!"

He is speaking extremely fast now. "The Chinese people and the American people are a great people," he says, in a tone which collides head-on with the meaning of his words. "The friendship between the Chinese and American people is . . ." He rattles on, but I can not follow him.

"I'm sorry to have caused this trouble," I say and put my camera away.

"Even the workers in the factory are not allowed to take photos," he says, relenting only slightly.

I beg his apology again and retreat, wondering whether it is a question of security, or a question of Chinese sensitivity over foreigners taking pictures of traditional or "backward" scenes in China.

I am shaken. I return to the dorm, fearing repercussions. In China, incidents are rarely just forgotten. China is a society where all acts have political significance.

Tonight we retire at the usual hour. Lao Chang, one of the interpreters who shares our room, carefully folds his gray cadre suit trousers and puts them under his pillow before sliding into bed. He is going to "Chinese iron" them by sleeping on top of them, a common practice.

As he readies himself for bed, Lao Chang seems to be trying to stir up a conversation. Given the slightest responsiveness, he sails right into a full-blown discussion of the Italian film director Michelangelo Antonioni's recent film on China, *Chung Kuo*, which has been severely criticized in the Chinese press. Lao Chang, who has lately been feeling poorly, is tenacious. His persistence in continuing the discussion finally draws me into it. Anyway, I have the strange feeling that it is aimed at me. Almost every day the interpreters meet, they discuss the trip, its problems, us and what political approaches are correct to follow. It is not uncommon in one day for two or three interpreters to find time to sit down next to the same person on a bus or during a meal, and all raise the same point. It is never crassly direct. But after a while, the process becomes inescapably clear. It is a kind of political education. If one is resistant, one feels a distinct coolness —a withdrawal of approval, and even friendship, during these probationary moments.

The incident at the river has apparently gotten back. There has evidently been a discussion of it. I feel singled out and somewhat trapped. My impulse is to try to explain my purpose in photographing in China. But I intuitively feel a sense of futility before I even begin.

"You see," says Lao Chang, lying down in the dark behind his mosquito net on an upper bunk, "Antonioni came to China, and he concentrated on the backward features of China. He showed old people straining to pull carts and old methods of plowing with water buffaloes."

I explain that perhaps he saw them as colorful or artistically pleasing, quite apart from the issue of China's astounding development.

Lao Chang remains silent for a moment. He does not believe in art for art's sake, or in aesthetics which are detached from politics. He does not understand or accept the notion of artistic self-expression.

"It's all political in nature," he says coldly and emphatically. "There is no such thing as a photograph or film without a political viewpoint. Why did he want to take a picture of a junk and not a new freighter? Why did he want to take a picture of an old peasant planting rice and not a tractor? Why do you want to take a picture of people in patched clothing?"

He is talking to me as though *I* were Antonioni. A hint of suspicion has crept into the conversation. Suddenly I am no longer sleepy. I find that I am girding myself for the challenge. I reply that Antonioni's film was viewed as most favorable to China in the United States and Europe. I half-heartedly explain that in nations like our own, there has been a disenchantment with industry and its benefits, and a nostalgic return in many instances to older, less technological ways of doing things.

"Listen, Lao Chang," I say, not without some irritation now, "you must understand that we are not Chinese. We are not always interested in learning lessons exactly the way you did. Our problems are different. Perhaps there is a wisdom in planting rice by hand, using sail-powered junks and fewer manufactured goods. Doesn't patching clothes to wear them longer show common sense, whereas throwing away half-worn-out clothes represents stupidity and waste? Doesn't the use of human waste as fertilizer show rational intelligence instead of backwardness? In our country we treat it and put it into the rivers and oceans full of chlorine."

My explanation now, as often in the past, does not seem to have clarified the issue. The object of a discussion in China is not always free give-and-take, but to provide the other person with a chance to reeducate him or herself to the "correct line." I wish I could end our discussion. I do not know how to handle it. Somehow it continues.

"We think Antonioni came to China looking for images of the past," continues Lao Chang. There is truth here, I think to myself, for foreigners do still superficially understand China through many of the old stereotypes. We are gratified by quaint, pastoral, peasant scenes, whereas tractors repel us.

"Yes," Lao Chang says emphatically. "You can take photos of anything you want. But they must show the future as well as the past."

"Lao Chang," I say, "many people in America are beginning to feel that in certain respects the past may be the future."

There is no reply for a long time.

Finally one of our roommates tells us to shut up. He wants to sleep. The room becomes quiet. I am relieved to be removed from the discussion. I hear mosquitoes trying to find a way into my mosquito net. Someone begins to snore.

Innovation

Each morning there is a new essay written in chalk on our work-team blackboard. Today it is entitled *"Let the Ancient Serve the Present, And the Foreign Serve China, Let 100 Flowers Bloom, Weed Out the Old and Let the New Emerge."*

Workers in the factory are possessed with the concept of innovation, or *"ko hsin."* The word turns up in many slogans, and is often the subject of some discourse in a B.I. The only notion which predominates even more in my discussions with Master Chang is that of self-reliance.

Today as we sit soldering, Master Chang explains in detail two innovations that have been made in our shop. One innovation revolves around a new method of bending the ends of the copper conductors on the rotors so that spaces are left between them. This prevents overheating, and has led to a ten-percent increase in kilowattage, while allowing for a decrease in size and weight.

The second innovation involves the use of spun-glass fabric rather than steel banding around a rotor, once the conductors are laid.

"It is cheaper, more efficient and lighter," says Master Chang, with an unusual amount of enthusiasm. Although he had nothing to do with their discovery, he seems to have thoroughly identified with these technical changes, and is quite pleased to represent himself as part of them.

"Every worker seeks to bring about these beneficial changes," he says, like a substitute who is pleased to be a member of a winning team.

Love?

This morning, I head for the shop a little early so that I can stop at the main bulletin board and glance at yesterday's paper, which is displayed in a glass case.

As I cross over the canal, I see P'eng Hung standing under a tree halfway down one of the side paths. He is wearing his overalls and is holding some books. Shao-feng stands next to him. They are talking. I stand quietly in front of the newspaper, watching out of the corner of my eye. And although I am not sure what is involved in "being in love" in China, it is suddenly clear to me that P'eng Hung has more than a passing interest in Shao-feng. And although I may never know, I wager that "at the proper age" they will marry.

They stand motionless next to each other and chat. Then, without touching, they smile at each other and leave for their respective shops.

"Criticize Confucius and Lin Piao"

At any given moment in China, there is almost always a nationwide political "campaign" in progress. They come and go, sometimes with an alarming suddenness which is indicative of the tenuous nature of any "line" in China. Today's "correct thinking" may become tomorrow's "erroneous viewpoint." Some of these changes are more intense than others, but none of them involves candidates or elections. The object of the campaigns is to raise political issues and stimulate people to reform their thought.

In the factory, as in the rest of China, the current campaign is called *P'i Kung, P'i Lin* or "Criticize Confucius and Lin Piao." All publications are full of essays which revolve around this campaign. Radio and television programs make constant reference to it. Slogans and banners all over the country repeat the catchwords, phrases and themes of the movement. Everywhere in China, people are "criticizing Confucius and Lin Piao."

Lin Piao, who was once Mao's chosen heir, disappeared mysteriously in a plane crash on September 12, 1971, while apparently trying to flee to the Soviet Union. He is compared to Confucius, the ancient sage, on whom the Chinese now heap nothing but contempt. Like Kung, or Confucius, Lin is pilloried as an idealist who opposed the true "revolutionary line." He is accused of believing in *t'ien-ming*, or the old Confucian concept that "heaven decides the way." Mao has taught that it is men who decide the future. Both Lin and Confucius are described as enemies of class struggle.

Here at the factory, groups have gone back and read some of the old Confucian classics in order to criticize them. They have read the *San-Tzu-Ching*, or *The Three Character Classic*, once studied diligently by all schoolchildren.

"*The Three Character Classic* claimed that man's nature was good at birth," says one worker, diving with relish into the subject at a special gathering called to discuss the Criticize Confucius and Lin Piao Movement. "They attribute no class basis to man's nature. Is an evil landlord the same as a hard-working peasant?" he asks rhetorically.

"We spent three weeks reading and criticizing this classic to better understand our old society and the mentality of Lin Piao," he continues. "We wrote hundreds of wall posters, trying to understand historical class oppression, idealist and reactionary educational ideas, because it was these ideas which taught the people to have feudal loyalty. *The Three Character Classic* taught how nine-year-old Huang Wang became loyal to his parents. It taught loyalty to a system which kept most people oppressed. This was the old Confucian system."

A young woman in short bobbed hair, with pink cheeks and a serious expression on her face begins to speak. She has a small notebook, which she refers to like a teleprompter as she talks.

"We also study the *Nü-erh-Ching,* or *The Guide to Women,* another classic, to understand the ideological basis of how women were kept inferior to men. There was an ancient expression, 'If a hen crows, the house will go bankrupt.' Women were meant to say nothing. Lin Piao also promulgated this line." She says this last sentence with conviction, but cites no source or quotation. She need not. Lin is now a pariah, one of the fountainheads of all things evil in China.

"Take me," she continues. "I was good at knitting. But until recently I didn't really feel strong in my ability to join in political studies. I just acquiesced. But after we read and criticized *The Guide to Women,* which describes the place of women in the old society, I changed my mind and saw how pernicious this kind of ideology was, and how it was influenced by Confucius. So I decided that we women should also pay great attention to politics. I ended up by applying for Party membership, and began to take an active part in theoretical discussion groups with men."

Suddenly, someone asks the assemblage of factory workers and cadres what actually happened to Lin Piao.

There is a prolonged silence. The question is so pointed and so specific that no general answer will suffice. I am reminded how much more comfortable the Chinese seem in the realm of theory.

"Lin Piao attempted to assassinate Chairman Mao," says an obviously high-ranking cadre. "He said that the dictatorship of the proletariat was a 'meat grinder.' He said that educated youth were just 'labor reform in disguise.' "

"How could Chairman Mao have picked a successor who ultimately proved to be so untrustworthy and counterrevolutionary?" asks someone else.

"Well, the exposure of Lin had to undergo a long process of development," answers the same cadre. "As a rightwing opportunist, he started very early, even in the twenties and thirties in Chingkang-shan, where he cast doubts on how long the red flag could continue to fly. Chairman Mao wrote *A Single Spark Can Light a Prairie Fire* to criticize him. Before Lin Piao crashed and died, Chairman Mao had tried to criticize him patiently and help. His crimes had been known and exposed earlier. But they needed a process to be completely exposed. We have a policy in the Party that when a person makes a mistake, we give him a chance to correct it. That's why we didn't say, 'Down with Lin Piao!' earlier. But Lin Piao took his chances and did not correct himself."

"Who exposed Lin Piao?"

"Well . . . he exposed himself."

"How did he die?"

"He exploded himself over Mongolia," replies the cadre implausibly after a moment of silence. (Lin Piao is generally believed to have been shot down by a Chinese Air Force fighter.) Then returning to less treacherous ground, the cadre continues, "His line was manifested in all levels of government. Lin called Chairman Mao an innate genius. But there is no such thing as genius which does not spring from one's class experience. Of course, we workers did not know all about his crimes until they were fully exposed by those who were privy to them in the Central Committee of the Party. It did, indeed, take time to see through them.

"Chairman Mao said that the Cultural Revolution is only the first one, and that there will be many more in which people like Lin Piao will emerge in their true colors. Without the Cultural Revolution, our economy would be stagnant. There would be no support for newborn things. After the Criticize Confucius and Lin Piao Movement began last year, we had eighty-two new Party members in the factory. Ten became cadres and Party secretaries of workshops. Twenty-nine became deputy secretaries. Ninety-five model workers emerged. Thirty-nine model work teams emerged." He treats these statistics as if they were magic talismans capable of warding off all doubts.

"So, in fact, the Cultural Revolution and the Criticize Confucius and Lin Piao Movement actually gave us and our economy a great boost. Total production value of the factory went up a hundred and five percent during this period. In effect, that means that whereas before the Cultural Revolution there was one factory, now there are two."

A Political Study Group

P'eng Hung sits with his hands clasped on top of his copy of *The Selected Works of Marx and Engels.* He sits at the table waiting for the last few people to drift in and for the clock to strike the hour. Meetings start punctually in China. P'eng Hung is the group leader of a Theoretical Contingency Study Group. It is composed of representatives from Workshop Eleven work teams who are readying themselves to serve as discussion leaders in their own groups.

The ten or so people settled around the table under a fluorescent light are primarily of the younger generation. Half of them are women. Each has a copy of the current issue of *Red Flag,* China's monthly theoretical journal. They are studying an article on the dictatorship of the proletariat by Chang Ch'un-ch'ao, who months later is to be publicly pilloried for belonging to the "poisonous gang of four." P'eng Hung opens the discussion. It very quickly becomes lively, if not confusing.

A woman launches off into a long explanation of "the principle of commodity exchange." She is groping for a conclusion, but sentence piles on top of sentence.

"Okay, okay," says a young worker in overalls and glasses somewhat impatiently. "But *what* is it? Don't use so many words!"

She tries again more succinctly. When she finishes, three people immediately begin to start talking at once.

"Okay," says P'eng Hung, trying to gather the reins, his voice rising without strain above those of the others. "What is the difference between why people work under capitalism and socialism?"

"Under capitalism, the purpose is to make money," answers a young worker. "Under socialism it is to serve the people."

"I read that in California one milk company poured thousands of liters of milk down the drain just to keep the price up," says a woman.

P'eng, who knows I live in California, turns to me.

"Yes. That's my home," I say. Everyone explodes with laughter.

"Is this true?" asks the worker next to me incredulously.

"Yes. I read about the same incident," I reply. "It happened in Los Angeles."

"Why do they throw the milk away?" cries one worker from across the table? *"Why?"*

"Because they want to keep the price up and make money," I offer.

"Why don't they just give it away?" Several discussants look in my direction.

"Because the poor people wouldn't buy anything else," volunteers an older man.

"I've also heard that sometimes in capitalist countries a woman will marry an old man just to get his money," says a young woman, jumping on the bandwagon."

"This is absurd," another woman almost shrieks, as everyone else laughs.

I nod, smiling, unsure of what to reply.

Someone suggests that there may even be a little capitalist-style mentality left in China. This remark provokes a veritable earthquake of debate. Surprisingly, no one disagrees with the remark. They argue about where and how these manifestations can be seen. Four or five people talk and argue at once. Several others busily thumb through their *Selected Works* for some irrefutable quote, like some fundamentalist Sunday school.

"Wrong!" someone yells. "Bourgeois outlook is not part of human nature. It is a class characteristic which must be rooted out."

"It's a force of habit—bad habits," shouts someone else. Several subdiscussions begin at the table. P'eng Hung raises his hand in a mock effort to quell the cacaphony.

"You know old Master Wang?" asks P'eng Hung, ending the previous discussion by beginning an anecdote. "Well, he gets paid twice as much as I do. I only get thirty-six yuan a month. Often when Master Wang gets sick I have to take over for him. But that's all right. He is older. Our relationship is that of comrades. It's not a question of money. It's a question of each doing what we can for socialist reconstruction."

"Oh, P'eng Hung. You're especially terrific," says the woman next to him humorously, provoking gales of laughter from the others. Shao-feng blushes.

"All right," says my neighbor, trying to steer the discussion back into a theoretical vein. "As members of the Party, we have raised our consciousness. We don't work just for ourselves. And because of the needs of the State, we even work voluntarily to fill our production quotas."

"There was the incident with the crabs," interjects Shao-feng, who has been quiet until now. "Remember those comrades who wanted to have their generator repaired quickly and offered us some crabs as a tip?"

"Yes. And I might add that they were tasty crabs at that," interrupts my neighbor humorously.

"But we said, 'No. We do not want your crabs,'" continues Shao-feng stalwartly. "'We will fix your generator for the revolution.' We must decide whether we are working for the workers and the revolution or for ourselves. We must work and forget ourselves."

This expression "To work and forget oneself" (*wang-wo-lao-tung*) is one of the leitmotifs of these young and politically ambitious workers. They seem to view sacrifice with the same relish that their Western counterparts view self-indulgence. They make sacrifices during the normal day which most men in our society make only at times of extreme hardship. They discuss sacrifice as a way of life for ordinary times, rather than as an unusual event.

A Professor at Work in the Factory

Today is my birthday. But since the Chinese do not celebrate birthdays (they all compute their age from the first New Year's Day they are alive), I say nothing. The day is marked, however, by the completion of the 750-kilowatt rotor which Master Chang and I have been working on. The crane comes and sweeps it away from our bench. Several minutes later it is back again with a bare spindle of a new 240-kilowatt rotor ready for us to begin the process of assembly over again. Master Chang cleans up for a few minutes. Then he sits back down at his bench, takes a deep breath, smiles and begins to work.

"How many rotors have you assembled in your life, Master Chang?" I ask.

He gives a smile, but no answer. Then he waves the question off as if it were a mere joke.

Lao Hu seems to be at loose ends today. He is a professor of English from Futan University. He has come to the factory with a group of students to accompany us and do a stint of manual labor. This morning he looks very unprofessorial in his baggy pants, several feet of which appear to have been rolled up into a lumpy cuff at his ankles. Lao Hu is short. He wears a blue cap which is so large that it comes perilously close to obscuring his vision.

He catches me looking in his direction, and walks over.

"Did you have a difficult time during the Cultural Revolution?" I ask, after we exchange pleasantries.

"Well, actually, it was not so difficult for me," he says. "I came from a poor peasant background. And, after all, I was still quite young during the end of the sixties." He smiles ruefully. "Others really did get criticized more sharply than I. And some didn't understand for a long time what it was all about. But it was not our intent to hurt these people or penalize them or throw them out of their jobs. Perhaps there was some of that . . . you know, old grudges or something.

"We had a series of policies at Futan to help different people reform in different situations. For instance, one policy was "to be patient and just help." Some comrades just needed time to change. They did not need serious criticism or pressure.

"Then we had another policy of 'criticizing to help someone change.' Some people just needed more awareness before they could change. Their tendency was to try to avoid the right thought if they could.

"Finally we had a policy of 'criticizing someone and putting him to work.' The idea was to let these people reform through the experience of work. Many people had just forgotten to ask the important question: 'Who are we working for? Ourselves or socialism?'

"Even now, I still have to struggle with myself," says Lao Hu in a somewhat gratuitous manner, as if there were a certain ideological necessity to recognize at all times that one is a part of the problem as well as the solution.

"Chairman Mao has said that as long as there are classes, there will be class struggle. And as long as there are classes, there will be class ideas which will create contradictions inside of us. For instance, some days I may just feel like telling my students not to ask questions and just do things the way I say. I may forget that I should listen and learn from my students. Perhaps I have selfish ideas. Maybe there are some jobs to be done, and I take one of the easy ones and let someone else do the hard ones. Maybe I just don't say anything about it, hoping no one will notice. You know how it is. Or maybe I take the easy job and am not even aware of it myself. I kind of fool myself.

"These ideas just sort of come into my head. And if I don't think about them and struggle against them, they will never go away."

Looking at Lao Hu in his ill-fitting uniform, it is difficult to summon up the image of him as a professor at one of China's most renowned universities.

"So sometimes we criticize each other," he continues. "We must! Chairman Mao says that we must criticize even friends. If we keep silent, we are not true friends. We don't wish to hurt each other, although that too is possible. We want to help each other."

Lao Hu sighs and smiles. "Well, this process will go on forever and ever," he continues. "Even under communism there will be bad tendencies. We must always guard against bad tendencies."

We Give a B.I.

Tonight is a special night. It has been set aside for us to give an introduction to the United States for factory workers. It was we rather than the Chinese who suggested the idea. They agreed, compelled by politeness and perhaps an acknowledgment that they had not been evidencing much interest in our country.

We gather in the large meeting room adjacent to the factory store. There are about a hundred Chinese present—mostly friends from the shops, factory leaders and various other cadres and workers. This time we give some prepared B.I.'s of our own on various political movements in present-day America. We cover subjects such as the labor movement, women, the counterculture, minorities and the economic situation.

Our presentations are often long, uninspired and rendered flat by the laborious process of translation. I am interested to note that the Chinese respond to our B.I.'s with just about the same low level of electrification as we to theirs. And I am again impressed by the apparent lack of interest these workers show in the United States. Our tales of social strife, cultural change and economic uncertainty seem neither to surprise nor please them.

I glance around the room during a delivery on the U. S. labor movement. People sit with their eyes out of focus, lost, staring off into space in some socialist reverie. Several comrades, kept up long past their normal bedtime, half-heartedly fight off fits of yawning. Only the most gung-ho pay full attention or take notes.

The audience evidences some signs of life as we ready the room to show them a series of slides on the United States. The large psychedelic portrait of Mao is unceremoniously taken down by two men when it becomes clear that it is occupying the only stretch of wall against which the slides can be shown.

The lights go out. Images of mountain landscapes in the Rock-ies, ghettos, wealthy suburbs, farms, factories and highways taken by various members of our group flash on the wall. One series on billboards showing advertisements for liquor, cigarettes, the Air Force and gasoline seems to impress us more than them: these banished images reappear before us as a shock.

A slide of a large illuminated outdoor advertisement for Canadian Club Black Velvet whiskey comes on. It shows a skimpily clad blond woman in a decolleté black velvet dress sprawled seductively across the length of the mammoth billboard. Beneath her body are the words FEEL THE BLACK VELVET.

I look around the darkened room. Faces are blank. People look as though they had been paralyzed by some new unknown force. What is filling the heads of these comrades?

I lean over to Hsiao Ti, who sits beside me. "What do you think of that?" I ask him.

He wrinkles up his face in puzzlement. "Why do they want to do that?" he whispers back.

Tonight I have the distinct sense that for most Chinese the outside world is still little more than a distant fantasy about which they get occasional predigested shreds of information in newspapers and on the radio—an unreal world. Since there is little fascination with the exotic or bizarre in China, people hardly appear titillated at all by a distant land with strange practices and problems. They seem to look upon us as some sort of retarded and essentially frivolous society—a society which is wallowing in complexity and confusion, but does not have the good sense to make a rigorous Marxist class analysis and get on with a revolution. We may be powerful, but we seem to appear to them as a side show devoid of inspiration. We are a model of decline, which, for those living in a land of socialist reconstruction, holds little fascination.

Factory University

"Our university is called 'May First University' because this was the date when Chairman Mao visited our factory in 1961," says a young teacher who was once a shop worker. He speaks with slight hesitation, and turns often to his comrades, who sit on either side of him, for affirmation. His openness and vulnerability lend an air of genuineness to his words.

"At first we only had courses in science and engineering at the factory university—all courses which related to technical production," he continues. "But then our Party Branch suggested that we should try to do more than just teach the workers how to produce generators. They felt that we should begin to train workers in various other fields as well, to help them master other aspects of their lives.

"The first year, our new liberal arts program graduated twenty-three students. Of course, the university still has the older departments covering engineering and science. There are also ten new night classes for workers in subjects like English, drafting and electronics. But still, not every worker can get into the university. What happens is that a worker who wishes to study applies for admission. Then the colleagues of that worker in the shops discuss whether or not he or she deserves to be admitted. If the worker is passed, then the Revolutionary Committee of the shop will send his name on to the leadership of the university. They must also give their approval. But we are still small, and can not yet meet the needs of the whole factory. We are trying to remedy the problem. We are thinking of ways to run even more spare-time and night-school courses to answer Chairman Mao's call to 'create vast ranks of proletarian intellectuals.' What we want to do is to train a grass-roots backbone of politically conscious workers who can go back to their shops, write articles, help hold discussions and lead study groups."

"We now have three courses in the literature field," says a young woman, breaking in. "One course is on Chairman Mao's thought on art and literature. Then we have a course on Lu Hsün, Finally, we have an experimental writing course in combining theory and literature. You see, most factory workers have never really written anything. So we run into a lot of difficulties at first, but we begin to overcome these by working in collectives. For instance, we wrote a collection of short stories called *Young Pathbreakers* by dividing the class into five groups. Each person discussed his or her ideas about how to write a story. Then if one person had problems, we would all help work them through.

"Finally, each person began working on his or her own short story. But they were rough and not very well written. It was not until after many discussions and some criticism that they improved. But then we still had too many stories. So we sent the students down to the workshops and let the workers read and criticize the stories. We even read the stories out loud to old workers who could not read. Other workers, who were too busy to attend a class, read them in their spare time, and then sent notes back with their suggestions. Anyway, it took half a year to work it all out. Some stories got discarded and others got improved.

"Then we decided to form a group and write a whole novel called *The Big Beam.*" One of the men passes around a copy of *The Big Beam.* It is a slender paperback, as are most books in China. The cover shows a drawing of a large metal girder being set in place. "It was a joint project of teachers, worker/students and people from a publishing house. It took over a year to finish the book. And it was not easy for these workers to write a novel, because most of them had only written one short story."

Some members of our group are giving one another looks of incredulity at the notion that the Chinese have collectivized even the writing of fiction.

"These stories are very important for younger workers," says a recent woman graduate, who has been sitting quietly at the table, taking notes with awesome thoroughness. "The younger workers never knew the old society. Now they can read about it. The stories are popular among the older workers too, because they can now read and are able to enjoy them.

"One of the main challenges in writing fiction is to work out the contradiction between realism and romanticism. Some works, of course, have good revolutionary content, but they are not written very artistically. They have no attracting power for the reader. We firmly believe that the artistic level must be just as high as the political consciousness. But we oppose counterrevolutionary works with high artistic merit. A work must be artistic *and* revolutionary.

"Take *The Big Beam*, for instance. It tells how a new cadre fought against capitalist restoration during the Cultural Revolution. It illustrates the vigor and spirit of youth. But it was not clear how we should put our experiences into writing, and properly portray proletarian heroic images. Granted, sometimes we might use darker figures to make our heroes stand out. In reality, a hero or person can not be perfect in everything. But since we are trying to create more perfect men and women in our revolution, the hero images in our literature must stand higher than reality in order to educate people. The heroic images should show the high aspirations of the proletariat. This is the function of art and literature. This you could call our revolutionary romanticism."

"Are there any just plain writers in China who remain unaffiliated with any kind of practical labor?"

"No," replies one of the teachers. "This is a thing of the past. Some may work in factories, and others in a university or publishing house. Everyone has a job. It is from these jobs that they get their practical experience and salaries. How could it be otherwise? A writer must 'go down' to the people to write a good book."

"What books by Western authors do students at the university read?"

There is a long silence. The four comrades at the table look searchingly at one another.

"Which ones?" asks the woman, her face breaking into a sheepish smile. "Well, you see, there are four periods in literature," she begins, but quickly realizes that her answer is heading for a dead end. "Mainly we've done critical work on Soviet writers," she finally says.

"Which ones?"

"Well, we have criticized some Gorki," says one of the men. "We don't view Gorki from the present, because conditions are different in China from what they were in the Soviet Union at the time he was writing. But he did reflect the struggle of the Soviet people to lay the groundwork for proletarian art. And, of course, Gorki has some weak points—perhaps some traces of belief in a basic human nature apart from class background. Often he just wrote about reality. He just wrote down what he saw. It was 'truthful writing.' He wrote about bad as well as good phenomena. And we find traces of naturalism when he describes situations.

"But we in proletarian art and literature should not indulge in this kind of 'truthful writing.' We do not see it as our role to portray the dark as well as the light. For instance, hungry people can not inspire others to socialist reconstruction. Why write about them? If we do write about people's faults, we must put the emphasis on their transformation. It is the heroes who provide a good influence. We want to write about the spirit of the proletariat. Only under these broad guidelines can we embroider on the lives of our heroes. Otherwise it is not permissible to write. One can not write a novel where the hero is an overthrown landlord. This is outside the main current."

Last Workday

I wake up just before six to hear the first static crackle over the loudspeakers before reveille is sounded by "The East Is Red." Puffy faces emerge from behind mosquito nets. The *flap*, *flap* of rubber shower shoes sounds on the concrete veranda outside, announcing the beginning of another morning processional to the washroom. Toilets flush. The sound of tin wash basins grating on concrete heralds the dawn.

The loudspeakers move on to the news—news about the "two-line struggle," "the dictatorship of the proletariat," "stamping out bourgeois rights." It echoes past the dorms as the workers rise.

It is our last day. At our special breakfast, the cooks are already talking about our departure.

"When are you coming back?" they ask.

"Please raise suggestions and criticisms about our cooking and work before you go," they say. Today, they have prepared an American-style white cake with thick greasy vanilla frosting and ice cream, apparently in honor of our departure. We are unclear how this bizarre birthday-party-like menu happened. Some of us fear that our reknown as consumers of ice cream has been interpreted as a national trait. The cake remains an unexplained gastronomical offering.

Workshop Eleven is unsettled this morning. Something about leave-taking has thrown everyone a little off pace. We stand in groups talking long after we should be at our benches working. On my lapel, I am wearing a photograph of my baby and his mother that has been stuck on a campaign-button-like pin. It is creating a mild sensation. People in China are enraptured by babies. Blond babies held by blond women are a fascination of irresistible proportions.

"Oh, so beautiful!"

"My, how fat!"

"Such white hair!"

Chang Kuei-li comes over. She stands right up close to it, and then arches backward to get it in focus.

"Oh! Your baby?" she asks. "How old is it?"

"Seven months," I reply.

"What kind of nursery does he stay in?"

I explain that nurseries are uncommon, and that consequently it is difficult for both parents to work.

Chang Kuei-li wrinkles up the bridge of her nose in displeasure.

"Aieeeyaaa!" she says. "Not very easy is it? Our nurseries cost one yuan a month. But that's outside the factory. Here it is free. But, anyway, my kids are eight and fourteen now. They're off at school all day." She smiles sympathetically, and then has another look at this strange family pinned to the chest of this "American friend."

Master Chang has begun to work by now. I walk over to where he is adjusting a large rotary metal saw. He stops work as I approach.

"So. Tomorrow you go." He takes one of my hands in both of his, and holds it for a long time without speaking. He looks at me, then pats the back of my hand with his palm.

"We've become good friends," he says. "We've made a step toward the friendship between our two peoples." There is a strange poignancy in this comment, which is at once so clichéd and so heartfelt.

Lao Hu comes over with a pair of pliers in his hand. He hears the tail end of Master Chang's remarks. He can not resist adding an embellishment in that manner of redundancy at which the Chinese excel. "We don't agree with the policies of your American government trying to take control of other countries. But we feel friendly toward the American people," says Lao Hu, invoking once again the magical—if poorly defined—concept of Chinese "friendship."

"You know," he says without malice after a brief pause, "it is the beginning of the fall. America's 'strength is not equal to its ambitions.' " He is quoting an old Chinese saying *(Li-pu-ts'ung-hsin)*.

"Do you remember what the Chairman said to the American writer Anna Louise Strong in 1936?" Lao Hu continues. "He said, 'All reactionaries are paper tigers.' They are paper, but still tigers."

Departure

The Chinese believe in symbolic occasions. Arrivals, departures, births, deaths are all duly noted.

Today we have a "gathering" with factory leaders and workers from our teams to mark our departure. The event is neither a party nor a meeting. It hovers somewhere in between, as close perhaps as the Chinese come to a party.

The leader of the factory Party Branch gives a short speech. Unless one had been previously introduced, there would be no way to pick him out of the crowd of other workers. He has a large patch that runs across the backside of his pants. He is slightly older than most of the other workers. There is an air of thoughtfulness and refinement about him. He need speak no more than a few words to make it clear that he is a personage of stature—a leader.

And yet, what he says is somehow not memorable. In one way or another it has all been said before many times. It is as though the Chinese had decided that their revolution will succeed through the sheer force of repetition. He keeps reiterating the point that "we have worked together, lived together and studied together." I wonder whether our short visit justifies such sweeping declarations of fraternity. The amount of work we did, for instance, was actually embarrassingly small.

Then, as one might remember just in time to thank some distant relative for an almost-forgotten box of Christmas candy, he says, "And we thank you for the better understanding you have given us of the American Revolution. Just as Chairman Mao has said," he continues, allowing himself to garner even the American Revolution under the Chinese political canopy, " 'The American people are a great people. And the American people want revolution.' "

The noises of people cracking and eating salted watermelon seeds, unwrapping candy and drinking tea continues throughout his speech.

"We ask for your suggestions and criticisms so that we may improve our work," he concludes. The sign-off is a familiar one, but one which usually does not release the great critical energies of anyone in the room.

The gathering provides one last chance for the Chinese to "put politics in command," as Mao has stressed. But I am seemingly unable to concentrate on politics today. My attention wanders. I find myself looking around the room and picking out the people I have come to know: Hsiao Ti, Master Chang, P'eng Hung, Shao-feng and Master Ch'en. Tomorrow the acquaintances we have so ardently cultivated together these past few weeks will be over. They will cease like brief love affairs calculated to end almost before they have even begun.

Were I Chinese, I wonder, would my involuntary and emotional reaction constitute a "wrong line"? It sets me to wondering about the role left for such feelings in the Chinese revolution. The Chinese are a feelingful but not emotional people. There is so often a formality about Chinese reactions that mystifies and troubles Westerners geared to catharsis and interpersonal drama. Perhaps our world of careless emotions is too frighteningly individualistic and somehow disruptive for the Chinese collective consciousness. It is at moments like this that I sense how different our life-style is from this Chinese socialist experiment.

Another speaker rises. He expresses gladness that we were able to spend such a long time at the factory, rather than just "Looking at the flowers from a galloping horse." He asks us to take "regards to the American people." He says that he hopes we will have a chance to return soon.

Gripped by some need to reciprocate, I lean over to Master Chang and say, "Perhaps some day you can visit us in America."

I am a bit stunned by my own words, Master Chang gropes for a response, but finds none. The idea is so remote. The Chinese we've met have repeatedly expressed the hope that we will return to their country; I can not remember anyone suggesting the opposite.

I turn back to Master Chang. He is unaware that he is observed. I try to envision him in America. I realize that were he, by some stroke of fate, to arrive at my American doorstep in his blue worker's suit and cap, I would not have the slightest idea of how to go about incorporating him into the life I lead.

III
THE FARM

Train Travel

The coal-burning steam engine in front of us whistles through green fields of winter wheat. Great clouds of black smoke belch out of the carefully cleaned and painted red and black engine. Outside, the flat plains and commune fields are blurred by a dust storm blowing in from the Mongolian steppe. The landscape is still bleak and gray, save for the early spring crops of young wheat, rape, and the almost imperceptible green of the budding trees which line the tracks and stand in single file along the edges of the fields.

The trains in China are superb. The rail beds are smooth. The car hardly sways as we head across Hopei Province to the rugged Taihang Mountains in Shansi Province.

Our compartment is spotlessly clean. But before we are two hours out of Peking, soot and dust have leaked in through crevices around the window and covered the fresh linen seat covers with grit.

Chinese trains are divided into three classes. Just how it is decided who rides where is a mystery to me. Although I have asked several times, no Chinese has even attempted to explain this apparent contradiction. The *Juan-wo-ch'e*, or "soft sleeping coaches," are much like first-class sleeping compartments on European trains. The *Ying-wo-ch'e*, or "hard sleeping coaches," consist of small doorless compartments in which there are eight hard bunks (four on each side) stacked as in a submarine. Finally, there is the *Ying-tso-ch'e*, or coach section in which one must sit upright in a hard seat.

We are guests, so we travel first-class. Prices vary according to the class. Compartments are almost twice as expensive as coach. There is usually no more than one such car on a train, and it is populated mainly by foreign visitors and a sprinkling of high-ranking officials and military men.

Every inch of land outside the train is under cultivation. Unused strips next to the tracks are being excavated for clay. Each work brigade or commune has its own kiln to fire bricks and roofing tiles. Farmhouses stand in village clusters. They are made of sun-dried brick or adobe blocks bound together with straw. Village walls, courtyards, corrals are made of stamped earth. There is a spareness but common sense in the way the Chinese build. They use virtually no materials such as wood, steel, concrete or asphalt roofing imported from other regions of the country. Glass is usually the only building material not locally made. As a result, everywhere houses vary in style and appearance according to what materials are locally abundant.

The countryside is alive with a kind of industriousness unimaginable elsewhere. Carts pulled by oxen, mules and camels crowd the roads, carrying wheat stalks, crushed rock, earth, coal and produce. Men and women on bicycle carts, pulling heavy loads, strain in the wind and dust. Occasional tractors whisk down the road past the slower-moving current of man and beast.

Teams of workers attack large, windblown, dunelike hills, pushing carts, carrying poles, hoes and shovels. They are reclaiming land. Through land reform the Chinese have pieced back together what was once a patchwork of privately owned fields into areas large enough to be cultivated by machines. They have diked the land, terraced it, built wells and pumps, composted and fertilized the exhausted earth back to a state of health. Even now, the land has a dry, desolate look to it. It is land which American farmers would doubtless have abandoned years ago. Looking out this train window, one easily conjures up visions of past China and this unblessed terrain before Liberation. Drought in the winter. Flood in the summer. In many places, earth so used and abused that one wonders how it could have yielded life to anyone. In the past, when the earth surrendered, so did the people. Today there is no sign of surrender.

    *   *   *

After a day on the train, we reach Anchuan, a railhead and coal-mining town in Shansi. A dust storm rages as we drive the last few hours to the Tachai People's Commune. The dust tints the whole landscape a strange magenta tone, as though we were viewing it through a photographic filter.

It is barely spring here, and still cool in these barren mountains. The rains have not yet come, and the newly plowed furrows in the minuscule terraced fields which have been carved out of the steep mountainsides are dusty as chalk. Each of the new terrace walls, which hold the fields hugging to the hillsides, is made from square hand-hewn stone blocks. They are constructed in crescentlike configurations which are stepped up the mountainsides much like box seats in old European opera houses. The curvature works on the principle of the arch, keeping mud slides and flood waters from pouring down the denuded mountains.

The older terraces, some from the pre-Communist years, are flimsy, half-hearted attempts consisting of round stones stacked one on top of the other in a crude, artless fashion.

The panorama is overwhelming. Mile after mile of terraces stretch up the hillsides as far as one can see. Everywhere, on the hewn rocks, adobe and brick houses and buildings are the characters "In Agriculture Learn from Tachai" *(Nung-Hsüeh-Tachai).*

All along the roadside, rows of poplars have been planted. I am just appreciating this new, aesthetic touch, and thinking of the cool shade they must afford passers-by in the hot summer, when we pass a crew of men sawing some of the older and grander trees down for lumber.

Nothing in China is done for purely aesthetic reasons. Almost everything has a practical or political justification. The trees are planted for lumber on the narrow road shoulders which normally remain unused. Often the fast-growing poplars are phased in staggered planting so that small young trees continue to grow in between the stumps of the older trees after the latter are harvested.

We pass some "less advanced" villages, where people still live in old-style earthen caves or in traditional brick houses with small courtyards and sloping tile roofs. The final tile at the end of each row is imprinted with a comical grinning face, a custom in these parts.

The classical bright red strips of paper with characters written for the New Year are pasted on either side of the doorways. Only now, instead of ancient Confucian or Buddhist couplets such as:

"Sincerity and honesty make the family long-lasting" . . . "Poetry and classics assure the generations" . . . "Filial piety and brotherhood are important measures for training children" . . . and others speaking of longevity, prosperity, and good fortune, the red strips now speak of revolution:

"Every household sings praises of the Communist Party" . . . "The red flag flutters over the four seas of spring" . . . "Long live Chairman Mao."

Donkeys, with sleepy eyes, slowly haul their carts full of coal, compost, earth and limestone. Drivers sleep on top of their heavy load, sprawled out in awkward battlefield postures, their mouths open, heads rocking gently in time to the motion of the carts.

Endless work, unbroken for most by the promise of weekends, holidays, vacations and leisure. Endless work that has been the peasant's lot since time immemorial. In the past it was work or die. Often both.

Today's peasants still work from dawn to dusk, with periods off for rest and meals. But work has lost its futility. It has been elevated from seasonal grind for subsistence to sacred calling. Work now offers satisfaction as well as food.

Arrival

We arrive in Tachai at dusk. We are scheduled to work at this model brigade for three weeks. The masonry and brick buildings clinging to opposite sides of a steep gully give the village a medieval appearance. We are lodged in the recently built reception center. It holds two hundred people. But tonight, the only other occupants are ten PLA soldiers and ourselves.

I feel a sense of disappointment at being in special quarters and eating in a special dining room. I wish that we could be living more in the midst of the people we have come to visit. But I can understand that a peasant village couldn't be expected to accommodate a visiting group such as ours, with a retinue of baggage, interpreters and guides, whose only connection is that of "world friendship." In fact, who can blame the Chinese for wishing to withhold some part of their private lives from an inquiring group of foreigners.

Almost everyone here lives in caves, the traditional dwelling in China's Northwest. They are dug into the loess soil banks, which have slowly been deposited by dust storms over millennia. Our caves at the reception center are of the newer variety, with arched, plastered ceilings, stone masonry facings, and wood and glass doors. The older-style caves are hewn out of the earth. The walls are plastered with mud and rice chaff. The windows are made of oil paper set in wood frames at the cave's mouth. But, in the past, though cool in the summer and warm in the winter, these caves were subject to flooding and collapsing during heavy rain. Now, in Tachai, the old caves are gone, save for one or two which have been left as reminders of the "bitter past." New caves, which stand in long rows parallel to the hillsides, have been built for each of Tachai's eighty-three households and four hundred and fifty inhabitants. They stand perched in long tiers, each one higher up on the hillside than the last.

Whereas the old caves used to be scattered about here and there on various rented or private pieces of property, the new caves are all centralized. The ambiance is that of a small housing development. People live cheek by jowl, but there is also a congeniality to this neighborhood. Children play out in front of the caves. Chickens wander in and out of the doorways. People chat at the communal water tap as they wait for their buckets to fill.

Working in the Fields

Today is windy and cool. The dust storm has subsided. The sky is clear, save for a reddish haze of Shansi dust. We walk up Tiger Head Mountain on a new tractor road which has been covered with cinders. We carry tools for the day: baskets and carrying poles, a broad hoe for weeding, a long thin mattock for trimming back earthen banks, and a large wooden mallet (not unlike those used at county fairs to test your strength) for smashing clods of clay and earth after the mule-drawn plow has furrowed them.

We work today with the older women's work team. There is some joking about this. They wear colorful red and green bandanas and traditional blue cotton pants and jackets. The blue is a perfect complement to the red-brown earth and gray-blue color of the terrace wall stones.

We stop at a series of quarter-acre terraces that have been reclaimed from a steep ravine. Like so much manual labor in China, our job is inglorious today. We pick up stones and load them into baskets hanging at either end of carrying poles (the standard tool of almost every peasant in China), and carry them to the sides of the field. Then we pick up the old sorghum stalks and roots and place them in piles to be burned. Ash is a key ingredient in soil management here at Tachai.

Lao Wang and I work together. He is about forty years old, a native of Hsi Yang County. He is in charge of visitors at Tachai, which means that he has little time to spend in the fields. As a result, there is a suggestion of corpulence about him. But today he works with great energy and good humor. He is a jovial man, who comes as close as any Chinese I have met to having a Western sense of humor. He is forever catching my eye with a kind of provocative comical gleam in his own. He is known for toasting at banquets with reckless abandon. He even gets into drinking matches with us on a competitive basis, often under the disapproving eyes of other cadres, who see his friendly sharing of libations as an unnecessary encouragement of our weakness for the same. In fact, I often marvel, as I watch Lao Wang operate, at how he has gotten to a position of such responsibility, when he is so manifestly undoctrinaire and expansive. It is not that he is not a deeply political person or unresponsive to China's revolutionary call, only that he seems to appreciate his life on a level which is not always so pointedly serious.

"Hey! Look here," says Lao Wang, leaning over a pile of rocks.

He has discovered a scorpion. Without further ado, he reaches down and picks it up, as those around him shrink back. He holds the head with one hand and the tail with the other, as though he were exhibiting a prize lobster. He is grinning as well as he can while still talking and holding a lit cigarette clamped between his teeth. With great merriment he points out the large stiff stinger protruding from the back of the scorpion.

"There are quite a few around," says an older woman looking on. "If they bite you, it swells way up and hurts a great deal. We are always careful when we reach into rocks and crevices."

With this said, Lao Wang unceremoniously crushes the scorpion between two rocks. Now we take a break—a regular feature of the work day.

The peasants here work long and hard: up at sunrise and home at sunset, with a two-hour siesta at the noon hour. The day is long, but the work pace rarely seems frenzied. It is uncommon to see someone angry or animated with frustrated rage at a job which is not easily done. The Chinese are slow, steady workers. Rarely have I seen anyone panting and exhausted. They take evenly paced rest breaks. The draft animals lie down, and the peasants sprawl in whatever shade they can find. The men take out their pipes and light up a bowl of homegrown, which smells like burning leaves. Throughout the countryside one sees people resting in the fields, sometimes asleep, head on a conveniently placed ox.

Pigs

Chairman Mao has made many pronouncements about pigs. Not only is pork an extremely popular meat in China, but as Mao has pointed out, "Each pig is a fertilizer factory."

The pigsty in the village is located alongside the composting operation. The pigs live in old earthen caves (once inhabited by poor peasants), which have been hollowed out of a small mesa-like tuft of earth which sticks up off the ravine floor. The operation itself is a stone's throw from the basketball court and exercise field, where the grain is threshed in the fall. The pigpens are fenced with stone walls. The farrowing shelters are also made of stone.

Two elderly men sit at the entrance to the sty beside huge iron cauldrons and smoke their pipes. Each day garbage is collected from the people's newly built caves, hauled to the pigsty, placed in the cauldron and boiled, both to kill bacteria and to improve the slops.

Ku Ping-yuan, a short, youthful-looking man, pokes his head out of one of the cave entrances to see what is making the pigs squeal and oink.

Ku was trained at the Institute of Microbiology, and has been "sent down" to the countryside by the Academy of Sciences. His job in Tachai has been to develop better pork production by bringing new scientific hog-raising techniques down to the lowest level. His salary is paid by the Academy of Sciences, and he has been here in the brigade for several years. Some years he will spend eight months here. Other years he will hardly be here at all.

Inside one of the caves at the sty, a bare light bulb hangs down from the ceiling. A fire is on in a small stove to take the chill off the room. Several vats line the wall.

"We are a breeding farm," Ku says. "Each year we raise about three hundred pigs. After they are weaned, we sell them to the State and other brigades which want to raise feeder pigs for pork. We only used to be able to raise a third as many pigs. But now we are using a special process for pig food." He takes the cover off one of the vats. There is a kind of porridge-like substance inside.

"What we do is convert waste cellulose into protein in these vats. We take millet husks, bean pods, bran, corn and sorghum stalks, grind them up fine, and add water, a special bacterial culture, and some urea. We are lucky here. In most areas people use this fiber as fuel. But here, there is an abundance of coal. We keep the vats reasonably warm, and just like in the intestines of cows, the enzymes and bacteria convert the mash into high-protein food. Although the protein content does not increase threefold, it does increase considerably. The urea decomposes the fiber, and the bacteria transform the inorganic nitrogen into protein. We brought the original culture from the Academy of Sciences in Peking. In the winter, when the weather is cold, sometimes the culture in the vats gets weak. Then we add a solution of horse or cow manure. Or if an ox is slaughtered, we will just dump some of the contents of its intestines into the vats. It's like cultured milk."

Ku pauses and puts the lid back on the vat. "Processes like these help people learn science," he says. "It helps narrow the gap between the scientists and the peasants. And, of course, it helps production. We used to feed each pig three pounds of grain a day. Now we only have to feed each pig two thirds of a pound of grain each day, and supplement it with this fermented food."

Two men now care for the thirty-six brood sows and two boars. They grind the fodder and make the food.

How does Ku, an educated man, feel about being off in the countryside away from his family?

"Well, my wife teaches in the biology department at Hsing Hsiang Teachers' College in Hunan Province. That's way down south. My children are in Soochow." And then, without any comment or hesitation over the separation from his family, he says, "I've learned so much from this experience. If intellectuals want to build their country, they should work with farmers and learn the real problems. It's not enough just to talk about patriotism. You know, in all the academies and institutes, it used to be that people just wanted to hang around and write learned dissertations."

Tachai As a Museum

Over the past decades the feats that the Tachai Work Brigade has performed have made it legendary in China. In a few short years, against all adversity, they have transformed these rocky hillsides into a rich food-producing area. Their spirit can only be described as dauntless, their works as almost unimaginable. Tachai is perhaps the most reknowned work brigade in China. A visit here is one of the greatest honors afforded to a Chinese.

Today a large group of PLA soldiers arrives to visit the brigade from Taiyuan, the provincial capital of Shansi. They travel in the back of army trucks made at the Shanghai First Truck Factory. All wear heavy greatcoats with fur collars. On this gray, cold morning, they file in endless columns up the barren mountain paths to visit the fields and various brigade operations. The peasants in the fields pay them little attention, inured by now to the many visitors who pass quickly through their midst. Though these people are on view every day, somehow their celebrity status does not seem to have gone to their heads. In many ways, the village still has a cut-off feeling. Although it is a living display, it remains somehow unaffected by the crowds arriving to study and admire.

At siesta time, the PLA soldiers sit around the main street near the cafeteria in their clean khaki uniforms, adorned only with red patches and stars which give no clue to the rank of the person inside. Many are in the Brigade Store buying souvenirs. They buy small china elephants which serve as teapots; the tea is poured out the trunks. Others buy tin teacups emblazoned with a red flag and the characters "Souvenir of a Tachai Visit." There is a large group of soldiers in front of the candy counter.

In a corner next to a window is a small table with a stamp and ink pad. Several soldiers are stamping red plastic books. This is an official testimony, a kind of certification like the stamp on a passport, of their Tachai visit.

I buy some cold cream which is packaged in two clam shells that open like a compact.

Siesta Stroll

Work has stopped in the fields at noon. People will not return to work until after their midday meal and siesta. The village is quiet now. Most people are resting on their *k'angs,* large clay platforms on which they sleep, heated by small fires lit underneath them. There are only a few people moving about as I walk out the main gate. I meet a man resting beside a cart hitched to a small hand tractor. The cart is full of rabbits in cages.

"Do you raise rabbits?"

"Oh, yes," he replies. "We raise a lot. We eat them. They're good. We can make sweaters out of the fur, or we can use the skin to line hats."

As we are talking, some stone cutters, who have been sitting and dozing near a pile of stone blocks, begin to wander over to see what is happening. They stand listening and smoking their long-stemmed pipes. They appear to think it somewhat comical that a foreigner is talking about rabbits.

"What do you feed your rabbits?" I ask.

"Well, see, this one's eating corn stalks. But they prefer green grass. If they can't get that, they eat dry grass, or anything else you give them. Each family can have rabbits just like chickens. But we like rabbits better."

"They don't lay eggs," says one of the stone cutters, doubling over in laughter, inducing some chortling from the others.

"No. But they reproduce and get big fast," says the rabbit man. "Some get huge. As big as a dog."

"So what are you going to do with them?"

"We sell them to the State, or eat them ourselves," he says, glancing at the crowd which is slowly growing around us. He is becoming more and more reticent about talking, as the throng of listeners and oglers increases.

I bid good-bye, and walk down the road toward the next village. A sheepfold is on the left. Like the pigsty, shelter is provided by an earthen cave. Outside, the shepherds have built a corral fence out of slender tree switches that are poked into the ground and bound together with straw twine.

During much of the year, the sheep, which are tough and scrawny by American standards, are led up onto the hillsides to forage for food. The shepherds follow the flocks all day, keeping track of them. They carry an ingenious device which consists of a small spoonlike implement fastened to the end of a supple stick about three feet long. With it, they can dig a small chunk of earth up off the ground, and then throw it with a whiplike motion at or in front of a sheep which is straying from the flock. They have learned to use these devices with deft accuracy. Seldom does one see a shepherd running about chasing a sheep.

But now it is late in the year. There is little to forage for in the mountains. The sheep spend more time in the corrals, which also serve as collection points for their manure. Outside the corrals are large piles of compost made from the sheep manure and shredded corn husks. They have been wetted and layered with human waste from the visitors' public toilet at the main gate.

Across the road, in front of a collapsed cave from the old days, there is a series of gravelike holes in the ground. They are covered by wooden platforms, on top of which earth and corn stalks have been piled for insulation. They look like primitive one-man bomb shelters.

An older man with a small child stands by one of the holes. They stare at me, temporarily distracted from the task at hand. The child, like all peasant children who have yet to be toilet trained, wears trousers with a slit which runs from front to back under his crotch.

The pants are designed to part when the child naturally squats to relieve himself, thus alleviating the necessity for diapers for some seventy-five million children.

The man wears a carefully patched pair of gray-blue pants. His pipe is slung around his neck and attached to a small leather tobacco pouch in peasant fashion. He wears dusty black cloth shoes with rubber soles. His face, lined and burned dark as the earth by the wind and sun, is unshaven. Tufts of whiskers bristle out from his chin and upper lip.

I say hello and ask him how old his child is. He continues to stare. Then suddenly a colossal smile spreads across his face, revealing a set of large brown-stained teeth.

He hears that I am speaking Chinese, but it is as though he can not quite conceive of communicating with a person of such a different physiognomy.

"What are these holes for?"

He begins to reply in his heavy Shansi brogue, full of gutteral sounds. "These holes are for storing vegetables in the winter . . ."

"What kinds?"

"Well, we can store turnips, potatoes, white radishes and white cabbage."

"Apples?"

"No. Well, you can. But it doesn't work so well. There is a special cave for storing apples."

"Do you ever cover the vegetables with sand or earth?"

"Some we do. But not all. It depends. But we cover the holes to keep the frost out. We put the vegetables in after harvest, and take them out as we need them in the winter and spring. It doesn't really rain here much in the winter, so they don't spoil." As far as I know, there is no refrigeration available to the peasants at Tachai.

"Does each family have a hole?"

"Yes. Each family. We dig these holes in the fall, and then we fill them back in in the spring so the earth can compact down again with the rain."

Two men with a carrying pole and baskets walk over. They remove some of the cornstalks from over one of the holes. One man disappears into the opening. Suddenly large white radishes come flying out of the dark hole. The other man loads them into the baskets. There are a few bruised spots, and they have begun to sprout feathery green foliage. Otherwise they are perfectly edible.

Nixon

At a small farm implements factory not far from Tachai, a long workshop wall is emblazoned with the characters DOWN WITH ALL AMERICANS AND THEIR RUNNING DOGS.

I maneuver myself outside of the main gate into a better position from which to take a photograph of this once-familiar slogan. A comrade comes up to me with determined agitation.

"Why do you want to take a picture of that?" he asks. This is an old slogan."

Indeed it is. Once current in China, it has seldom been in evidence since Nixon's 1971 trip. I diplomatically agree that it would be pointless to memorialize its message on film.

"What do you think of ex-President Nixon?" I later ask Lao Chang, one of the interpreters accompanying us.

"He's a two-bit crook and a liar," says someone from our group sitting behind us. There is laughter.

"Yes," replies Lao Chang seriously, "but I think what he did with U.S.-China relations through the Shanghai Communiqué was quite significant, don't you?"

"Sure, but Nixon spent most of his life hating the Communists and the Chinese," I reply.

There is a confused silence. It is a familiar moment in China, when an all-too-bold comment runs headlong into official orthodoxy.

"Yes," says Shih, another interpreter, without any humor, "but he was still correct in his line toward China. And the Shanghai Communiqué was a step forward."

Children cultivating walnut orchard

Stone masons carrying building blocks

Older women's work team assembling to go to the fields

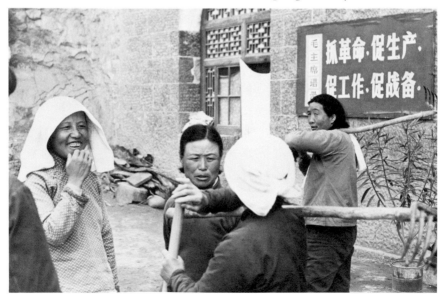

*Child with bubble maker
at Tachai day-care center*

Children at Tachai day-care center

Spring planting at Tachai

Peasant children playing

*Children standing at cave window
in Shansi Province*

Tachai peasant in traditional headgear

Peasant leaving for fields

Peasants gathering vegetables from underground storage

Ch'eng-yüan and two of his brothers

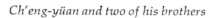

Hua-ming (right) and friends with the author

Ch'eng-yüan's mother and her grandson

Nixon probably has more friends in China than in the United States. It is not that the people "love" him here, or revere him the way they do Chairman Mao, for they know that he is at heart a dark imperialist. But he has received favorable mention in the mass press when he has visited China. The same press carried little detailed discussion about Watergate and his subsequent resignation. His preeminence just dissolved without comment. Most peasants are utterly unaware of what happened. Most cadres and educated city people who read the papers seem to explain his sudden disappearance as "just another split in the American ruling class." Nixon is remembered here for that small part of his career when he came in contact with China. It is said that when Chairman Mao wrote Nixon a letter a year after his resignation inviting him back to China, he called him "One of the greatest leaders of our time."

Toilets and Fertilizer

There are no private toilets here at Tachai. Whereas in the old days every house had its own (usually unsanitary) arrangement, now even defecation has been collectivized. Public toilets stand at the end of the rows of stone-faced caves. The outside structure of the building, like everything else, is masonry. Inside there is a plaster wall down the center of the room, dividing it into two chambers. The character for "man" is painted on the lefthand side of the entrance; on the right side, the character for "woman."

The toilets themselves are functional. A concrete slab has been poured over a large underground holding tank. On each side of the dividing wall, there are five narrow slits over which people squat to relieve themselves. When peasants are in the fields high up in the mountains, they simply dig a small hole.

The average peasant does not use toilet paper, although it can be purchased at the Brigade Store (Peony brand). Instead people make do with any kind of paper scraps available. There are shreds of the

People's Daily and *Liberation Army Daily* scattered around the room. And since there are no individual booths, there is a certain amount of conviviality to the process of elimination. There appears to be little inhibition, and from time to time a *bon mot* or two are passed. There is even an occasional bit of graffiti, mostly children's names scrawled in awkward characters.

One morning in a community toilet, a comrade was concentrating on his labor, when a friend came in through the door. He looked at his crouched friend, stopped, laughed and remarked, "Well, Comrade Li. I see that you are making your daily contribution to building agriculture."

It is now *chung-t'ien*, or spring planting time here in Shansi. The fields are being plowed, fertilized and readied for sowing. All human waste is used as fertilizer at Tachai. It is collected in the underground holding tanks, and then periodically pumped or ladled into tank carts, in which it is transported to maturation ponds. These ponds are usually large holes dug in the earth. They are often lined with stone or clay, and have thatched A-frame roofs over them to keep out the rain. Here the sewage is anaerobically digested, a biological process in which parasites and pathogens are destroyed. (The Chinese also use excrement, or "night soil," hot on the fields, although this practice is not as common as in the past for health reasons.) The digested night soil is usually then layered into shredded agricultural waste products like stalks, husks, bean pods and chaff to make compost.

China is also making great efforts to increase its production of chemical fertilizers. Leaders speak of decentralizing production so that every county (of which there are more than twenty-two hundred) will have at least one chemical fertilizer plant. Here in Hsi Yang County, they produce enough fertilizer at the local plant to each year provide approximately 54 chin per mou—(or 432 pounds per acre). (There are 1 1/3 pounds to one chin, and six mou in one acre.) This fertilizer comes from an ammonia nitrate plant built at the county seat during the Cultural Revolution. It supplies all the county's fertilizer, and rather than using petroleum or natural gas, it uses locally mined coal for fuel. Although the factory is working three eight-hour shifts a day, and produces 3,000 tons a year in excess of its designed capacity of 5,000 tons, the plant is still unable to produce anywhere near enough fertilizer to adequately cover the county's 400,000 mou (66,000 acres) of cultivated land.

Most work brigades are thus still largely dependent on organic fertilizer. And although eager for more inorganic fertilizer, they know that the soil needs as much organic humus as it can possibly get. Painful experience in the past has taught the peasantry that unless their soil is light and spongy, it will compact on the terraces, causing floods and sliding.

"Yes, we use chemical fertilizer," says one peasant. "We use it separately from the compost. We alternate organic and inorganic fertilizers. Often we work the chemical fertilizers deep into the ground around the roots. But the truth is that many older peasants prefer organic fertilizer. If we use too much inorganic fertilizer, it destroys the tilth of the soil. Our problem is simply that we can not make enough compost. In some places they use sediment from riverbeds. Or they use sludge from city sewage treatment ponds. It's rich in all sorts of organic things left over from dishwashing and human waste. Actually some cities even raise fish in these ponds.

"Do you know about the two-line struggle?" he asks after a brief pause. "Well, we have a two-line struggle in the fertilizer business too. It comes down between the conservatives and the nonconservatives. Because in the beginning, many of the peasants didn't want to use any chemical fertilizer. They just didn't know what it was. But they learned. And now only the diehards refuse to use it. But still, we don't want to become dependent on anything we can not make ourselves. There is a balance. But, of course, the simple problem is that chemical fertilizer is in short supply. So even if we wanted to, we could not totally rely on it."

All human and animal waste is treated with great respect. It is not uncommon to see an ox or a donkey going down the road with a burlap manure catcher fastened beneath its tail, or to see a man with a pair of bamboo tongs picking lumps of manure off the roadside and putting them in a basket. As the Chinese tirelessly point out, "All waste is treasure."

The Aged

Every morning we walk through the village to pick up our tools. Always we pass the same old Granny with bound feet. Binding feet was an old tradition in China which was considered to make a woman more desirable. She sits outside a brick house, just down the courtyard from a large weeping willow dubbed "the Tree of the Unfortunates" by village residents. It is the tree from which peasants were hung and beaten by landlords and gendarmes before Liberation.

This Granny sits on a stool with a small boy, who usually retreats wide-eyed to a position of safety between her legs as we go by. Each time I pass her, it is jolting to see her feet—scarcely four inches long. In a way, these tiny feet, once painfully bound, evoke the China of old so much more poignantly than all the lectures. They tell of a world that is past now, erased, the traces of which are just barely visible. The Chinese are aware that the past which compelled them so resolutely toward communism is fading as a reality, even in the minds of the older people. For the young, it is merely a series of recollections passed on by grandparents. But the Chinese use these recollections as teaching devices.

When some members of our group ask whether they can talk with this old Granny, the idea is met with enthusiasm by our Chinese hosts. She spends most of her day around the house of her son and daughter-in-law, attending to their small children while they work. Chickens cluck and run in and out through a small hole made especially for them in the wood frame door. Inside the warm room, some newborn chicks chirp from the confines of a basket.

"I had my feet bound when I was nine," she says. "I don't really remember much about it. But, you know, if I hadn't got my feet bound, I couldn't have gotten married.

"I got married for the first time at the age of fifteen. My mother-in-law was not a good woman. If I came in late, she would scold me. Women always moved into the house of the husband's parents, where the mother ruled in old China. She made me bow and kowtow to her, and then she would put this big brick on my head.

"My mother-in-law made me cook all the food. And when guests came, I was told not to speak. If I spoke one or two words, she would beat me after the guests left.

"After the death of their son, my mother-in-law sold me away. But I couldn't walk because my feet were bound and then frozen one cold winter earlier. My mother-in-law told me that she would not feed me, and that if I wanted to live I must go out and beg on crutches.

"All in all in my life, I was sold four times—the first time for three hundred fifty yuan, then the second time for a hundred fifty yuan."

The old woman's story begins to ramble. Sometimes it is confusing and contradictory. At one point, she is near tears.

This morning we walk past her, nod and smile. She sits with her grandson in front of a new house, having bridged one of the great transitions in history.

Spreading Compost

Today we climb the mountain to several broad terraced fields which overlook the valley below. It is time to fertilize the fields and make them ready for sowing. A thirty-horsepower Chinese-made East Is Red tractor, and a thirty-five-horsepower Bountiful Harvest tractor have brought the compost up and dumped it in huge piles on the edge of the field. It is loamy and odorless.

We work with a team of younger women today, spreading the compost with carrying poles and baskets. They break into fits of uncontrollable laughter as we shoulder our heavy loads and stagger out across the fields to dump the baskets in neatly spaced smaller piles. The women load our baskets with pitchforks, careful to put less in ours than in their own.

Nonetheless, we are beginning to get the hang of the carrying pole. I have learned a special technique to ease the pain on my already-aching shoulders. Although some of the women wear shoulder pads made of layered cotton, the real salvation of the basket carrier involves taking light, quick, rhythmic steps that set the two baskets bouncing in cadence. If one breaks out of this cadence, the feeling is not unlike that of coming down on a stiff diving board just as it is on its upward stroke. It induces a mild shock in one's body, which, if repeated, is exhausting. For the first time I understand the strange prancing step I have seen peasants use throughout Asia as they carry a heavy load with pole and baskets.

We soon have our first field done. We sit down for a rest. There is much chattering with the peasant women, who have lost some of their initial reserve. Two small boys arrive with carrying poles. One carries a bucket of steaming hot water (*pai-ch'a,* or white tea). The other brings a basket of porridge bowls. We sit near an embankment on the brown dusty soil, and drink the hot water.

The faces of the peasant women are sunburned and red-cheeked. They sit close together, leaning on one another, with hands on the knees of their neighbors, or arms around the shoulder of a friend. Their wide, unqualified smiles burst out effortlessly over some small detail about us which strikes them as amusing or unusual.

An explosion goes off on a far hillside. A cloud of dust billows up. A wall of rock crashes down, the raw material for a new masonry aqueduct which is being built to irrigate yet another part of the hill. All day, and deep into the night, we hear these explosions as rock and earth are blasted loose. The earth is frequently blasted off cliff sides to fill in behind newly built terraces.

We resume work. Suddenly a group of peasants, visiting from Honan Province, come down the trail beside our field. They are here for two days to "learn from Tachai." They visit the terrace-making teams, the vast network of waterworks and land-reclamation projects. They watch planting and plowing. They study the Tachai horse-and-pig-breeding operations. In the evening they see movies describing

Tachai's new agricultural techniques and spirit. It is like an elementary school class trip.

Heads snap around as the Honanese pass our field and see people with white faces carrying compost. Some stop briefly and stare. When they are greeted their faces dissolve into awkward smiles. Then they quickly continue down the hill, laughing and chattering, casting furtive glances backward up the hill to affirm that they have not seen apparitions.

Landholding

Looking down from Tiger Head Mountain, the eroded land of Hsi Yang County looks similar to the Badlands. It is strange to see all this land and to recall that there are no deeds, no title searches, no real estate companies, no insurance companies, no tax assessors, no property tax, no speculative holding and selling of land in China.

When land reform was implemented in the 1940's, the village of Tachai had been divided into four thousand tiny plots, creating a web of land ownership and tenancy so complicated that it is a wonder that it could work at all. During land reform, peasants were actually given title to the newly divided property of the landlords. As land was collectivized in the fifties, families continued to hold title. But the titles quickly grew into vestigial documents, as more and more of the land was communized during the Great Leap Forward in the late fifties. Finally all private ownership of land was terminated. All titles reverted to a production group, work brigade, commune or State-run enterprise.

One often hears stories in China about former landlords who, even today, hide their old deeds, in case some sort of reversion comes. Many of the Chinese who fled the Mainland with Chiang Kai-shek in 1949 still cling to old deeds in Taiwan, waiting for the long-heralded "counterattack on the Mainland."

Visits

Our work days in the fields are punctuated with trips to surrounding brigades and other points of interest. Some of the trips are interesting, others distracting from our experience at Tachai. Some are both.

Today's expedition is to nearby Shih P'ing, which, like so many other brigades in Hsi Yang County, has been gripped by the call to do the impossible. In what must surely be one of the world's most ingenious feats of engineering, the people have run a river underground by means of a vast and elaborate system of masonry tunnels which stretches over 7,000 meters. They are 5 meters high and 4 meters wide, and are built without the benefit of any mortar. The main object of the project was to provide an underground channel for a river which was once a yearly flood hazard. But not only has Shih P'ing put the river underground, it has filled in on top of it, creating 500 mou of prime flat farmland.

We sit in the brigade meeting room, and are bombarded with statistics. The village masons have hewn some 14,000 cubic meters of rock out of their quarries for the tunnels. There are 27 stone blocks in a cubic meter of rock. The villagers figure that one good mason can make about 40 rough blocks a day. This means that this village of 480 households has hewn, carried and laid some 378,000 stone blocks. The work took the villagers five years.

"The tunnels can be used as air raid shelters too," says the chairman of the Revolutionary Committee.

As we get up to leave, I notice that my parka beside me on the bench has been reduced to a strange tight little knot. Someone has snapped all the snaps on the cuffs, collar and around the zipper together with one another in a hodge-podge.

I look up and see Lao Wang, my benchmate, grinning deliciously at me from the doorway.

It takes me about five minutes to get it unsnarled.

Money

The people of Tachai receive a salary according to the number of work points they get. Each brigade gets together either once a month, once every few months, or even once a year to decide how many work points each member should receive. The "less advanced" brigades might meet each month, and the worker's point allotment is carefully computed according to the tasks he or she has performed, and by adding the sum total of the points awarded for each task. By this system, the more one works on a piece basis, the higher the number of points, and the larger the share of brigade revenue due the individual.

Although this system is still widely in use in China, it is now considered backward and unprogressive. It stresses piece work, and puts a premium on everyone working for himself, often by choosing the easiest jobs with the highest number of work points affixed to them. Like private plots (which exist elsewhere, but not at Tachai), this system is considered to smack of bourgeois vestiges.

The system used at Tachai emphasizes the need for people to work for the commonweal rather than themselves, and is considered to be "more socialist." No strict accounting of the number of tasks done by an individual is kept. Instead the brigade holds meetings once a year at which each person is asked to assess his or her own performance, and to suggest how many work points he or she thinks are appropriate. It is then discussed by the group, and either agreed upon or adjusted.

Of course, a person is not judged solely on work, but on political viewpoint, willingness to study, willingness to help others, and strangely enough, on whether or not one is a man or a woman.

"Yes, there is a difference between men and women," says one Tachai cadre. "The men do most of the lifting of the large stones and things like that. The highest number of work points a man can get is ten. The highest number a woman can get is eight. But in actuality, men get as low as five, and some women have gotten four and a half.

"But women share in other hard tasks, because since 1949 women and men are equal. Women hold up half of heaven, and no longer just work at home the way they used to. But yes, there is a difference in this wage scale. We do have shortcomings here. We are not yet a communist society."

"Do you know what people ask after you have had a baby?" asks Lao Chang, smiling at the dinner table.

"Well, when your wife has just had a baby, your friends ask, 'Hey, what did you get? Eight or ten points?' "

Local Opera

The theater in the city of His Yang is packed when we arrive. The more expensive seats in the front center are filled with PLA soldiers this evening. The back and sides are filled with young people, peasants and factory workers. Since it is not easy for most peasants to make the journey to the city, the county troupe spends much of its time on the road, playing at communes and brigades.

There is a feeling of familiarity and informality among the audience, as well as much talking and some craning of necks to see the foreigners. The lights dim. A woman in costume slides through the slit in the curtain. In the stylized falsetto voice of traditional Chinese opera, she recites a quote from Chairman Mao on the importance of class struggle. The curtain rises. An orchestra in the stage wings, composed of both Chinese and Western instruments, begins to play.

The plot of the opera revolves about the "two-line struggle" during the 1950's. The good revolutionary comrades favor collectivization of animals and the building of a new bridge. They are pitted rather starkly against the "bad bourgeois elements" who are conniving to ruin collectivization by dividing up all the livestock among private owners.

The actors are dressed in colorful stereotypical Tibetan costumes. The Chinese are fond of plays, operas and ballets about their minority people, since one of the added bonuses of such subjects is a chance to dress up in the eye-catching costumes of Mongolians, Tibetans and Moslems.

The "good" elements are played by handsome actors and actresses with ruddy rouged cheeks. They use stalwart, resolute gestures—such as thrusting one arm defiantly up into the air, and looking past it piercingly skyward while delivering a line. The "bad elements" are played by unmistakably evil-looking reprobates. These caricatures are invariably somewhat comical. For instance, the revisionist cadre (bad) shows up wearing a neatly pressed powder-blue Mao tunic and carries a brief case that fairly reeks of bureaucratic officiousness. He wears dark-rimmed glasses which are set off by his sallow made-up face. He is the epitome of the arrogant bookish intellectual who disdains manual labor—and everyone in the theater knows it.

At one point, this antihero extracts a silver cigarette case from his spotless tunic, with grand gestures. He lights up, and the crowd goes wild. Make no mistake about it: this man is bad!

The revolutionary cadre (good) is a fatherly, upright man with a face not unreminiscent of Chairman Mao's. His rouged cheeks make this slightly rotund actor look like a benevolent Chinese Santa Claus. His clothes are modest. He exudes kindness and fairness and listens intently to the problems of the "people."

Then there are the running-dog accomplices of the revisionist cadre. These full-tilt villains include an ex-prisoner and a scheming reactionary land profiteer who wears a regulation "poisonous weed" mustache. Instead of walking with proud, defiant steps, he walks all hunched over, as though trying to hide his indelible evilness. These villains usually dress in a quasi-Western manner. One of the favorite villain props is a felt fedora pulled down over the eyes in a sinister fashion. Just where the Chinese get these hats is unclear, but they seem to have an ample supply.

There is also a plethora of in-between characters who start off being uncommitted and confused. There are the rich and middle peasants (Mao said that they could "go either way," to either side) and the trusting brigade leader, who is not clear about which is the correct line. In the end, of course, the bad elements are purged in an orgy of scowling and vindictiveness—furies swept away in a whirlwind of righteousness, while the uncommitted see the light.

Getting Sick

There were flurries of snow last night, which left the tops of the higher mountains a dusty white. The air is uncharacteristically damp and cold.

My neck is painfully stiff for the third day. Our caves do not have *k'angs* and are unheated. I go up to the clinic for treatment.

The waiting room and consultation room are one and the same. It is uncluttered and sparsely furnished. An old peasant sits on a stool. He cradles his unshaven cheeks in his hands and rocks back and forth very slowly with his eyes closed. Several women, one with a small child, sit on a wooden bench quietly and wait. I am immediately seated in front of a table—immune, as a guest, to the waiting line. A woman in a white gown, surgical mask and cap asks me what is wrong. I explain.

"Have you ever had acupuncture before?" she asks.

I reply that I have not.

"All right," she says. "Then I think we'd better use the short needles."

She unrolls a cloth case that has rows of thin, shining needles stuck into it like a pin cushion. She selects several, sterilizes them in alcohol, and without hesitation begins to stick them, with a wiggling motion, into the muscles just below the back of my skull.

"Is there any pain?" she asks.

There is a slight but even sensation of pain which is difficult to distinguish from the pain of my stiff neck. She twirls a needle and forces it in farther.

"Now do you feel anything?" she asks.

It hurts more, but I derive a sense of satisfaction from the needle, now that it is reaching the source of the pain; the sensation is something similar to the relief felt as a painful boil is lanced.

She inserts three more needles with great care. They slide in almost painlessly. "Fine," she says. "Have you any medicine? No? Good. I don't think you'll need any. Just sit here now for a few minutes or so, and then I will remove the needles."

A little while later, she returns. She twirls the needles one last time, and then removes them. She puts on an herbal aromatic compress which gives the sensation of Ben-Gay, but smells like Tiger Balm.

I gyrate my head. There is no pain.

The Tachai clinic has twenty-eight beds, a staff of eighteen, and treats sixty or so outpatients a day. The attached hospital, like the examination room, is spare but adequately equipped. There is a large operating room with overhead surgical lights and anesthetic equipment for basic operations like Caesarian sections, hysterectomies, tonsilectomies, appendectomies and tumor removal.

"Most of our patients can be cured here at the hospital," says one of the staff doctors as we walk around. "For rare diseases, complications and operations on organs like the heart and brain, we send for specialists from other areas, or refer the patients elsewhere."

The hospital wards are simple whitewashed rooms, accommodating two to six patients. The beds are wood and covered with straw mats. Since the hospital is so close to the homes of the patients, family members are able to spend a good deal of time here. As a result, during recovery a hospitalized person remains within the fabric of the community.

Toward the end of the hospital complex, there is a one-room dental clinic with a brick floor. The dentist is a small, silent man in his thirties. When we enter, he is sitting at a wooden table reading a book, *Prevention and Cure of Common Diseases of the Teeth and Mouth.* There is one dental chair constructed of painted pipe, an electric motor fixed with a belt which drives a drill, and an overhead floodlight that looks like it might once have belonged to a photographer. On a nearby wooden counter is a rather terrifying collection of plierlike instruments, presumably to pull teeth. In one corner is a wooden bed, a quilt neatly folded up at its foot. There are some health propaganda posters above it.

"I live in the dental room," says the dentist. "It is convenient, because people can always find me."

Further down the line is the hospital's own pharmaceutical factory. In one room, two women in white gowns and masks run a hand-cranked pill machine, which stamps pills out of powdered herbs and makes them into small tablets. They are making an herbal diuretic, part of the research and experimentation that goes on all across China to combine Western and traditional Chinese herbal medicine into a new synthesis. The Tachai Commune raises seventy mou of herbs for the pharmacy. About sixty percent of all prescriptions written at the hospital are for herbal medicines.

As we look on, the women continue to crank the machine, which spits out khaki-colored pills, made from the herbs which stand in burlap sacks around the room.

It is not always easy to tell just how people are ranked in a Chinese organization, in terms of responsibility and authority, since they are usually introduced with vague titles like "responsible member," "comrade," "member of the Revolutionary Committee." But Dr. Liu radiates a sense of confidence. He has a kind, softspoken, almost gentle authoritativeness that makes one instantly want to trust him. His hands are surprisingly rough for a surgeon. But it is not uncommon for even surgeons to participate in manual labor.

Dr. Liu's wife is the doctor who treated me with acupuncture. Both have an air of cultivation about them. Their accents are more Peking than Tachai's rough peasant *t'u-hua*, or argot (literally, "talk of the earth"). In fact, they did spend some time in Peking before being transferred to Tachai by the Provincial Board of Health ten years ago.

Like so many others in China, Dr. Liu is a city person who has been sent to the countryside to "serve the people." It is not clear how Dr. Liu and his wife made the adjustment. When asked about it, he just smiles. But ten years later, his dedication to the people in this commune seems boundless. He speaks of Tachai as his *lao-chia*, or "old home."

"Before Liberation, the only way to see a doctor was to go to a city," says Dr. Liu, speaking so softly that one has to be completely quiet to hear him. "People without money had no such hope. The death rate here at Tachai was very high. The middle of the village was a stinking mess. People had poor sanitation facilities, and they lived in old earthen caves that often collapsed. Mosquitoes bred rampantly.

"Since the Cultural Revolution, Chairman Mao taught us that we should put more stress on providing medical care for the rural areas. Right here, the number of our medical personnel jumped from three in 1966 to eighteen now. In fact, you know, there have been no contagious diseases over the past six years. Our health conditions improve each year. And we will continue to try to implement Chairman Mao's directive to raise the level of health care in the countryside."

Someone asks who pays when a doctor has to be brought in from the outside on a special case. Dr. Liu listens patiently to the question in a manner which suggests that he has answered it before but is still a little confused about the obsession of foreigners with figuring out who pays for everything.

"No one pays," he replies. "You see, we all serve the State and the people. Every doctor has his salary from some organization. So whether he comes here to Tachai or elsewhere, he just continues to get his salary."

Then Dr. Liu switches to a subject which seems to have more meaning for him. "We do have a division of labor here, but not in terms of who has a high position or an inferior position. The wages of doctors and nurses are different, although, in some cases, the older nurses with a lot more experience get more than the doctors. But after a nurse has had several years of on-the-job experience, he or she can become a doctor. Many doctors here started off as nurses or 'barefoot doctors' who served as paramedics. They can become doctors by being approved by the medical leadership at the county and provincial level without actually going through formal medical school. A nurse or a barefoot doctor is recommended by his or her comrades if they think the person has the experience, dedication and skill.

"We believe that practice makes perfect," says Dr. Liu. "Truth comes from practice. Some nurses know more about medicine than people who have graduated from medical school. We really don't have blind faith in people who have degrees from medical colleges."

At Tachai, there are three levels of medical training. There are the barefoot doctors, who take short courses in hygiene and basic health care, and fill elemental medical needs at the lowest level. They give shots, dress wounds, minister to simple illnesses, write prescriptions and help with emergencies. There are forty-two barefoot doctors spread out over the twenty work brigades of the Tachai Commune. Barefoot doctors, however, are primarily workers just like other peasants. They are expected to do a minimum of two hundred days of manual labor each year.

Then, there are paramedical courses which students can attend while in middle school. Finally there are the full medical school courses of study, which last from three to five years. These have been considerably shortened since the Cultural Revolution, and students are expected to spend half of their time actually practicing in hospitals and rural areas.

"Most of our work now goes on in preventive medicine," continues Dr. Liu, throwing a glass of cold tea onto the brick floor. (Floors in rural China are considered to be part of the ground. People usually do not try to keep them clean. Throwing tea on an earthen or brick floor is deemed to have the added feature of settling the dust.) "Most of our medical problems here are respiratory and digestive, because of the high elevation and severe weather changes."

"Do the respiratory problems have anything to do with the large number of cigarettes consumed?"

"No," says Dr. Liu. "We do not attribute these problems to smoking. We feel that they are due to the dust and weather." (This is a familiar refrain in China.)

"Our barefoot doctors and medical personnel spend a good deal of time out spreading propaganda among the masses. They advise people on personal hygiene, and why it is important to keep the area around their houses clean. We have succeeded in putting a lot of the old putrid drainage ditches underground. Each week the children go out and help clean up around the brigade. And, of course, everyone is given a physical examination and inoculations on a regular basis. For these physicals, the medical personnel go right to the people's houses."

"What about birth control?"

"We usually consider two children per family enough. We give contraceptive devices free of charge to these people, as well as to any other couple who wish to delay having children. And generally speaking, those who have had three children ask to be sterilized. Chairman Mao has said that mankind must control its birth rate. [Chinese policy on population control has changed several times over the past twenty-five years.] So we tell people that they must act according to Chairman Mao. Anyway family planning is beneficial to everyone, because it enables women to work and join political activities. And this helps men and women to be more equal in what they do."

"Can unmarried women get contraceptives?"

Dr. Liu pauses. He gives the smile of someone who knows that sooner or later these visitors will be unable to control themselves and will ask this question.

"We have never encountered this."

"What if an unmarried woman has a baby?"

"We have never encountered that either," says Dr. Liu as two women doctors further down the table look at each other and only partially succeed in suppressing smiles.

Work with the Children

Today we work again. We begin our day with the usual trek through the village. Overlooking the pigsty, we meet our workmates for the day. They are a group of twenty-five boys and girls from the sixth grade at the brigade school. We walk together up the mountain for about a mile through winter wheat. On the stone terraces that rise all around us, peasants with teams of oxen and mules are planting, usually in groups of four: one man with a draft animal to plow the furrow, a second to lay a bed of compost in the furrow, a third to drop the seeds and kick in the earth on top of them, and a fourth to walk on the furrow and pack the earth around the seeds.

We each have a mattock on our shoulder. The children walk in two columns. The girls are dressed in bright reds, pinks, greens and purples. Their pigtails are tied with bright-colored plastic thongs. The boys wear blue or khaki tunics. All of the children are a bit shy. They give perfunctory, polite one-word answers to our questions.

As we walk higher and higher, the path narrows, and the terraced fields grow smaller and smaller. Where the terraced fields stop, the walnut orchards begin. The trees are just beginning to turn green after the winter. Our task is to cultivate, and make small circular berms around each of the trunks to hold the summer rains.

Each child carries a mattock belonging to his or her family. They wield these adult-sized tools with ease and coordination. They work as if they were playing. The girls are as adept as the boys. There is something about this kind of work which makes conversation come more easily. As we hoe, the children begin to laugh, talk, stop to dig up insects, worms, wild garlic. They joke. But there is no meanness. No one sticks a worm down the back of a class sissy. Their merriment seems to exclude no one.

Toward midmorning, we sit down to rest. They begin to tell us various English words that they have learned in school. "Gooda-by," "Mappa China" (map of China), "peng" (bench). They repeatedly ask how to say certain words. Several children seem to have no intention of learning these words, but just enjoy having something to ask. They want to know how to say "work" and "Long live Chairman Mao."

About eight of us sit under some walnut trees on the earth. The children start singing. Like all children in China, they sing continually—and invariably in a group. Their songs are all *ko-ming ko-ch'ü,* or "revolutionary songs."

They begin to teach us a current favorite, "I Love Peking's T'ien An Men, which refers to the large Ming Dynasty gate guarding the Forbidden City, which is now used as a reviewing stand. Over and over they sing it.

> *I love Peking's T'ien An Men*
> *There the red sun rises high*
> *Our great leader Chairman Mao*
> *Leads us marching on.*

We make a few lame attempts to sing some "representative" American song for them. We finally end up singing "I've Been Working on the Railroad," painfully aware that there are almost no songs written in America in the last twenty years with which these youngsters would feel comfortable. Names flash through my head: Janis Joplin, Bob Dylan, Alice Cooper, Merle Haggard, the Beatles, Ike and Tina Turner. None of these seems right for China.

Work starts again. Slowly we move up the mountain. There are walnut trees tucked into every tiny flat crevice. One small girl sticks a mustard-weed blossom in my hatband. A short while later another small girl in a bright-red plaid jacket bounces up the rocky thorn-covered mountainside and returns with some small red wild-flowers. Soon all the boys are dashing about, grabbing flowers and insisting I put them in my hat, which is beginning to resemble an Easter bonnet from the thirties. The children stand around, leaning on their mattocks, doubled up with laughter, pointing at my hat. A girl comes bounding along the rocky slope with some branches from a flowering thorn bush.

"K'o-i ch'ih! K'o-i ch'ih! You can eat them! You can eat them!" she says, passing some of them to all of us. They taste like honeysuckle.

At midday, we stack our tools, and begin to walk back down to the village. All across the mountainside, men and women are winding their way down, carrying tools and leading animals. We rest until two-thirty, then head back up to the orchard. It is hot in the afternoon sun. The dry mountain air holds no moisture today. It has a thinness to it. We work slowly now. We do as much talking and joking with the children as work. More flowers are presented. I am beginning to feel somewhat self-conscious. I dare not remove the flowers from my hat for fear of offending the children. But in the village during siesta, other peasants look with wonder and bewilderment at this strange display of millinery.

In the late afternoon, as the sun is beginning to turn orange, we take another rest. On the stone terrace behind us, Richard, a member of our group, begins to walk on his hands, which sets all the kids off scrambling for a good view. Richard's spontaneous performance demands a reply. The teacher (who usually works in the fields with the children) quickly organizes them into putting on a short display of *wu shu* (martial arts), which is a brigade activity for Little Red Soldiers.

We finish around six o'clock. The children walk down the path in their usual orderly line. We tag along in disorder like gypsies. Amused peasants watch us pass.

Music Teacher

It is evening. I am sitting outside the Ping-Pong room, having played several games with some of the children. A man comes up and introduces himself. He is short, wears glasses and speaks in a Peking dialect. He looks like an intellectual. He walks hand in hand with two small children. We begin to talk, and he tells me that he is, in fact, a violinist who was sent from Peking to teach music at the brigade.

He invites me into the music room, which is adjacent to the Ping-Pong room. It has a piano in one corner and shelves of numbered instruments in cases against the walls. No child owns his or her own instrument. They all study and practice on instruments bought by the brigade.

"These are my students," says the teacher, introducing the two children on either side of him, who look about eight years old.

"How long will you stay here at Tachai?" I ask.

"As long as I am needed," he replies.

"Is your family here?"

"No, they are not."

"What would happen if they never allow you to return to Peking?" I ask, feeling almost instantly as though I have posed an unfair question.

"Well, then I will gladly stay here," he says. And then, with no sense of strain or ingenuousness, he adds, "Under the leadership of Chairman Mao, we are willing to go anywhere to serve the people." He puts his arms around one of the young students who have been waiting patiently beside him.

We walk back out into the darkness.

"If you have time, you must come again and talk," he says, shining his flashlight on a building, indicating the doorway of his living quarters. And then, as he shakes my hand good-bye, he says in perfect English, "I'm so glad to have met you."

Ch'eng-yüan

Li Ch'eng-yüan stands about three feet six inches tall. He always wears a blue cap. He has a crew cut. His small face is flatish and burned brown by the sun. He has pink cheeks and dazzling white teeth. He is eleven years old.

Ch'eng-yüan usually wears three faded-blue cotton jackets, one on top of the other. The necks and cuffs are frayed. In his breast pocket he carries a key ring with a small pocketknife affixed to it, a key to his chest back at his family's cave, and for some obscure reason, a nail clipper (with which he has several times tried to clip my nails).

His hands are unmistakably those of a little boy. His cuticles are ragged, and his nails invariably have dirt under them. His palms are calloused and rough from working. His meticulously patched blue corduroy pants sag clownishly around his waist. They are held to his hips by a belt almost twice the circumference of his waist, the end of which hangs down like a long tongue.

He wears khaki-colored sneakers and no socks, revealing several inches of brown ankle between shoe and pants. This gap is forever widening as Ch'eng-yüan grows. To temporarily postpone the purchase of new pants, his mother has sewn on several inches of green cloth below the blue cuff.

Ch'eng-yüan climbs around the rock terraces like a goat. He holds people's hands with reckless abandon, and chatters away full speed in his heavy Shansi dialect, oblivious as to whether or not he is being understood. Sometimes if no answers to his questions are forthcoming, he will answer his own questions, and then continue his monologue.

There is a toughness in his lack of inhibition. But it is a childish, gentle toughness. There is no posturing or game playing for attention. When Ch'eng-yüan wants attention, he runs over, puts down his tools, grabs your hand and starts chattering.

In the fields, he grits his teeth as he swings his oversized mattock. He often stops to inspect a grub, a spider or a worm, sometimes holding them up, and asking with a rakish grin what the word is in English. His finds are usually preceded by "Aiyaaaa! Hey! Look at this!" at which point he drops to his knees in the earth to watch the insect.

When asked what they want to do when they become adults, most children reply, "Whatever the Party wants, I will do" or "I want to serve the people."

When Ch'eng-yüan is asked, he jumps right up, and with boyish cockiness says, "I want to join the PLA and get the bad guys!"

Ch'eng-yüan is only vaguely aware of the United States. He asks me where it is. I tell him that it is thousands of miles away across the Pacific Ocean. But the expression on his face shows that he can not visualize the distance. I trace our journey backward from Tachai to Anchuan by bus, from Anchuan to Peking by train, from Peking to Canton by plane, from Canton to Hong Kong by train, and from Hong Kong to America on a long plane ride that took almost twenty hours.

He squints his eyes as though trying to grasp the magnitude of the distance, then he breaks off a piece of grass, puts it between his teeth, and says, "When are you going to come back?"

I try to explain that we probably will not come back.

"All right," he says, as though the whole subject were too elusive. "Let's rest." He takes his mattock, digs the end into the rocky earth on the terrace so as to make a small bench, and sits down beneath a walnut tree.

"Tell us another story or sing us a song," he says. The children often ask us to tell stories and sing songs while we work. They listen to "Froggy Went A-Courtin'," "There Once Was an Old Lady That Swallowed a Fly," "The Wizard of Oz" and "Snow White" (sung and told in abridged form) without fascination. They seem bewildered in a way which transcends the shortcomings of my extemporaneous translation. The fact is, they have never heard stories about talking animals, frog-marrying mice, giants, fairy godmothers, ladies swallowing flies, spiders, birds, dogs and horses.

Sometimes they laugh wanly. But one can see by the tentative expressions on their faces that they are on unfamiliar ground. They are not used to fantasy stories. Fantasy is too close to superstition. And for the Chinese peasant, superstition is almost coterminous with "the old society."

I find that the children enjoy hearing historical stories better. I begin to tell them a rough history of how black people got to America. They are curious; they stop work and listen in rapt attention.

Chinese children's stories are all practical in nature, and invariably political. They tell of young children who perform incredible feats to help the revolution. The messages are always indelibly clear at the end. The plots always resolve with a decisive catharsis in which good wins over evil.

In movies and plays, as well as books, the children always know how it will end. Such endings seem to reassure them that their universe is in order. There is no escapist literature for any age. Children's stories are not supposed to transport a child into his own world of fantasy and imagination. They are supposed to transport a child into the practical world of "building socialism."

Distractions

Although we are here at Tachai primarily to work and observe this one brigade, the Chinese arranging our trip seem unable to control their urge to continue the dizzying pace of outside excursions to dams, rug-factories, canals and other communes. There is a repetitiousness about these trips. Even the startling successes recounted begin to seem routine.

Today, although many of us beg to be allowed to stay and work in the fields, we are shipped off to a neighboring commune with the usual explanation that "it has already been arranged," "the comrades expect you and will be disappointed," etc. Protestations seem not only impolite but futile. I can not help wondering whether or not these side trips, which I find essentially distracting, do not serve as much to give the local peasantry and leaders a chance to sound off and be on exhibit, as to give us new information.

I feel this centrifugal force trying to spin us away from Tachai as inexorable. The formal meetings and receptions, even with the simplest peasants in a small out-of-the-way brigade, often grow exhausting and boring. My notes are full of statistics. They are dull. I have never even bothered to write up most of them. Sometimes I sit in the meeting halls listening to the platitudes, the "welcome of foreign friends," the "B.I.," the blank recitation of how many tons of grain have come from how many mou of land after Liberation and the Cultural Revolution, the stories of rooting out "those who have taken the Capitalist road," and "the wrong line," and find myself yearning for a more tangible kind of contact; something warmer, more real, more human; something which we seem to be on the verge of grasping when we stay put in one place and work without interruption. Most foreigners who visit China never leave the meeting rooms, theaters and historical sites. It can not help but influence their perceptions.

Today the "responsible member" drones on. Even the interpreters are dropping like flies—heads banging on the tabletops in bored stupor. The comrade has it all written out in front of him. (How many times has he used it?) I see people staring at the pages of his monologue, trying to divine how many sheets are still left unrecited. We are served the usual endless cups of green tea poured from thermos bottles. This meeting room, like all others, sports the same boiler-plate portraits of Mao, Marx, Engels, Lenin and Stalin looking off the walls; the beards of Marx and Engels providing the Chinese peasants with their only tonsorial connection to the various long-haired Europeans and Americans who have sat around their hall, listened, and later asked too many loaded questions, often fixated on pleasing their generous hosts rather than eliciting an often complicated reality.

I wonder how many Chinese and foreigners have visited each place we go, heard the same spiel, been served tea from the same thermos bottles by the same rosy-cheeked peasant women. For Hsi Yang is a "model" county, and much on display. I wonder what the members of each Revolutionary Committee really feel about yet another group to lecture to—people whom they have never seen before, and will never see again. People who come from a land that they can hardly imagine. People who will disappear in a few hours . . . forever. I can see how some reporter from *Time* magazine might feel manipulated or conned if he got all the way to China and ended up on a tour full of B.I.'s. And I begin to wish that the walls of these meeting halls could speak, letting me hear the real struggles and human drama which must have gone on within.

But then I look at the hands of some of the people talking with us. I recall one man with large, calloused, gnarled hands with dirt under the nails, and earth ingrained seemingly permanently into the print lines of his fingers. I asked what he now eats each day. He said a few bowls of gruel, some corn meal, and meat three times a year on holidays. Then he told about his life before Liberation, a life of starvation and misery. The room was absolutely silent. All eyes were fixed on him.

We are a society that is fascinated with the power of personality. The Chinese are a society fascinated with the power of a political system, and they do not seem to understand the deep yearning of Westerners to put faces on the facts and statistics, and to give personalities to the people who are making their revolution. Or perhaps they understand the yearning, but reject it as a bad tendency.

Dreams

There is a large theater in the brigade. It is used for movies, large political meetings and cultural events. It is also being used during the day by four old men who weave straw mats in the vestibule. The mats are used to cover piles of adobe bricks to keep them dry.

The men are from another commune. Mat weaving is their speciality. They have come to Tachai to work for ten days. They weave effortlessly. Their only tool is a small sharp knife with which they split the reeds into long sinews and trim the edges.

Old Hsieh wears a thin wispy beard. He squats over his mat, his fingers deftly creating an even pattern from the reeds. He is smoking his pipe and humming in a high-pitched voice as he works.

He looks up, and his fingers go right on working, the way someone might look up from the piano yet continue to play. "What am I singing?" he asks. "Oh, just a song from the old society." He looks down again, his face creased into a grin—the grin of a man caught in the act.

We talk. It is much easier to talk to the Chinese when they are working. The silences do not weigh heavily. Conversation is less pointedly didactic. Questions seem less jarring.

"Do you dream?" I ask, as he returns with a new bunch of reeds.

The question seems not to strike the old man as odd. He stops working for a moment. "Yes," he says. "I dream often."

"What do you dream about?"

"Oh, I think everybody dreams about the things they want," he replies.

"What things do you want?" I ask, accentuating the word "things."

"Well, it's not things so much . . . things you can pick up, that is. Actually, we don't have so many things. Like food, fuel, a place to live—we are given all that."

"Then, what do you dream about?"

"I dream about making mats. I dream about my work."

The Chao Family's Cave

It is raining. The main street and the courtyards between the long lines of caves are empty. The outdoor loudspeakers continue to play some final evening music and an occasional political message. But there is no one to hear them.

Inside the Chao family's cave it is warm and smoky. A fire made with dried corn cobs is just going out in the *k'ang*. On the walls, along with the usual household mirrors and slogans, are several large photos of a handsome middle-aged man.

"Is this your husband?" I ask Mrs. Chao, a short roundfaced woman in her fifties.

"Yes," she replies. "He was killed while they were blasting rock and earth for the terraces." She does not appear eager to pursue the subject of her departed husband. He has died "serving the people" and is a hero. This seems to take the edge off the loss.

Mrs. Chao reaches over and turns on a small turquoise plastic radio. It is a prized possession, although by now most families here have one. Some martial music issues forth from it, making it somewhat difficult to talk. But it is a special offering for the guests, and there is no question of asking her to lower the volume.

We sit on the warm *k'ang*, next to a large flat basket of cornmeal, which is drying before being stored. Children wander in and out, going from one family cave to another. The eldest son, named Tiger Chao, is thirty. The youngest is in his second year at primary school. There are other children, some of whom are married and have children of their own. It is not easy to figure out just who is who in the

Chao family in the endless procession of young people and small children who come in and out through the cave door; some are even neighbors.

The youngest son wears a blue sweatshirt with the characters for TACHAI on the front. He has just come from *wu shu* practice (martial arts). He is reserved and observant. His mother finally coaxes him into saying "Long Live Chairman Mao!" in English, a phrase which he has just learned at school.

The eldest son works repairing the stone terraces, as his father did. He shows us the earthen grain-vats neatly stored along the wall at the back of the cave, under a large picture of Chairman Mao. The vats are filled to the brim with corn, millet and wheat.

"We have enough here for a year," he says. "Then, we have an emergency reserve for another half a year. And if that is not enough, the brigade also has a large reserve supply." As he talks, he picks up handfuls of grain and lets them slip back through his fingers into one of the vats.

"We get as much grain as we feel we need for the household. We pay the brigade for it out of our yearly income, which is figured according to how many work points each family member gets."

These tall vats of grain, standing reassuringly at the back of the cave, radiate a sense of security. They represent a life-sustaining certainty. They are proof of the revolution's efficacy. There is something touching about the way Mrs. Chao's son stands in this warm, simple cave and runs his fingers through the grain which will feed their family until the next harvest.

We sit and eat on the *k'ang*. The meal consists of flat tortilla-like cakes made from corn meal, an omelette made with green shallots, and a large bowl of soup with noodles and bean curd. For dessert we have apples that have been stored over the winter in a special dark, cool cave.

In the kitchen across the courtyard, the daughter is baking corn cakes *(wo-wo-t'ou)* over a coal-fed brick stove. In the corner beside the *k'ang* (the whole family sleeps on the two *k'ang*'s, one of which is in the kitchen room) are two clay crocks. I lift the lid of one. There is a large stone sitting in a sea of drab-green spinachlike vegetables.

"That's pickled green vegetables—*ch'ing-ts'ai,*" says Mrs. Chao. "We pickled it last fall, and eat from it every day."

"What's the big stone doing in there?"

"It keeps the vegetables from spoiling," she replies.

"Do you add salt or vinegar?"

"No. We just pour boiling water in," she says.

"What does the stone do?"

"It keeps the vegetables from spoiling," she answers. "All winter," she adds with enigmatic but humorous finality, as though to say: Anyone knows that if you put green vegetables in a crock with a large stone they won't spoil!

Back in the cave, Mrs. Chao prepares cups of hot water and brown sugar for us to drink.

"We don't grow sugar here," says Tiger Chao, with his arm around his younger brother. "We must buy it from the Brigade Store."

Mrs. Chao brings out a plate of corn kernels which have been roasted in sugar. They have not been popped like popcorn, but have a nutty burnt flavor.

It is nine o'clock, late for people who rise with the sun. We bid the Chaos good-bye. As we step back into the rainy darkness, Mrs. Chao forces several extra corn cakes on us. I put mine under my parka to keep them from getting wet.

Washing

The rain has stopped. A lovely warm sun has appeared. My sock situation is desperate. All laundry washing has halted during the poor weather.

I put my soiled clothes in my tin wash-pan, and head for the reception-center's boiler room with a large brown cake of soap each of us has been given. I take along a towel, intending to launder myself as well. (The peasants in these parts rarely take baths.)

There are no windows in the boiler room. Across from a pile of large chunks of coal are several taps over concrete sinks.

Four young women are washing clothing and bedcovers. They squat on the floor, gossiping and scrubbing their clothes on wooden washboards in tubs.

"Do the men do much washing in your home?" I ask. They stop washing and talking, and look at me as though the wall had just spoken.

Then one woman regains composure and laughs. "Oh, not much," she says.

"The young ones do," says one of the other women, brushing a long braid back over her shoulder. "Especially the single ones."

"Are there any washing machines in China?"

"Any what?" asks the first woman, vigorously wringing out a bed-cover.

Just then, Lao Nieh comes in. He is a nineteen-year-old all-purpose factotum around the reception center, where he lives. He is followed by Shih, one of the woman interpreters accompanying our group. Lao Nieh swaggers up to one of the young women, and picks up one of the tubs of wrung-out laundry with a jaunty serve-the-people-machismo. The woman laughs and shrieks a protest. She grapples with Lao Nieh unconvincingly, and then lets him go. It is Chinese courtship. In any event, Lao Nieh seems to be cock of this roost.

I finish my laundry while talking to Shih. She is about thirty, mother of two. She inquires after my seven-month-old child, about whom she is warmly curious and always eager to see photographs. She tells me about her children—that one of them is "very naughty," and the other lives with his grandparents in Shanghai because Shih and her interpreter husband are often away from their Peking home on trips such as this.

I finish my laundry and take off my shirt to wash myself down a bit. Shih is silent. Conversation ceases. I begin to gather up my face pan and soap, and to head shirtless out into the sunny courtyard to dry off.

Shih looks up from one of the sinks as I move toward the door. She waves an index finger back and forth in an only half-humorous manner.

"You know," she says, "we do not think that it is correct to walk around without any clothes on."

Hua-ming

We work again today with the children, hoeing and banking walnut trees. At break we sit on the freshly turned earth and make shadow pictures with our hands. Several of the girls sit off together and play jacks with a bean bag and several small pieces of bone painted red. Instead of bouncing a ball, they throw the small red bean bag into the air and catch it before it hits the ground. I watch them as they play. There is only a single moment of mild disagreement—and that dissolves with ease as one of the girls smiles and acquiesces.

I find myself working beside Hua-ming, who several days ago gave us the *wu shu* demonstration in the fields. Her mother and father are the two doctors. As this poised young girl hoes the earth and lifts rocks, we talk.

"My father and mother are always busy. They go all over," says Hua-ming. "Sometimes my father has three meetings in one day. They are not home much. But neither are we children. I don't get home until seven o'clock after my *wu shu* practice. It's just before dark. Sometimes my brother cooks. Or sometimes, when everyone is busy, I cook for my mother and father."

"What do you want to do as an adult?" I ask.

"She stops hoeing and stands motionless for a moment. Then giving a radiant smile of beautiful, straight, white teeth, she says, "Whatever the Party needs, I will become."

When we rest again, Hua-ming sits next to two girl classmates. Bien-chih leans on her knee. Hua-ming has an arm draped around the shoulders of Yang-erh in a manner that is poignant in its lack of self-consciousness. They live in the same village, are in the same class, and work in the same fields. They are at ease with each other. But there is a difference between Hua-ming and the sons and daughters of the Tachai peasants which is at once subtle and substantial.

Bien-chih is a solid, small girl with a chunky round head. Her cheeks are red. There is a coarseness to her features. Her teeth are slightly yellow. She does not speak much. There is an unmistakable sense of the countryside about her.

Hua-ming's whole presence gives off an aura of cultivation and ease, traits which have traditionally belonged to the children of educated urban parents in China. She is tall and slender. Her face shows a quality of being well-bred but not spoiled. She laughs easily, and asks questions with a directness and confidence uncharacteristic of many peasant children (Ch'eng-yüan being the exception). She has a winning way of looking at you, laughing nervously and then grabbing your hand. There is a sovereignty about her which bespeaks what the Chinese would call a "different class backround."

As the daughter of two doctors, she lives in larger rooms than the normal family. They have a sink. There is a newspaper rack on the wall. The living quarters are better lit, more spacious and refined than those of Ch'eng-yüan's family.

And yet, for all the differences, I find that what lasts in my mind is the way in which this pretty and able twelve-year-old girl fits into the routine of peasant life. It is at once incongruous and reassuring to see her working beside Bien-chih. The distinct contrast between the two is surprising, not because it exists, but because it is not greater.

Incident

We go into Hsi Yang, the county seat, to walk around. It is another gray day, with the sky the color of stone. As we disembark I notice a brick wall which is covered with the tatters of hundreds of posters which, over the years, have been pasted up on it. In the middle of this shaggy flapping collage of half-ripped posters, there is one gleaming bright proletarian face looking out. It is in reds, yellows and blues. Its edges are ripped, but it shines out amidst the other shreds as though a spotlight were upon it.

I have an irrepressible urge to take a color slide of it. I raise my camera. But some inner mechanism tells me that the Chinese might not understand. I decide to wait for a less public and more auspicious moment.

Later, just before we leave, I sally up to the wall alone, set and focus my camera, and shoot four or five shots. I am pleased. Then I turn around. Hsiao Yao, the head interpreter, stands behind me. He confronts me with a scowling look of displeasure. I walk over to him.

"Why do you wish to take a picture of a dirty old wall?" he asks accusingly.

"I'm not sure I can explain," I reply. Nonetheless I begin to try to tell him that artistically speaking I find such colors and textures interesting and appealing. I mention that Chinese standards of art are not the same as those in the West. Hsiao Yao is intelligent and an excellent interpreter. He has been to Australia, Hong Kong and the Mideast. He served as interpreter for Gerald Ford when he first visited China as a Congressman. But I can see that nothing I am saying is capable of allaying his suspicions.

"And why do you take all those pictures of toilets and compost piles?" he asks, finally letting out another grievance. "Many of the local comrades do not understand this. They think that maybe you only wish to show how backward China is."

I try to explain my interest (and that of many people back home) in waste management and reuse. But I feel a sense of futility in pursuing the discussion. There is a value at issue here which we do not share.

Facts

Li Hsi-shen is the chairman of Hsi Yang County's Revolutionary Committee. He is an important and busy man. He gives us some statistics on this model county.

The population is 200,000.

There are 20 communes and 460 production brigades in the county.

Every commune has its own hospital.

There are 586,000 meters of new stone terrace.

There are 220,000 meters of river dikes.

Forty percent of the land is already under mechanical cultivation.

There are 420 scientific teams circulating around the county, comprising 2500 people.

In 1966 the county had a total output of 80 million chin of grain. By 1974 total output had climbed to 340 chin.

In the past eight years 352.9 million chin of grain have been sold to the State (at relatively low-pegged prices; this, rather than taxes, is the main means of accumulating State capital in China). In 1974 the county communes sold seven times as much grain to the State as in 1966.

The State has invested 6.9 million yuan in some 700 county projects, although most projects are done without State aid.

A campaign against graft and corruption was conducted in 1968.

Almost every Chinese statistic is impressive. If statistics were as gripping as matters of life, love and death, the cause of the Chinese revolution would long since have spread throughout the universe without a shot being fired.

Transform Heaven and Earth

On a cliff so sheer that one can only speculate on how it was done, someone has painted large neat white characters which read: TRANSFORM CHINA BY LEARNING FROM THE OLD MAN WHO MOVED THE MOUNTAIN. The slogan refers to the much-studied popular legend about an old man who commenced to move two mountains in front of his house a little bit at a time. People laughed and said that he would never succeed before he died. But he persevered, claiming that if each generation would continue, ultimately the land would be flat.

And indeed the land in these narrow Shansi valleys has been transformed in ways which leave me wondering just how to convey the magnitude of the change.

China is obsessed with transformation and development. TRANS-FORM THE MOUNTAINS AND CHANGE THE EARTH, says another slogan, on a stone dike several miles long, which squeezes a river from its once-broad bed into a narrow, deep channel. The rest of the flat bed (hundreds of acres) has been plowed and planted. And rising around this strangely out-of-place flat field are stone terraces clinging to the steep, rocky mountains. Every stone is hand-hewn and hand-carried up the mountain. We visit one brigade where they have rerouted a river four hundred meters through a mountain.

It is not as though there were only a thin dusting of these spectacular projects to serve as a public relations veneer. They are everywhere. Communes and brigades compete with each other to complete new and ever more unimaginable projects to make the landscape more hospitable. There is a kind of insatiable pride in each village which will not allow it to be outdone in good works by another. Brigade members give these projects as much energy and enthusiasm as an American town might give the local ball team.

Our bus bounces down a dirt road, leaving a billowing cloud of dust behind us as we wind through the Shansi countryside. It is truly spring now. The brown hills are splashed with pink and white blossoms of the flowering apple and walnut trees. The rape is bright yellow in the fields. The poplars along the roadside have just begun to sprout fresh green leaves which contrast strikingly with the blue sky. Small towns perch on hillsides looking down on wide new fields instead of the bed of some uncontrollable river. We pass no other cars all day—just a few trucks, tractors, and an endless procession of animal carts. The Chinese are proud of their tractors, bulldozers and other machines. They can not understand why foreigners prefer to take pictures of mules and oxen pulling carts and plows. They visibly wince when insistent shutterbugs relentlessly take photographs of quaint old walled houses from former times, or old-style caves without the new trim masonry façades. The Chinese have no nostalgia for their past.

But there is indeed a timeless quality to these mountains and back valleys dotted with villages and stone watchtowers from the T'ang Dynasty. During the last thousand years before Liberation these villages changed little. The people living in the earthen caves remained fixed as the floods and droughts came and went, as men lived and died, sometimes going no farther than their county seat, and as the dynasties rose and fell. There is an old peasant saying,

> *I plow my ground and eat,*
> *I dig my well and drink.*
> *For king or emperor,*
> *What use have I?*

The constants were the summer rains, which cut these villages off from the outside for months at a time, hunger and the landlords in their walled houses. They ruled as petty tyrants over a peasant population described by one historian as being like a man standing up to his neck in water, so that one ripple would drown him.

The landlords are gone now. The rivers are tamed. A new web of organization has been woven throughout each village. The change is everywhere, even though visually many of the projects seem to blend into the landscape in a way which not even the most skillful architectural planner could attain.

Socialist Distillery

For 1.60 yuan, a bottle of Hsi Yang Pai Chiu (Hsi Yang White Wine) can be purchased. It is made from fermented sorghum, and is 65 percent alcohol, or one hundred thirty proof! For 2.30 yuan, a bottle of Gai Chih Chiu can be purchased. It is made of twelve different kinds of fermented herbs and grains, and is 45 percent alcohol, or ninety proof. Both kinds of wine are available from the Hsi Yang Huang Shih Distillery.

It is the end of the day, and by the time we arrive at this regional distillery, we are all dusty, tired and thirsty. We are squired into a large bare room furnished with chairs and tables. Our hosts graciously place a bottle of each wine on every table. There is a briefly awkward period. Finally the ice is broken when some workers snap off the pop tops of the wine bottles. Small glasses of wine are poured for each of us.

Soon everyone is gagging and recoiling in horror at the potency and taste of this local brew. The clear sorghum wine is so offensive-smelling that it is virtually impossible to get it to my lips without reeling under a wave of nausea; this is not an exaggeration.

I see Lao Wang drifting around the room holding a glass aloft. He has a large provocative grin on his face. He challenges Richard (a fearless drinker) to *kang-pei* (bottoms up). Richard downs his glass. There is a cascade of astonished voices from others who by now have found that hot tea is also available. Lao Wang does not follow suit and drink, but instead laughs at his clever prank, and departs in search of other prey. Some, who have frequently been participants in Lao Wang's jests, shrink under the tables to avoid being similarly challenged. Our wine-tasting session seems to be on the edge of breaking down into buffoonery, when much to our astonishment, a B.I. begins. By now, even the fumes have begun to get to me.

The cadre who is speaking tells us that our "presence is a great inspiration." The B.I. is mercifully short.

I ask the comrade if he feels it is a good thing to inspire the workers to make more alcoholic beverages. The question goes unanswered.

"Do you enjoy drinking?" I ask the comrade.

"Yes," he says.

"What is the policy on drinking in China?"

"People can buy wine according to their needs. A little wine is good for their health. And, no, they won't get drunk."

"Does wine-making contribute to building socialism?"

"Yes."

"How?"

There is no immediate answer. By now our meeting is collapsing. People are laughing and joking, making only feeble attempts to whisper. Several interpreters are talking with distillery workers, trying to form some coherent answers.

The meeting just frays off, and we begin a tour of the plant. Hsiao Yao comes up to me as we go out the door. He is accompanied by the vice-chairman of the distillery's Revolutionary Committee. Hsiao Yao has a weary, troubled look on his face. He has apparently not appreciated the directness of my questions.

The vice-chairman is smiling. He good-naturedly begins an explanation. "Actually," he says, "producing wine is just one part of what our plant does. We also make full use of grain residues after the wine is produced. We raise about 50 pigs on the grain wastes. We also raise some 20,000 chin (about 27,000 pounds) of beans for noodles each year. And although we do buy some grain from the surrounding brigades, we also have our own land and fields. You can see it out there." He points across the road. "We reclaimed all that land from the riverbed over the past few years. We did not do this before because of Liu Shao-ch'i's revisionist line. Eventually we want to raise our pig production to 1,000 head, and raise our wine production to 1,000 tons a year."

This gracious man guides me by the shoulder through a doorway into a room where the grain is being shoveled into vats. "So you might say," he continues, "that we have multiple use of the grain from which we make wine. Wine is just one of our products."

Returning home in the microbus, I sit next to Lao Chao, one of our interpreters. "You know, I used to be an alcoholic," he says. "I used to work as an interpreter for Russian technicians before they pulled up and left in the late fifties. My case was quite severe. I also have hypertension. But I succeeded in overcoming it. And the peasants . . . Well, they might drink a bottle on a special holiday with friends. But there are not many alcoholics in China any more.

Ch'eng-yüan's Family

The sun is glaring, hot and bright. It is midday siesta. The village is quiet.

Ch'eng-yüan and Hsin-kuo come up the hill to find us as soon as they have finished school and eaten lunch. They arrive while I am asleep.

I wake up to find Ch'eng-yüan pulling at my arm. His head is cocked to the side like a bird, looking at my face for any sign of life. Hsin-kuo stands in the cave with an awkward look on his face, not quite as confident as Ch'eng-yüan of his prerogative to wake up foreigners.

I get up. We walk along the steep cobblestone roadway to the third tier of caves, where Ch'eng-yüan's family lives.

I ask him whether his family is resting.

In his cavalier manner, he says that it doesn't matter, throws back the rattan curtain which hangs across the doorway to his cave, and drags me inside.

His father is indeed asleep on the k'ang. He immediately wakes up. I apologize for disturbing him. He presents a large sleepy smile that immediately puts me at ease, and urges me to sit down.

Ch'eng-yüan's father is about fifty. His head is close-shaven. His skin is coffee-colored. There is dark stubble on his chin. His hands are large and strong, but so calloused and gnarled from work that they look like the claws of some ancient reptile. He wears his brass-stemmed, soapstone bowl pipe and tobacco pouch slung around his neck. His patched, faded cotton jacket lies beside him on the *k'ang*.

Five of Ch'eng-yüan's seven brothers and sisters suddenly appear in the cave. Ch'eng-yüan's mother comes through the door with a stack of corn-meal pancakes in her hands. She nervously proffers one in my direction. Ch'eng-yüan seems oblivious to the uproar he has created. In the manner of the lord of the mansion, he urges all to eat.

The cave is neat, but crammed with grain vats to feed this large family. There are a few photos on the mirrors, which abound in every cave. One shows an old peasant couple. The woman has bound feet. The man sits expressionless. He is wearing an old-fashioned round hat and has a long wispy beard. They have been posed in front of a roll-down, romantic, turn-of-the-century backdrop at a photography studio.

"Those are my parents," says Ch'eng-yüan's mother. "They're dead now."

Two of Ch'eng-yüan's brothers are climbing around on the *k'ang* like monkeys. When I look at them, they grin and retreat behind their father, who sits trying to think of something friendly to say. But Ch'eng-yüan's father is not a man for whom words seem to flow easily —at least when talking to a foreigner.

Two more daughters-in-law walk in, holding two more babies. Our presence is beginning to attract attention from the adjacent caves.

I mention that I have a small son just about seven months old.

"Was he born at home?" the daughter-in-law asks.

"We started to," I reply, "but there were complications, and we had to go to the hospital at the last moment."

"I see," she says. "We had this one at home. Most people here in the country give birth at home. But it's up to the individual. Some people go to the hospital."

"Will the doctor come to your cave for a birth?" I ask.

"Oh, yes—a barefoot doctor or a midwife."

The baby she is holding in her arms is naked from the waist down. She wears an almost comical pink and white wool ski hat, which sits over her two coal-black eyes, incredibly fat cheeks and chin, creating a J. Edgar Hoover-as-a-baby effect. She suddenly begins to cry.

Ch'eng-yüan's father remains quiet and smiling, but siesta time is a time of rest. The quasiconscious expression on his face suggests a bear disturbed from its normal seasonal hibernation. I express apologies for barging in, and suggest that before departing, the children come outside for a photograph. Ch'eng-yüan's father sparks briefly to life. He shakes my hand vigorously between both of his, and says that I should come again.

The children pour out of the mouth of the cave in gleeful anticipation of having their photograph taken. The older women hang back uncertainly just inside the doorway. It is clear that they would love to have a picture to place in their mirrors. But they are shy, and come only reluctantly.

I take several photos, and Ch'eng-yüan walks me back up the hill, immensely satisfied with himself and the success of the visit.

Brigade Store

The Brigade Store closes at seven o'clock each evening. Tonight several of us slip off after dinner on a candy run.

The Chinese are intrigued by our buying habits. The woman behind the counter has grown somewhat jaded by our almost nightly visits. She countenances our seemingly insatiable passion for sweets with a tolerant indulgence reserved for guests from a "different society." Peasants from the village look on, as startled by the ease with which we spend our money as by anything else.

On those occasions when several emissaries arrive at the store five minutes before closing time to make a group purchase of wine and beer, the crowd is even larger. Whichever Western reprobate has been chosen to make the run leaves the store bulging with bottles, and feeling very much on the wrong line. The Chinese accompanying our trip rarely join us in these evening bouts of libations and conviviality. They seem both suspicious and disturbed by our inclination to "relax." They look with horror on our more flagrant displays of indulgence. One senses that they fear that at some point we might become completely dispossessed of our senses, and create some unimaginable scene of great embarrassment.

I recall one incident when many members of our group were in one cave late at night, smoking, drinking and (Oh, God!) dancing to the one cassette of rock music that someone had providentially brought on the trip. One of the Chinese comrades drew back the curtain to the smoke-filled cave at about eleven o'clock, looked at the wanton spectacle, and withdrew mumbling something about two factories and a water conservation project to visit tomorrow, and that we should all go to bed.

Tonight while waiting for our order of candy, I strike up a conversation with a middle-aged man who is waiting to buy some shoes. He has an unmistakable dignity. He speaks softly and intelligently. He wears a cotton tunic and faded khaki cap. He tells me that he is a fruit tree specialist with the province, who has been "sent down" to Tachai.

"I am here to work and study. I spend most of my time in the orchards, caring for the trees and doing some research on diseases," says Comrade Huang in measured tones, suggesting that although he agrees in principle, his exile to the country has not always been easy. "Now we are checking the trees for bark rust, other diseases and damaged branches."

We talk for almost half an hour in front of the stationery counter until the store closes. Because we have fruit trees on our farm at home, I am interested in what he says. He in turn is curious about what kind of trees we have in California. Do we have dwarf stock? How do we fertilize and cultivate? What is the weather like?

"Yes," he says. "California is famous for its fine soil and fruit."

A small crowd has gathered around us, listening. Comrade Huang cautiously suggests that maybe we could talk again. I am delighted at the prospect. I ask him where he will be working tomorrow.

"I'll be up behind the new caves tomorrow, working on some apple trees." And then hastily he adds, "Of course, you should make arrangements with your group leader."

We shake hands, and bid each other good night.

I am excited by the encounter. I am curious about his work. But I am equally eager to have a chance to work alone with Comrade Huang, and to be able to talk with him in a leisurely, informal manner. There is something about individual encounters which seems to make the Chinese uneasy. Why? I'm still not sure.

I speak of my experience with our group's leaders, who in turn discuss it with Hsiao Yao. I sense a coolness. I am asking for exactly the kind of individual dispensation that does not rest easily alongside the group ethic.

In a day, word comes back that it has been arranged for me to leave our work group and work with Comrade Huang. I am surprised and pleased.

A Sleepless Night

Slowly people start moving out of their caves and houses toward the theater. There is a movie tonight. It is a special event. We too are supposed to be attending. At least it is on our schedule. But feeling tired, and having a slight headache, I return to our cave to write and sleep.

At eleven-thirty the overhead fluorescent light suddenly blinks on. I am half asleep. Hsiao Yao has entered without knocking. He stands over me. He is agitated about something.

"I have already told Comrade Huang that your work trip to the orchards is canceled tomorrow," he says coldly and with deadly seriousness. "Since you are sick, tomorrow you will not go out at all. You are to stay indoors and get well."

I sit up in bed, still somewhat disoriented. I protest that I am not sick, only tired. Hsiao Yao is unmovable. Then, almost as suddenly as he arrived, he departs.

I am stunned. I lie awake the whole night trying to fathom what tensions have culminated in this stark moment. I recall a comment by Hsiao Yao some days earlier about writers rarely getting visas to visit China for as long a time as two months. Hsiao Yao seems wary of the backlash that the printed word might entail. And then there is the question of distrust that seems to generate around the taking of certain photos, asking certain questions, seeking individual experiences, not bending totally to the schedule arranged for us.

I spend a sleepless night, trying to string all these things together coherently in my mind.

Working

We continue to work almost every day with the children. We have broken ourselves down into small work teams of eight to ten people each. Today, at one point, our small group temporarily merges with another group. We meet them as we hoe our way down a terrace, coming from the opposite direction. Hua-ming and I begin to talk with some children from the other group. So deep are we into our conversation and hoeing that we do not notice the rest of the group gradually hoeing themselves away from us and disappearing. When we realize we are separated, we strike out to find them. Upon regaining their midst, we are criticized in a friendly, but nonetheless serious way.

"This is the way the Chinese used to be," says one comrade. "No one could stay organized long enough to get anything done. We must stay with our work groups."

The Bank

There is only one bank in China. This is the state-run Bank of China. It has branches in almost every small brigade or city neighborhood in the country.

In Tachai, the office is a spare, sparsely furnished room across from the store. There are two tellers who live and sleep in the bank. They rotate. And when not working in the bank, they work in the fields.

There are no bars on the windows. A rifle hangs on the wall, suggesting that one or both tellers are in the militia, rather than fearful of robberies. There are a large desk, a big safe and sleeping platforms for the two tellers.

The bank handles the payroll for the brigade. It also makes loans to organizations, although after the Cultural Revolution it ceased making loans to individuals. The loans are decided upon after consultation with local and county officials.

Most of the peasants in this village have their salaries deposited directly in the bank. There are two kinds of accounts available. A person can accrue interest of 3.24 percent per annum on deposits left for more than a year, or 2.16 percent per annum on deposits in an ordinary account.

The money that is secured in the bank is both loaned for local projects, and invested through the bank network in national projects.

School

Keng Chu is the Chairman of the Tachai Brigade School's Revolutionary Committee. He, like other teachers, lives in a cave dormitory, and returns home to his family only over long national holidays.

Keng shares a cave with one other roommate. It is raw and cold out today, but inside the coal-burning cast-iron stove makes the cave warm and cozy. There are several copies of the Army newspaper, *Liberation Army Daily*, hanging in a wall holder. There is an Air Force calendar on the wall behind a small desk. It shows a smiling pilot in a leather helmet silhouetted against the sky. On the opposite wall, there is a map of China. Two pieces of plywood supported by sawhorses serve as beds.

Keng was a beggar before his village was liberated in 1945. In 1946 he entered school for the first time. In 1952, he began at teachers' school. He has been teaching ever since. Now, like all the other teachers, he draws a salary from the brigade (between thirty-five and forty-five yuan a month), and teaches in this school of two hundred forty students, which provides nine years of primary education. During the Cultural Revolution, the course of studies was shortened from twelve years.

"We shortened it," says Keng, "because Chairman Mao told us to shorten our classroom education and allow the children to learn more from the outside." He lights up a cigarette.

"Of course, you must know all about this," he continues, "because you work with some of the children. Usually each class will work about a hundred days of physical labor each year. Even some of our curriculum is related to work. Our school has a small farm where the children can have gardens and do experiments. Last year, for instance, they did some experiments with fertilizers. They tried to make some chemical fertilizer themselves."

A bell rings outside. Suddenly there are hundreds of cacaphonous voices coming from the block of previously silent classrooms.

"Would you like to come to a class?" asks Keng. "What kind of a class would you like to see? Perhaps you would like to go to a class of your young workmates?"

Word travels fast in this village. By the time we reach the classroom, the kids already know we're coming. They are elated at our presence. They keep turning around in their seats, smiling and looking to see who has come. They are about to have an English class.

On a wall board hangs a series of small children's stories in paperback comic-book form. The children may borrow them and take them home. There are bright-red quotes from Chairman Mao all around the walls. On one side of the room is a map of the world. On the other side, a map of China. As usual, a portrait of Chairman Mao hangs over the blackboard. Characters on either side of this portrait read: "Unite, pay attention, be conscious, happy and gay." The floor is earthen; the walls are whitewashed plaster which leave great powdery-white smudges on blue tunics when leaned against. Behind us, on another blackboard, are essays written by the children on squared blocked paper in their childish but fine calligraphy.

The teacher is a young woman. She stands before the children, and in Chinese she apologizes for not knowing English well.

Keng leans over and whispers, "There used to be no teacher of English. But the county organized a six-month course, so one of our teachers went to it last October. She taught a class last year for only two months before the harvest break, but then she had to stop because she was going to have a baby. So she has only taught two months of English. She really isn't used to it yet. But she will go to the continuing English teachers' course at the county."

Meanwhile she is writing sentences on the blackboard in Chinese. Then beneath, she writes them out in English, and begins to read them out loud.

"Zoza ara desk." ("Those are desks)."

Her pronunciation is not easy to follow. The children repeat in unison after her.

"Is this a desk?" she asks.

No children's hands fly up in response. They are unusually uncertain.

"Is this a bench?" she tries.

Since no child volunteers to answer individually, she cues them to respond in unison. The children respond with great volume and gusto, relieved of the burden of going it alone.

The class is obviously not very advanced. The teacher never strays from the book. And it is evident that, although teaching, she can not herself speak English. But she imparts what she knows to the students with a confidence that is impressive and surprising. She seems not the least bit fazed by the two English-speaking foreigners sitting at the back of the room. It is as though she has decided that it does not matter so much how well she knows English, as how well she teaches the little she does know.

The children sit on wooden benches, three and four to a desk. At this age, boys and girls still mix freely and share desks. Each student has his or her own copy book. But they share textbooks, which are thin paperbacks. In the usual careful Chinese manner, they are printed without error.

HANDWRITING

The sun is red.
The sun is bright.
The sun is Chairman Mao.
The sun is our Party.
We love Chairman Mao.
We love our Party.
Long live Chairman Mao.
Long live our Party.

NEW WORDS

Sun, Chairman Mao, bright, Party.

EXERCISE

These are Chairman Mao's works.
Are these doors?
The workers make chairs and doors for us.

What are these?
These are works of Marx and Lenin.
We study the works of Marx and Lenin.
We study Chairman Mao's works.
We study hard.

The teacher writes several English phrases on the board for the children to copy. Quiet descends over the room. Clutching their pencils, the children begin laboriously to write out the phrases.

I walk down the aisle between the desks, watching and correcting the children as they work. Ch'eng-yüan has his tongue firmly clenched between his teeth as he writes large ungainly looping letters. Hua-ming gives a shy smile as I look over her shoulder at her copy book. She has made no mistakes. Her writing is as graceful as she is. Hsin-kuo, a young boy with a crew cut and large ears, thrusts his paper out for me to see. He has left out a whole word, and commences erasing busily to make a space when I point it out.

Are these chairs?
Yes, they are.
Are these benches?
Yes, they are.

When they have finished copying, there is a brief period when every child practices saying the written phrases out loud. They all practice together, although not in unison. The room is filled with an indistinguishable din.

Finally, like an orchestra conductor, the teacher gathers their concentration together again. For ten minutes they recite over and over in unison, "Are these doors? Yes they are . . ."

Martial Arts

It is dusk. In the half-light, a group of children are doing *wu shu* exercises on the threshing field. They seem secretly pleased that several of us are there watching them. (They practice twice a day, from six to seven o'clock in the morning and evening.) They execute their steps with exquisite form and balance—kicking, swirling, jumping, turning. There is no sign of clumsiness. Their talent is awesome, all the more so for the unselfconscious manner with which they perform.

I watch carefully. The children line up behind their coach. One after another they step out in turn and do a series of fast steps and swirls. There is very little gap between the best and the worst. In fact, the evenness of talent is astonishing, reflecting the concern of the Chinese with developing the backward as well as the advanced. This has been one of Mao's passions: all-around equal development of every sector of Chinese life. It is perhaps for this reason that he first called attention to this once-impoverished desolate village, which has now succeeded in such a dramatic way. It was a village with no unique talents and no lucky breaks. Yet it transformed itself.

The Media

It is evening. I have washed up after work. I walk down to the store to see what is happening. The *People's Daily* is posted across the square on a kiosk under a small roof. The headlines tell of a recent banquet in Peking, held for North Korean Premier Kim Il-sung on a state visit. News of the visit almost fills the front page. The Chinese have determined that his visit is a political event of significance. It receives a commensurate amount of coverage, even though by our standards the events may seem dull.

It is strange to see this spare, functional paper. There are no stories on cult slayings, bombings, speculations on Kissinger's comings and goings, no news on governmental corruption, or tales of heartbreak and desire in filmland. The *People's Daily* is both unexciting and a relief. Its function is to propagandize, not to induce anxieties and fears, or titillate with the bizarre or horrible. People in China are not expected to absorb or deal with two hours of the world's latest disasters each day.

At the far end of the square, a young man sits out in front of the dormitory for work-study guests in the last rays of evening sun. He is knitting.

Watching

We sit high up on Tiger Head Mountain under a walnut tree, looking out across the red, eroded Shansi hills. It is break time. Ch'eng-yüan sits beside me on some freshly turned earth. He wears a plastic army canteen slung across his chest, like a military hero from the Long March. For the moment at least, he is silent, absorbed in some hand-clapping games Hua-ming and two other girls are playing.

Beneath our perch, a work team of women slowly hoe their way down rows of green winter wheat, which has begun to grow with the new spring rain. "Spring rain is more precious than oil," goes the old Chinese saying. A man with a team of oxen clucks and coaxes his animals on as he harrows a freshly ploughed field. His harrow is made in the village from poplar wood and willow branches.

As I look downward, I can not help feeling sad that so soon we will be leaving.

Rehearsal

Word has been out for several weeks now that on our last night there will be a joint performance in the auditorium. We and the children will each perform. An excitement over this event builds in the days which precede it. This evening, some of the children sneak in to watch us rehearse. Ch'eng-yüan falls off a chair and cuts his forehead. He sits quietly in the front row, crying, and pressing a bloody paper against the gash until he is taken to the clinic.

Performance

Tonight the auditorium is packed to capacity with people from Tachai and the surrounding work brigades. Everyone is curious about what the American Work Group will do at its performance. Our interpreters have also been curious. They have asked for the words to all our songs and dialogue so that they can translate them. They find some of the acts politically unsuitable, and suggest some changes. We make no effort to resist, realizing that true contemporary American culture and art forms would only confuse and upset the Chinese.

The lights dim. The Tachai children, of all ages, begin the performance. They sing, dance and play instruments. There are the usual choreography, costumes and political themes. But the performance is greatly enlivened by all the familiar faces.

There is an orchestra in the wings of the stage, composed of both Chinese and Western instruments. I see Ch'eng-yüan's head in the back row. He is holding an oboe-like instrument, which he very occasionally raises to his mouth. It emits a harsh, bleating tone. His role in the orchestra seems to be equivalent to that of a cymbal player. He waits patiently for his chances. At one point he lets out a horrendous quack at the wrong time. But he seems unfazed by it, and the music, which is otherwise quite professional, goes on. Almost every child seems to be worked into the performance in one way or another.

One dance shows a boy transporting manure in baskets on a carrying pole. A whole phalanx of brightly costumed girls follows him, sowing wheat. My first impression is that the theme of the dance is somewhat comical. But I look around the theater. The room is filled with peasants who have spent their whole lives in the fields. They watch intently.

The high point of the performance is the *wu-shu* exhibit, in which Hua-ming participates. The performance is exquisite. It starts with simple exercises, then solos, and finally group performances. The bodies of the children move with such adult grace and coordination that one forgets their age. The thought that they are the sons and daughters of peasants seems utterly remote.

We perform after the *wu-shu.* As we file up onto the stage, to much approval from the audience, I feel a little like an anesthetized elephant in comparison to the children.

We sing listless versions of *"Joe Hill"* and *"Follow the Drinking Gourd,"* which provoke only a polite response. We sing a Chinese song we have learned called "Hsiüng Mei K'ai Huang," and receive a thunderous ovation.

Several of the blacks on the trip have worked up a blues-rock tune which has been slid past the review committee because it has words from the civil rights movement. It is very rhythmic, and several of the group begin to rock and boogie very timidly during the song. The Chinese seem nonplussed.

The big hit of the evening is a skit several of us have worked up about inflation (which many of the older Chinese remember from the forties, and which we tell them the Americans are now experiencing in a less severe way). The climactic scene is one in which a poor worker, who is forced to carry his many sacks of inflated money in a wheelbarrow, gets robbed on the way to the store. The robber ends up pausing in front of the commandeered wheelbarrow of money, scratching his head, throwing the money away, and taking the wheelbarrow. The crowd loves this twist, and cracks up.

I play the evil boss, with a fat pillow on my stomach, a black villain's mustache, a bottle of liquor, and a slouch hat. I sit at a desk in front of piles of money, reading a newspaper (clearly marked with a felt-tipped pen for all to see) called the *Fa Ts'ai Jih Pao (The Strike It Rich Daily)*. My function is to dispense laundry bags of inflated currency to the worker, at pay day.

Like all Chinese dramas, it must have a happy and politically instructive ending. After the robbery, I get decked by an incensed worker, who has been reborn in a whirlwind of anti-inflationist righteous wrath.

The audience enjoys the performance. It is not so much that they appreciate our jokes or our talent (of which there is little), but they seem fascinated just to see Americans on a stage.

Leavetaking

I awake in the first gray light of morning to see three small faces in blue caps peering past the curtains in the doorway. It is Ch'engyüan, Hsin-kuo and another friend. This morning we will leave. They have come to see us one last time.

I tell them to go next door and wake up Andy and Richard, which they do with great delight and enthusiasm. I splash cold water on my face and dress groggily.

We walk hand in hand down the hill to the caves to say good-bye to others. Smoke is curling up from the kitchens. It is not yet six o'clock. But most people have already been up an hour, though we all went to bed after midnight last night. The men and older children have already left for the fields. The women are in the kitchens cooking corn mush and millet gruel for breakfast.

We stop at Jui-lan's cave.

"She's not up yet," says her mother, from over the stove. "But please come in."

We go into the kitchen room, where Jui-lan is sleeping on the *k'ang* with her little sister. She wakes up and sees us. She gives a sleepy smile. Her face is still rouged from last night's performance. We sit down on the edge of the *k'ang* while Jui-lan dresses.

The sound of chirping chicks comes from a basket beside the door. Jui-lan opens a small wicker gate, and a fleet of fledglings fans out across the floor, peeping and searching for kernels of spilled grain and scraps.

Some neighbors from the cave next door wander in without knocking. They stand, eating bowls of corn-meal mush with chopsticks. They watch our awkward good-byes.

"If you have time, come again," says Jui-lan's mother, unable to fully grasp the chasm that our departure signifies.

"Yes, of course," I say, even though I know we shall not return.

She approaches each of us in turn and takes our hands in both of hers.

Jui-lan is silent. There seems to be no easy moment to leave the room. It is not until words fail us that we back out the door.

Ch'eng-yüan is not at all subdued. He leads us on fearlessly to the next cave, where he just barges in with a sense of disarming familiarity and welcome.

Several stops later, we leave Ch'eng-yüan and his friends to *"sung fan"* (take breakfast to the adults in the fields). They promise that they will return in an hour or so to see us off at the bus.

We return and pack. Everyone is tired and quiet.

It is midmorning when we finally stack our luggage out in the courtyard of the reception station. I walk outside past the brick archway for one last look at the village. The whole sixth-grade class is coming up the stone steps from school.

We stand around together for a while. A few people take pictures. Very few of the children say anything. Someone tries half-heartedly to get the group singing. The effort fails.

Ch'eng-yüan has a subdued blank look on his face now.

"When will you come back?" he asks without looking up, searching for some finite, clear statement.

I tell him that I will write him a letter.

"In Chinese?" he says, brightening only a little. These are the last words he says.

Hua-ming still has traces of blackened eyebrows and rouge on her face. She holds my hand and looks at her feet. She begins to cry. I find myself giving her a hug. The un-Chineseness of it frightens me a little. For a moment, our strange disorderly group seems suspended above the normal Chinese routine.

Ch'eng-yüan's eyes remain averted, but he does not cry. Even in China tears seem to come easier to girls.

Our bus pulls out down the road. The children stand under the poplar trees and wave. As we bump down the hill past the neighboring village, the children already seem like a poignant but distant memory.

About the Author

Born in New York in 1940, ORVILLE SCHELL graduated from Harvard University, and then spent several years in the Far East studying Chinese, and later covering the war in Indochina. He returned to do Ph.D. work at the Center for Chinese Studies at the University of California at Berkeley. He has written for *The New Yorker, The Nation, Atlantic Monthly, Look, Saturday Review* and many other publications. He was coeditor of the first three volumes of *The China Reader* and coauthor of *Modern China;* his other books include *Starting Over* and *The Town That Fought to Save Itself.* He now lives in Northern California.